MW01615696

A. Ramana

AMERICAN MYSTIC

MEMOIRS OF A HAPPY MAN

As recounted by Arunachala Ramana in
interviews with Saroja G. Poilblan from 2008
up to early 2010
Edited with additional text by Daniel Tigner

American Mystic: Memoirs of a Happy Man is a joint publication of
Inquiry Books, Gatineau, Quebec, Canada and
AHAM, Asheboro, North Carolina, USA.

Saroja G. Poilblan, Inquiry Books
35 Hawthorne Street
Gatineau, Quebec, Canada J9H 3Y2
www.inquirybooks.com
Email: info@inquirybooks.com

Interviews for this Book by Saroja G. Poilblan
Edited with Additional Text by Daniel Tigner
Cover and Book Design by Daniel Tigner
Cover Photo of Ramana by Saroja G. Poiblan
Book Layout ©2015 BookDesignTemplates.com
Interview transcription: Paulette Hayes

American Mystic: Memoirs of a Happy Man / A. Ramana. -- 1st ed. POD-CS
ISBN 978-0-9683658-9-2

ACKNOWLEDGMENTS

Thanks to Gayle Leona Jabour for her assistance in proofreading, and to Enid Page for reading every draft of the manuscript and providing valuable comments and advice.

Contents

PREFACE xv

PROLOGUE xix

PART 1 - From Childhood to Young Man (1929 to 1953) 1

1 The Accident 3

2 First Experiences 17

3 Teen Years 21

4 A Young Man Goes Out Into the World 31

PART 2 - The Pursuit of Happiness (1953 to 1973) 61

5 The Salesman: Pursuing the American Dream 63

6 Kicked Out of Heaven 89

7 The World Is Not the Cause of Happiness 111

8 Flashes of Success 117

9 History Repeating Itself 129

PART 3 - Self-Realization (1973 to 1978) 141

10 Awakening 143

Dialogue on Awakening 1 - Our Higher Nature 149

11 Giving It All Away 151

Dialogue on Awakening 2 - Getting Your Sea Legs 159

12 Teaching Meditation 163

Dialogue on Awakening 3 - Seeing "Others" 169

13 Gurus 177

Dialogue on Awakening 4 - Freeing Ourselves from Entanglement 190

14 Will You Marry Me? 195

Dialogue on Awakening 5 - Liberation 209

PART 4 - A Vision of Happiness (1978 to 1984) 217

15 AHAM (Association of Happiness of All Mankind): A
Wonderful Vision 219

Dialogue on Awakening 6 - The *Sense of I*..........................229

16 Early Years of AHAM (1978 to 1981)..............................235

Dialogue on Awakening 7 - AHAM's Core Teaching......................246

17 Encountering Resistance..251

Dialogue on Awakening 8 - Who Is Ready for the Spiritual Path.....263

PART 5 - Sacred Journeys (1984 to 2009)............................271

18 Arunachala Ramana in India for the First Time 273

Dialogue on Awakening 9 - Grace 291

19 Satsang (Spiritual Talks) 299

Elizabeth - A Pilgrimage to India..................................313

Dialogue on Awakening 10 - Some Final Words 317

PART 6 - Completion: Remembering Ramana (1929 to 2010) 325

Stan: My Journey with Ramana.......................................327

Vivian: Taking Care of a Master 335

Jan: Completion - Arunachala Ramana's Passing......................345

Arunachala Ramana's Samadhi - Creating a Sacred Place for Meditation ..352

Ganesan Speaks about Arunachala Ramana's Passing...................357

Saroja's Experience of Meditation in Ramana's Samadhi 365

Glossary for American Mystic 371

References, Suggested Reading and Websites 375

Arunachala Ramana Books 375

AHAM Contact Information 376

Videos of Arunachala Ramana and Osho 376

The Writings of Bhagavan Sri Ramana Maharshi..............................377

Writings about Living with Bhagavan Sri Ramana Maharshi..........378

Picture Books 379

Websites of Interest...379

Recommended Spiritual Biographies...380

Books by Authors Mentioned in American Mystic 381

Books on India 382

List of Images

Arunachala Ramana, born Dee Wayne Ray, early 1990s.....................xiii

Ramana, circa 1950.. 1

Texas 1935, in the midst of the Great Depression..............................2

Ramana with black dog...4

Tent home of migrants near Harlingen, Texas, 1939.........................6

Ramana around eight years old...9

Dust storm approaching Stratford, Texas, April 18, 1935.....................16

Dust Storm, Amarillo, Texas, 1936..18

Ramana in ROTC..22

Ramana aged fifteen..25

The Trammells - Ramana with his father and mother............................26

Ramana with his father and a girlfriend..27

Ramana at eighteen...33

Ramana near age twenty...37

1951 Chevrolet Deluxe Bel Air Hardtop Coupé.....................................50

U.S. troops in Korea, August 6, 1950.................... 54

Advertisement for Arthur Murray's dance system, January 1922 56

Veloz and Yolanda in a scene from the 1937 film Champagne Waltz...59

Ramana late thirties..61

The movie *Giant* playing in Dallas, circa 1956...................................62

Napoleon Hill, 1937...67

Ramana in his late twenties or early thirties...79

Unity Tower, Unity Village, Missouri...95

Ramana, circa 1965..110

Neville Goddard as a young man...115

Mankind First Lands on the Moon, July 20, 1969................................128

Earthrise over the moon..138

Bhagavan Sri Ramana Maharshi, circa 1949, "Tilted Welling Bust" ..141

Portrait of Arunachala Ramana in Meditation, Pencil on Paper.......142

Bhagavan Sri Ramana Maharshi, circa 1949, "Welling Bust"..............146

Ramana greeting people at a Satsang with Namaste...........................149

Ramana and Saroja greeting with Namaste...161

Ramana and friends, "conscious company," in dialogue.....................171

Ramana singing during a Christmas celebration 172

Ramana in his mid to late forties, with friends...................................181

Ramana at dinner in Gatineau, Quebec, Canada.................................191

Ramana in dialogue with Jason, age 11...192

Ramana in dialogue with a student at mealtime,.................................211

The logo of AHAM (Association of Happiness for All Mankind)......217

Ramana, 2005...218

Bhagavan Sri Ramana Maharshi, circa 1942.......................................224

Elizabeth..227

Ramana wearing shirt with AHAM logo..249

Ramana giving AHAM seminar, 1981................................254

The main building of AHAM, Asheboro, North Carolina.................261

The lake at AHAM, Asheboro, North Carolina....................262

Ramana speaking at AHAM, Asheboro, circa 1993...........267

Arunachala, The Sacred Mountain, Tiruvannamalai, India.............271

Ramana in his fifties.. 272

Bhagavan Sri Ramana Maharshi, circa 1949......................274

The Arunachaleswara Temple complex seen from Arunachala..........275

Inside the Arunachaleswara Temple complex....................276

The Adi Annamalai Temple..............................277

Ramana in his mid fifties..281

Sri Ramanasramam, Tiruvannamalai, India...................282

Annamalai Swami and Ramana, circa 1992......................286

Maniswami, circa 2005..289

Bhagavan Sri Ramana Maharshi in Lotus pose, 1915-17.............291

Ramana and friends, 2008 293

White Peacock, a symbol of grace, at Sri Ramanasramam.............296

Patricia..302

Elizabeth, Ramana and Swami Ramanananda......................304

One of the towers of the Arunachaleswara Temple 306

Friends attending Ramana's fifth Death Anniversary (2015)............309

Kumarasamy during construction of AHAM Ashram, India..........310

Charlotte...311

The Sanctuary in`the AHAM Ashram, Tiruvannamalai, India.........312

Elizabeth, Ottawa, Canada, 2001.............................313

Elizabeth and Ramana, circa 2008.............................315

Ramana and Saroja, Ottawa, Canada 2001...................318

Ramana's resting place (Samadhi)..324

Flowers around the photo of Ramana at his Samadhi........................325

Performing Puja rituals..326

Stan, 2015...327

Stan and Ramana saying hello...332

Vivian reading to children, 2008...335

Students at the Arunachala Village School listening......................336

Vivian, beside Ramana, taking notes during Satsang, 2008.................339

The day following Ramana's passing (February 16, 2010) 340

Ramana coming out to the portico for Satsang.............................344

Jan and Ramana enjoying children 345

Ramana Washing Car, Ottawa, Canada 2001..................................347

The AHAM logo carved into the wood of door panels 348

Bhagavan Sri Ramana Maharshi, 1940-42....................................349

Ramana's room, AHAM Ashram, Tiruvannamalai, India........................351

The hole for Ramana's Samadhi is being lined with brick..................353

Vivian and Jan watching the placing of the Shiva Lingam..................355

Ganesan at the fifth celebration marking Ramana's passing................357

Arunachala...359

Ganesan putting flowers into the burial chamber of Ramana................362

Ganesan in a moment of prayer by the burial chamber of Ramana....363

Arunachala seen from the roof of the AHAM Ashram.........................364

Saroja at the Sri Ramanasramam in 1998...................................365

Saroja helping with the morning Puja at Ramana's Samadhi.................367

Saroja with basket of flowers for morning Puja 368

Arunachala Ramana, 2008..370

Bhagavan, circa 1949...377

.

This book is dedicated to all those
seeking true and lasting happiness.

"All that I have told you about my life - as it unfolded and ultimately resulted in my awakening into the awareness of being - has been to share aspects of my awakening with those who would find it of benefit to them in their own awakening."

—ARUNACHALA RAMANA

Arunachala Ramana, born Dee Wayne Ray, early 1990s.

AHAM archives.

"We hold these truths to be self-evident, that all men are created equal, that they are endowed by their Creator with certain unalienable Rights, that among these are Life, Liberty and the pursuit of Happiness."

UNITED STATES DECLARATION OF INDEPENDENCE

PREFACE

Normally, the author of a memoir writes his own preface, but in this case, Arunachala Ramana has passed on (1929 to 2010). Since I interviewed him and recorded his life story for *Ramana - American Mystic: Memoirs of a Happy Man*, presenting the scope and purpose of this book falls to me. I write it with both pleasure and trepidation, because Ramana was a big man in every way, a beautiful man, and a true mystic. As a young man, he was handsome and, growing up in Texas and spending most of his life in the southern states, he spoke with the charming accent of the American South. I have always envisioned Ramana's life as a movie, a feature film about an independently thinking man, who spoke his mind and lived life to the fullest - and, as unlikely as it might seem, pursued and found a permanent and lasting happiness.

Spiritual biographies are a popular genre - I surmise, from my own reading - because they have the power to help people connect with their own quest to find out who they are. That is, after all, the *raison d'être* of the spiritual search, and, Ramana's story is particularly worth knowing in that regard. His story is gripping, frankly told, providing a fascinating glimpse into American culture and history beginning in the Great Depression and ending in the new millennium. His struggles, adventures and inner search, culminated on June 4, 1973 in his having a homecoming, an Awakening with a capital A. How many people can actually say that they have "awakened" or "found happiness?" Ramana did – and in these memoirs, he shares his journey and his thoughts about how this can happen for all of us.

The memoirs were extracted from more than twenty interviews I had with Ramana in 2008 and 2009. Our conversations mostly took place via Skype (online, digitally recorded as we sat face to face in front of our respective computers) while he was in the United States or India and I was in Canada. The last interviews, though, were in person; I spoke with Ramana on my last visit to the Arunachala Ramana AHAM Ashram in Tiruvannamali, India from December 2009 to mid-January 2010. Ramana's memoirs are also an international love story between two worlds, India and America. Ramana attributed the spark for his awakening to his seeing a picture in a book of the great Indian mystic Bhagavan Sri Ramana Maharshi (1879 to 1950) and it is Bhagavan's teachings which are at the core of what is taught at AHAM (Association of Happiness for All Mankind), the spiritual institute Ramana created.

The first five chapters of his memoirs had been completed by the time of my arrival in India in December of 2009, and, hence, I was able to read them to Ramana. This was just a few months before he passed from his body on February 15, 2010. I am immensely grateful that he enjoyed them and gave his blessing and full support to the work. He told me clearly that he wanted to see the project completed and a book published. It was Ramana's conscious intention that his memoirs transcend the personal and bring people to the spiritual Journey. "I'm sharing this story - and it's important that it is authentic and true – but it is still not who I am," he said. "It's a history of the body-mind... It's the spiritual quest that is important."

Ramana would love it if many people read this book, especially if in doing so, they feel invited to probe more deeply into who they are, the nature of the true Self, and discover the possibility of spiritual awakening.

Namaste,

Saroja - 2015

PROLOGUE

The accident occurred during the winter when I was five years old. I was sitting in a little rocking chair next to the stove to keep warm, while my father was boiling water for coffee in a tin saucepan, which held a quart and a half or two quarts of water. It was badly banged up, did not sit well on the stove and wobbled as the water heated, but it was all we had. When the water was boiling, my father inadvertently hit it with his arm as he passed, knocking it off the stove onto my lap, burning my left leg all the way from my thigh down to my ankle.

It was a terrible burn.

In that small town, there was no hospital, only an itinerant doctor, and he was not in his office. That's when they went to get Uncle Billy, a hermit living way back in the woods.

Uncle Billy was considered to be strange by all the people in the area. In reality, Uncle Billy was a *Jnani* (an awakened one) and his treatment was of a psychic nature. He rubbed his hands back and forth about an inch above my leg and whispered something in my ear, and, just like that, with a snap of the fingers, the pain left me and I was out of my body. I was no longer identified with the body, even though I was connected with the body, and I saw the body, and was aware that I was in the body. I remained in that state for perhaps another two or three years, I don't remember exactly; but, then I lost that state…

PART 1

From Childhood to Young Man (1929 to 1953)

Ramana, circa 1950. *AHAM archives.*

Texas 1935, in the midst of the Great Depression. Old time professional migratory laborer camping on the outskirts of Perryton, Texas, at opening of wheat harvest. *Photo: Dorothea Lange, Library of Congress, Public Domain.*

CHAPTER 1

The Accident

I was born in El Paso, Texas on November 1, 1929. Three days before I was born, the stock market crashed, beginning the Great Depression (October 28, 1929, "Black Monday"). My father had a problem finding work as there was not much to be had. Also, he was not well-educated, never having completed high school, although he was capable of reading and writing, and doing arithmetic. He had a functional education, but not enough to get meaningful, gainful employment and he always had to rely on his wits and innate abilities to earn money.

I remember a picture of my dad squatting, holding my hand. I don't remember when it was taken and I don't remember it being taken; but he's wearing a revolver, a gun he'd had for many years as a Deputy Constable in El Paso, where my parents lived when they adopted me.

My birth mother was unwed. Her name was Rachel Elizabeth and her maiden name was Taylor. I only learned that when I was sixteen and got a copy of my birth certificate. My birth certificate showed John Sylvester Ray as my father, but I learned much later he was not my true father, but my birth name was given as Dee Wayne Ray (Ramana's last name became Trammell, the family name of his adopted parents, so his full legal name was Dee Wayne Trammell. *ed.*).

In 1929, when a woman had a child out of wedlock, she was pretty much branded, so my birth mother, Rachel Elizabeth Taylor, was not considered to be a "nice" woman. But she was friends with the people who became my parents. My foster mother, whom I always felt to be my real mother, used to babysit me when my mother was away working; sometimes she babysat me for days at a time.

Now, the first thing I actually remember is a photograph being taken of me when I was just a little boy, somewhere around the age of two or three, probably in Dallas, Texas (After El Paso we moved to Dallas). I was standing in a "window seat," wearing a little overcoat. It was convenient for my mother to dress me in the window seat, as it was probably two feet deep. That day I was dressed in my good clothes. Most of my early life I had about three sets of clothes: those I wore to school, those I wore after school and could get dirty or do anything in, like chores ... and special clothes I wore only on special occasions, such as going to church, so I wouldn't wear them out.

Ramana with black dog. *AHAM archives..*

Another memory I have is of a beautiful dog I used to play with, a collie. Somehow or other that dog contracted a type of rabies called "dumb" rabies, meaning that the dog's mouth was locked and it was not capable of biting people as a dog with rabies would normally do, but they were concerned that I might have gotten infected with the rabies virus. So, I had to have rabies shots for two weeks in my stomach. I would first take shots on one side one day and shots on the other side the next day. These shots were very painful.

I remember having to go to the doctor. I'd start crying as soon as I was in his office, because I knew what was going to happen, but the doctor made up a game for me that helped overcome my dread. He would take the syringe used to inject me, remove the needle, and fill it with water, then squirt the water across the room. He'd then pass it to me and let me squirt the water.

In Dallas my father was not able to work, but then he got a job, along with his brother, my uncle, working in the salt mines in a little town in East Texas called Grand Saline, a Spanish name meaning "great salt." The Morton Salt company had what was considered to be the largest natural deposit of salt anywhere in the world. It was huge, and all of the mine was underground.

So, we moved from Dallas to Grand Saline; that would have been about 1934.

That is the first time I remember having any friends. I remember one in particular, a boy about my age whose name was Freddie Lee Tippit. My parents used to call him Freddie Lee, but he was called Fred as he got older. He had an older brother and two older sisters. They, along with other neighbors, lived up the road at the edge of the woods.

There was a trail we used take to go between houses, as there were no roads. The house where Freddie Lee and his family lived was really a shack with tar paper on the walls. They were very poor - like my family: it was the depression and we had little or no money, in fact, we didn't even have a house to live in.

My father got permission from our neighbor, Mr. George, to squat on his property, which was right at the edge of a woods. My parents built a floor base which had sides on it going up about four or five feet.

Then my dad bought a canvas tent for the top. You had to step up to go into the tent, but there was a regular front door to it.

So, that was where we lived, that one room tent. Inside was a wood stove with four burners and an oven. We cooked on it and, in winter, used it to heat the tent. There were poles at each of the four corners and during the summer, we would roll the canvas up so that the breeze would blow through and it wouldn't be so hot.

Tent home of migrants near Harlingen, Texas, 1939.
Photo: Russell Lee, Library of Congress, Public Domain.

And, it was there, living in that tent that the accident occurred.

When I got burned, when the pot of water fell into my lap, it didn't take long for our neighbors to hear about it. Right away, some older boys raced on their bikes into town to tell the doctor to come. It was seven or eight miles. This was a very small town with only three streets: Main Street and two streets on either side of it with US Highway 80 running perpendicular to them.

The doctor had a car and would make house calls; as it turned out, he wasn't in. He was somewhere else making a call. There being no other doctor, and no place else to take me, the neighbors suggested getting Uncle Billy, the hermit, who was rumored to have the ability to take the heat out of fire. My mother and father had heard about him, although, no one really knew him.

My mother was beside herself, as was my father. They were under such stress due to the pain and suffering I was going through; I was just screaming with every breath, the pain was so intense. So when a neighbor said to go get Uncle Billy, my mother said, "Anything, anything."

And so, they went to where Uncle Billy lived a couple of miles or so down a foot trail, way back in the woods. There was no way to get to his home other than by taking this trail.

He lived in a small shack. It was November and the weather that day was cold rain and sleet. I remember that. The Harvel and the Tippit boys went on horseback and on bike to get him as quickly as they could, and a couple of hours passed before they returned to the house. The accident happened early in the morning and now it was late morning.

In those days, all the neighbors would pitch in and do whatever they could to help one another out. When Uncle Billy arrived neighbors were already there and there wasn't room for more than two or three in our house, along with my mother and father. Uncle Billy just motioned everyone out of my room, out of the tent, with his hand, shooing them away. He did not say a word to anyone.

I was in my bed, which was an old army cot with a canvas top. I slept on a couple of quilts and blankets, as a base for a mattress. Uncle Billy sat down on a crate by my left side. As I was lying there, he just moved his left hand back and forth about an inch above my leg, very slowly, never touching the burn. His right hand he moved over my chest and sometimes up on my head, back and forth between my chest and my head, touching me in my heart area. At the same time he whispered something in my ear, I don't know what exactly, maybe a mantra. I was the only one in the room, as everyone else he'd shooed out. So, no one saw what happened to me, but I remember. Snap, just like that, the pain was gone!!! I suddenly was floating in the room.

I felt myself as Being, in Being, in my own Being; knowing my own Being was not different from his own Being and that the Being I Am was the Being in which everything is and was occurring. I knew all of this without words. I had no words in those days: as a child, I couldn't explain it. It was going on, but I had no way of explaining it. And, I stayed in that knowledge, that state, for about two or three years.

It was extremely delightful.

This new 'state of being' helped me deal with all the excruciating pain that resulted from the accident; because I was able to feel a "gap" between me and the pain.

My mother bought a supposed burn remedy, an ointment called 'Unguentine,' and put a whole large tube of it over my leg. She shouldn't have used it. The burn was too extreme; my whole leg formed into a solid blister.

I was wearing long corduroy winter overalls, the kind that have a strap over the shoulders and buttons on either side. Well, when my mother realized what had happened, she tore them completely off me.

It didn't take long for those blisters to burst, and, as a result, I got blood poisoning and it took months of treatment before it healed. For a long time, I had to go daily to the doctor's office to have my bandages changed. The bandages would stick to my leg, and he would remove them slowly until he reached a point where he could more or less just rip them off. The doctor was very compassionate, it was the best he could do. I would cry and scream; and, when that particular pain would finally end, I would fall back to the Awareness that had awakened in me where I was free of the body, prior to the body.

After my awakening, it was impossible for me to communicate with my parents or with anyone else around me about my experience. I didn't have words to put to it. On occasion, I attempted to explain where I was and where I was coming from, but there was no one who could understand. I remember saying to my mother, "Can you see this or that?" and her getting frustrated and saying, "Oh, you're talking crazy."

Ramana around eight years old, during period of being awakened. *AHAM archives.*

I went in and out of that state - it wasn't constant - I could more or less just recall it by simply relaxing into it.

I had a couple of places I enjoyed going by myself back behind our house.

Our house was up high and in the back there was a decline. Being a kid, the decline seemed like it was very big. It was grassy and there were a couple of huge trees and I would lie on that decline and see through the trees into the sky. While lying there, I would sense that I was abiding in Awareness and I was really no different than the trees. It wasn't an objective experience; it was subjective - because I could feel myself, in a manner of speaking, as being no different than anything around me.

I would watch the birds in the trees. A lot of Blue Jays and Sparrows would come and I would watch them as they'd fly and I'd have this great desire to fly with them. It was almost as if I felt I really was flying myself when I watched them.

I'm telling you now how I felt then, but at that time, I had no way of describing it, words didn't come to me. Any time I'd say that I felt close to the trees, or like the trees, my mother would tell me I was talking crazy.

In a way, my father was more understanding. He loved just to sit still. He loved to fish and he had built a small row boat that he kept at Carrington's Lake. We would have to row a long distance from where the boat was kept to our fishing spots. We'd fish with poles and line. My dad would occasionally use a rod and reel, but I would always use a pole. While sitting there fishing, I was able to go into that state of Awareness. I felt my father did, too, in his own way.

We very seldom carried on a conversation, because we were so involved in the fishing. My dad would look at the cork in the water and when a fish would bite, he would be ready. We'd fish all day long from early morning to late afternoon, we'd just sit there. I think my Dad was meditating. He didn't really know that was what he was doing. When we were out there on the lake fishing, and I was trying to explain to him my state of Awareness, he would only say, "Be quiet."

So, I never really had anyone to whom I could describe this state. Perhaps Uncle Billy may have been able to help and probably would have if I'd been able to talk to him; but I didn't have the opportunity. I went back to his cabin in the woods two or three times. I remember that he was very kind and compassionate to animals. He had several cages of animals that were sick or wounded and he would nurse them back to health.

Uncle Billy was so different from everyone in that area. He had a thick, long beard and long hair. He never shaved nor ever cut his hair; and he wore old tattered clothes. There was a creek, not too far from his cabin, where he got water. He had buckets of water and he didn't take many baths: he didn't smell very good and he didn't look clean. So, yes, he was kind and compassionate; but, because he was considered to be so strange, everybody in the area looked at him as suspect, without understanding. So, I only went a few times to see him before I was told not to go there anymore. I had to obey my mother and father. After that I never heard anything about him or what happened to him.

I was somewhere around five years old when the 'Awakening' happened. And, I must have been somewhere around seven or eight when I lost it. And, on the occasion of losing it, it was in the evening and my father was not home.

My mother, who was an excellent cook, had fixed dinner. We were meat eaters in those days. We didn't have a lot of meat, but occasionally my mother would buy ground beef from the grocery store. We also raised our own chickens. On this particular evening, my mother made homemade chili, a Mexican-style chili with beef and chili powders. I remember this occasion pretty much like yesterday.

I was an extremely slow eater.

The reason I was slow – and I could never describe this to my mother – I saw no difference in the food I was eating and my own body.

Anything objective was just an expression of the Awareness I was, knowing really that I was not my body. But in those days I didn't know how to say that, and this would cause me to eat very slowly, because I delighted in watching myself eat. I was eating me. I was watching the fact that the food I was eating and chewing and taking so long to eat, was me eating myself. And I couldn't explain that to anyone.

My mother was always wanting me to hurry up and finish my meal, because she wanted to clean up and be about other things she had to do. So, when I would take so long eating, she would get very impatient, irritated and upset with me. And, on this one occasion, I was, as on many other occasions, enjoying the taste and the sensation of my food, when my mother came up behind me (the table was off to the side of the room and I had my back to the room) – took her fist and banged it very hard on the table crying "God dammit!!! Will you hurry up?"

She had already asked me a couple of times before to hurry up and I didn't, but the combination of her banging on the table, the tableware jumping off and my cup falling on the floor and breaking, shocked me so much I lost that state of Awareness.

I just started gobbling my food down and I finished the whole bowl in five or six bites.

After losing that state of Awareness I fell back into the soup of ordinary life - like my mother and everyone else. I was no longer able to regain that state as I had before. Each time I tried, I couldn't get it to come back. I completely lost it except for on rare occasions, when without my doing anything, it might come back momentarily, just enough to keep me frustrated.

That state of Awareness was now in the past. I became desperate to have that state again, it was so blissful. I would pray for it. I was in the turmoil of the ordinary life everybody else was going through, with all the typical upsets and complaints, likes and dislikes. And there was nothing I could do about it. I just had to live through it like anybody else.

From then on my quest began - to regain that Awareness I knew intuitively to be my true natural state.

It was probably in my first year of school that I lost my state of Awareness. I was very frustrated by this loss. I began to wet my bed and I was punished severely for it, as though I'd done something terribly wrong. It would scare me if I woke up in the night knowing I had wet the bed, because I knew I was in for it – I would be beaten for doing it.

I'd also sometimes soil my pants in school.

My first grade teacher, Mrs. Rayburn, was very kind and I think she sensed there was something different about me. I would talk to her and she would just nod her head, even though I don't think she knew what I was talking about. She was very encouraging and compassionate.

Still, I was afraid to admit to her that I had wet myself. She would take me out of the room or send me home. And I knew when I'd get home I'd probably be in for another beating. That was a terrible time in my life.

My father was a World War I army veteran and he received what was called a mustering out check that had been owed to him all the way back eighteen or twenty years. There had even been a time when veterans from World War I marched on Washington - soldiers, sailors, and marines. Finally, when my father received the check, he used the money to buy lumber and build us a house. He bought about four or five acres of property near to where we lived in the tent house. You could actually see it from there. My father did a lot of work on the house, my uncle helped, as well as neighbors, some with carpentry skills. Everyone worked together and finished building our house.

When I was around the age of seven in 1936, my father had a very serious accident and was almost killed. He was unconscious and in a coma for fourteen days. We didn't know whether he was going to come back or not.

I was never able to communicate with my father about what he experienced in the coma. I understood that his state was similar to the state of Awareness that I had experienced. He was reluctant to talk about it. I believe he had a near-death experience, and that resulted in a state of consciousness that he neither fully understood nor could explain and which caused him fear. When he came back to regular awareness, his whole disposition, his whole manner, his whole outlook changed. He got what you call religious.

The only religion he knew anything about was from when he was a boy, which happened to be a very fundamentalist church: the Church of Christ, which is pretty well known in the South, in America. I was required, as well as my mother, to start going to church because my father did.

My parents were extremely strict: I'm not saying this in criticism or judgment. They were always afraid something might happen, that I might do something I shouldn't - yet I was not a bad boy. I was always a good child. I never did things I shouldn't do. I was not a delinquent child. I was very well-mannered and respected my elders. I was always taught that when walking down the street in the small town, where I grew up during my formative years, if I was on the sidewalk and an adult was approaching, and there was not enough room for both of us, I was to step aside and make room for the adult to pass - that kind of thing. I was reared with rules that I lived by. I was taught all these by my parents and I am grateful they did that.

I got interested in the Bible. I asked for and was given one that is called The Red Letter Bible. It was thick and huge, with big type and had all of the words spoken by Jesus in red letters. It was really easy to thumb through the New Testament and pick out at a glance when Jesus was speaking.

I was in love with Jesus. I intuitively knew that Jesus was coming from where I was coming from before I lost the experience of Awareness. The fundamentalist Christians called him the "only son of God" - which I somewhat accepted - but I also felt that his work was to bring people into the Awareness that I had experienced and that I was trying to experience again. And so that was how my spiritual quest continued, even though the fundamentalist Christians of the churches that I went to could not understand where I was coming from. I felt that they were not understanding the real message that Jesus was sharing. I enjoyed going to church and I continued to go to church even beyond what my mother and father did. It kept alive the memory of the consciousness that I had experienced when I had the burn.

There was a long period in which there was no experience of the state of Awareness, but remembrance of the state stayed with me like a very vivid dream, except I knew it was not a dream. Remembering and trying to regain it, was always in the back of my mind, in the background. Occasionally, the memory of it would come into the foreground, although the actual state of Awareness did not come back until I was much older.

Dust storm approaching Stratford, Texas, April 18, 1935.
Photo: George E. Marsh, National Oceanic and Atmospheric Administration's
(NOAA) National Weather Service (NWS) Collection, Public Domain.

CHAPTER 2

First Experiences

Every year at Christmas when I was just a kid, we would stay with my grandmother who lived in the little town of Slaton in West Texas. We were still living in the small town of Grand Saline, and one year my grandmother was not well so we stayed with her during the summer school break.

My grandmother actually owned and lived in an old hotel near a train station that was built away from the town. It was the only hotel, but times had changed, and it didn't have many regular guests. It was three stories tall and the top floor was no longer used. A lot of things were just stored in the rooms up there. The second floor was also used partly for storage and the main floor had a big kitchen and dining room because a lot of people used to stay there during the oil boom when the hotel was built.

I don't think the hotel still exists, though I've never been back there.

My Uncle Henry and his wife, my Aunt Sally, lived there and took care of my grandmother. He was my favorite uncle - my dad had three brothers and a sister – and he happened to be my dad's next to youngest brother. There was my Aunt Lilly, who was older than all of them, my Uncle Pat, my dad, my Uncle Henry and my Uncle Jess. I thought they were my blood relatives - and I was included as one of the family - except that I was adopted. I told you already that I didn't know that I was adopted until I was sixteen years old; it was a tremendous shock when I learned about it. On the other hand, it was also a relief, because I was always feeling so out of place.

Dust Storm, Amarillo, Texas, 1936. Slaton was affected by the dust storms that struck in the Dust Bowl in the late 1920s and the 1930s. *Photo: Arthur Rothstein, Franklin D. Roosevelt Presidential Library and Museum, Public Domain.*

I remember running around and playing mostly in the hotel that summer. I hardly went away from it, but there were some boys - a few about my age, and one, the leader of the group, was a few years older than me - who I occasionally played with away from the hotel. My mother didn't particularly approve of me playing or associating with them, but it was okay to a point.

These boys used me as a whipping post so to speak. Not literally, because they were not beating me, but they would play tricks on me and get me to go along, because I was just a kid who didn't know differently. I wanted to be accepted and be a member of the club and so I agreed to go along with whatever they told me to do. Each one of them wanted me to do a little something and some of those things had a sexual connotation.

Well, I had never even thought of such things before. After doing what they asked me to do in order for me to be in the club, they turned on me and started ridiculing me. I didn't even know what I had done. I didn't know there was anything wrong with it. I went running home crying - not because of what I had done – but because they had lied to me, and they weren't going to let me be a member.

I told my mother and my aunt what had happened and later they told my uncle. He really got all over the boys next time he saw them, as did my aunt and my mother in their own way. Of course, I was no longer allowed to have anything to do with them. They were the only boys around, so I didn't have anybody to play with for the rest of the time we were there.

That was the first time I knew anything at all about sex and when we got home, I told my buddy Fred Ely and his sister, Janita, about my adventure. They laughed at me, and Fred's sister, who was about two or three years older than both of us, and was already beginning to have her own interest in sex, started teaching us and playing around with me.

I enjoyed the sensations I experienced, and that was it. One day, when we were a little older, I was down at a little pond near their house fishing for crawfish when Janita came by. I was there by myself and I didn't know where her brother was or anyone else.

Janita saw me and said, "Would you like to jig?"

I knew what she meant and I said, "Yeah."

She said there's no one home at her house so we could go up there.

That was the first time I had ever done it in a bed - all the other times it was somewhere in the woods - and I had my first orgasm. It was a delightful experience of course, and it also scared the daylights out of me.

I thought, "What is this?" I didn't even know what it was.

It felt good and then I ran home. It really scared me, and of course I didn't tell anybody, but went to my spot on the deep decline where I often used to lie and remained there just considering it.

That experience of orgasm had begun to bring back the qualities of the transcendental experience that I had had in my accident and it was the first time I began to link the sexual experience, sexual ecstasy, together with the spiritual experience.

CHAPTER 3

Teen Years

As a teenage boy I felt like a fish out of water, displaced. I had a very strong feeling of incompatibility with regard to my life and my relationship with my parents. I didn't know why, I just did. I also felt out of alignment with everyone in the world. There was no way I could frame that in any way that I could communicate. I felt they were in another world than the one I was in and this was one of those things that had carried forth from those two or three years in which I was in a state of awareness.

We had moved from the small town of Grand Saline to Dallas where my father got a job as a security guard. We bought a small modest house in a new development and watched it being built. Here I lived most of my life when I was in school. I was a little freer, I had a few more friends, though none of my friends knew about that state that I had been in: I may have talked about it to one or two of them, but they didn't understand what I was talking about.

I wanted to play the trumpet, and so my parents bought me one. I took lessons and played in the Junior High School band. The band marched and played at football games. I even gave a concert. When I graduated to High School I had to choose between entering the Reserve

Officers' Training Corps (ROTC) and being in the band. I chose the ROTC because a number of my friends had chosen it and one of my friend's brothers was an officer.

The ROTC was typically offered in USA high schools and colleges, so that a young person could participate in it and get training to go all the way through into the military, potentially becoming a commissioned officer. Well I never went that far. I only received the rank of a Sergeant in the ROTC. Frankly, I didn't like the structure, but still I remained in it up through my senior year.

Ramana in ROTC. *AHAM archives.*

Much later when I joined the Army, ROTC was of great assistance through basic military training. I got the temporary rank of a Sergeant because I knew how to train people in close order drill and I wore Sergeant stripes on my arm outside the sleeve of my garment.

I was among the first high school students in the state of Texas to take driver education in school and get a driver's license through the Driver's Education Program. My father's and my picture were in the newspaper. It made my father's chest about to burst to have his picture in the newspaper even if it didn't make that much difference to me; what was important to me was I had my driver's license and I was now able to drive. But my father would not let me drive our family automobile, because he thought that I would be using it to get into trouble. Here I was the first one in the state of Texas to get a driver's license through driver's education, and my father would not let me drive the family automobile, even with him and my mother in the car! My dad was very controlling.

The summer when I was sixteen, I went to summer school and also got a job working for the Neiman Marcus Department Store, a small but highly exclusive chain. They had the most expensive items and only the well-to-do, the rich or upper-middle class were customers. A high school friend also worked at Neiman Marcus and after finishing school we would rush to catch a streetcar, which had cables and ran on tracks, to go downtown to work. We worked throughout the summer and did such a good job that we were asked to continue even when summer school was finished and we went back to ordinary school. That gave us both some money. I could save and use my money for whatever I wanted.

Well, it was during that period of time my father put some strong after school restrictions on me. After work I would have to rush home to do chores. My father felt that by having the responsibility to do home chores, I would keep out of trouble.

I was not a delinquent, yet my father still insisted on this strict discipline, and the restrictions became too intense. He would just create work for me to do, things that didn't make any sense, just so that I would remain busy. It reached the point that I said to him I didn't think it was fair and he replied, "Well, you can take it or leave it."

I began to feel that I could not tolerate it any more. I wanted to leave home and was in the process of packing a suitcase when my mother confronted me in her frustration and anger, "I'm going to tell you something you do not know, something your father and I never told you. We are not your real parents."

I had always felt something in my life was not right. I did not know what it was, so I thought, "My God, that's what it is, these are really not my parents."

The way my mother told me about my having been adopted was not very positive nor gentle. I am sure, even though she never said it, that later on she regretted the way she had told me, but on that occasion, she defended herself and dad, saying how they had sacrificed for me, did without, so they could provide for me, give me a home and the things that I wanted. It felt as if I had done something wrong in being adopted. We both began crying and so I didn't leave home, though the pressure was never really relieved until I finally did leave a while later.

That came about one day when I was late getting home after work. I had to rush to get the trolley car in order to catch the transfer to a bus that went to our part of town, and I missed the bus. In missing the bus I didn't get home in time to be able to complete the list of things my father wanted me to do and again when I said something I was told I either had to take it or leave it. I answered by leaving.

I had a job and I figured I would be able to make it on my own and still continue to finish school. That day I went to work with my suitcase and told my buddy, Joe, that I had left home. He thought I was kidding at first, until I showed him my suitcase and he knew I was serious. He had known about my situation and my dissatisfaction. So he called his parents and asked them if I could come to their home and share his bedroom.

Ramana aged fifteen. *AHAM archives.*

I stayed with them for about a month, paying them for the room and for meals. His mother would make Joe and me lunches that we would take to school. I was pretty happy living there (I tried to find Joe years later, I asked about him at the high school fifty-year reunion, but nobody knew what happened to him), and during my stay with him, I felt liberated from my parents. Joe's parents were communicating with my parents attempting to tell them that I was considerate and courteous and that they needed to ease up on me and allow me more freedom, which they finally agreed to do.

And so when my father came to get me in the car, he handed me the keys and let me drive home. After that, he would allow me to use the car on special occasions, even to go out on dates, for example, to my senior prom.

I wanted to go to the prom with Marietta, my high school sweetheart, but someone else had asked her. That kind of crushed me, and I ended up going with a girl who didn't have a date with whom I was a pretty good friend.

The Trammells - Ramana with his father
and mother. *AHAM archives.*

Marietta and I were not destined to have an ongoing romantic relationship, even though we are still in communication with each other today. She was an entertainer and very popular and was working on a career after school. Her mother was a stage mother and constantly pushing her. Marietta had a very good voice and not only sang in school functions but worked as a singer at a nightclub. Her mother would go and sit the entire time in the clubs as a chaperone and a number of times I would sit with her while Marietta was working, and when she had a break, she would come and sit at the table with us. In her senior year, she was a singer with the Tommy Dorsey Orchestra, a world famous Big Band. Later she went on to have her own television program called "Midnight with Marietta." She married a producer of that television show and was in quite a number of movies. The most popular one was "The Texas Chain Saw Massacre," not a pleasant movie - I wouldn't watch it - but it brought her a certain amount of notoriety.

Ramana with his father and a girlfriend. *AHAM archives.*

I saw her again after forty-five years at our fifty-year high school reunion in Dallas in 1997 and we now email and talk occasionally over the telephone.

During high school I dropped going to the Church of Christ that my parents attended. It was a relatively small church and did not have much in the way of activities for young people, other than traditional Sunday school. I lost interest in it and finally I told my parents I wanted to go to another church. There was one in a part of town called Oak Cliff, a considerable distance away. The Trinity River runs right through the city of Dallas and Oak Cliff was on the opposite side of the river in downtown Dallas. To get to the church I would have to catch a bus then a trolley car.

That church in Oak Cliff was a large church. In the basement, they had youth activities, Sunday school, recreation rooms and a cafeteria where they had fellowship and occasionally meals. I enjoyed that church more because of the youth activities available, even though it was unusual for a teenager to go to a church by himself.

It wasn't very long after I started going to that church when I met a girl, who happened to be the minister's daughter. There was mutual attraction and we began to sit together.

Now, back when I first started going, I would always sit right up close, usually in the front row of the church. I liked to hear what the minister had to say, but his daughter did not like to sit in the front row and she kept inviting me to sit with her in the back rows. Hence, as we sat together regularly I was less and less involved with the sermons.

Her family had two automobiles and her father and her mother would usually go to church earlier in her father's car. She used to come later in her mother's car and we would go to Sunday school and then attend the service. After church I began to leave with her and we would go for a drive and then park somewhere… That went on for quite some time.

Then it progressed until - instead of going from Sunday school to church service - she suggested not going to the church service at all. At first I was reluctant, but I agreed anyway and so we started going out. Instead of leaving after church, we would leave before church ended and go out in the park for a drive. On Jefferson Avenue, not too far from where she lived, there was a drive-in grocery called Cabel's Drive-in where you could buy bread, milk, groceries and beer. In those days, beer was not sold on Sunday and, as now, not sold to a minor. We were both minors but she knew the young guy that worked there quite well. So we would buy a six-pack and we'd go out in the park and drink our beer. It didn't take long before we were having sex. So instead of being in church on Sunday morning, we would go to Sunday school, leave early and not go to church. Then we would buy our six-pack and go out to our favorite spot in the park or somewhere else we knew about.

That was my Sunday event. So all of that dovetailed together and I began to feel pretty bad about our making out, and didn't know what to do about it. And so I went to the assistant minister, a young guy, and said I would like to talk to him very confidentially. I asked him about what if someone did this or that, what would be the results in their after-life? The assistant minister confirmed my greatest fears that you would go to hell for doing such things.

Hell was a strongly held belief in the church.

Now I didn't know about what would happen to you in your after-life. I had had transcendental experiences almost a decade back, but I didn't have any alternative beliefs or proof of anything else. I did understand that their religious beliefs were their religious beliefs, and I didn't necessarily go along with the notion of there being such a thing as hell fire where you would end up for eternity. After asking the assistant minister about it, I went to the minister himself, the father of the girl I was having this affair with. He relayed the same notions of hell. As a result, I quit going to that church, because I was not able to withstand the temptation of his daughter.

After that I started going to all kinds of churches, a different church almost every Sunday: Baptist, Methodist, Presbyterian, Lutheran, Catholic... I was trying to find something or some teaching that connected to the experience of awakening that I had had.

I was still pursuing my own reconnection, if possible, with the state of consciousness that I had known in my younger years. That was my real interest. I was looking to better understand God, Jesus and spirituality and for how to live in the world in a spiritual way.

CHAPTER 4

A Young Man Goes Out
Into the World

When I graduated from high school (circa 1947, *ed.*), my dad was a Deputy Constable - he always wanted to be a policeman but never qualified education-wise. He wore a uniform as a security guard and that's what he did most of his life. He always wanted me to do that which he was never able to do himself, so when I graduated from high school, I got a couple of menial jobs, and I applied for a position in the Federal Bureau of Investigation, the FBI. I was accepted and moved from Dallas to Washington D.C. and worked for the FBI for about two years in the Identification Division.

I was a fingerprint analyst. When someone had their fingerprints taken for a job application or the police department had arrested someone and sent in their fingerprints, my job was to search throughout all the fingerprint files to see if there was a match. If we didn't have the fingerprints on file, I would mark that fingerprint card as a new master card and then it would be added to the files.

In those days, my ambition was to be an agent for the FBI - because it was what my dad wanted- but I didn't have the education. I finished high school, and hadn't gone on to college.

31

It was possible for me to go ahead to college and get the degree that I needed in order to become an agent, and there were two ways to do it. You had to have a degree either in law or accounting. I thought accounting was not as much work and didn't take as much time as law, plus, I didn't have the high school credits I needed for law school. So I enrolled in the George Washington University night school to take accounting but I went for only one semester as I didn't like it at all. It was just not for me.

I got to the point that I didn't like working for the FBI. The reason was the structure of it, the seriousness of it.

Working as a fingerprint analyst was also tough on my eyes. You would set the fingerprints on the table and look very closely using a magnifying glass that was only three inches from the fingerprint. I have a stigmatism in my left eye, so I would use my right eye, which was better, then I would get headaches. Along with eye problems were the intense working conditions. We had breaks once in the morning and then again once in the afternoon and occasionally I could take a break to go to the dispensary for eyewashes. All of us had the opportunity to do that, and I did it a little more often than anyone else because I was having headaches. Frankly, it was just unpleasant work with no leeway; if you were a couple of minutes late, then you were put on report, things of that nature.

My father had a grip on me, which eventually he loosened and became more liberal in his way of dealing with me. I came to love my father very much. My mother's grip on me was even more than my father's. She lived in a constant state of self-pity and paranoia. The world and everyone, including me, was against her. I lived through all of that in my childhood years. My parents were poor and uneducated people who lived in a state of limitation and restriction and all of that caused me to take on the same self-image and identify with it. I had to live with that and work to finally overcome all of that in my own consciousness.

When I was accepted into the FBI after high school - after having gone through a background investigation (I was very young so I had no background of significance, no problems, no difficulties, no bad situations or experiences) - I received a letter, handwritten and personally signed by J. Edgar Hoover, the head of the FBI, its Kingpin until he died. Working at the FBI, I met Hoover in person on occasion - that was something quite special, though at the time it did not seem to be a big deal.

Ramana at eighteen. *AHAM archives.*

When it came time for me to go from Dallas to Washington D.C., my parents purchased a ticket on the bus. Back in those days, only the wealthy could afford to go via an airplane, and I intentionally chose the bus over the train, because I felt it would give me an opportunity to see parts of the country that I had never seen before. For such a young man, still a teenager really, taking the bus from Dallas to Washington D.C. was quite an adventure.

In Ohio, a sergeant in the army got on the bus and sat next to me. He was going to Pennsylvania to his home near Pittsburg. He recognized that I was just a green kid with no worldly experience and, in a manner of speaking, he took me under his wing.

He asked me, "How much money do you have?"

I had enough, I thought, to take care of my needs. I told him how much and I pulled out my wallet and showed him. He said to me that was a mistake. I should, if anyone ever asked how much money I had, tell them it's none of their business.

The sergeant asked me where I was going. I didn't know even where I was going to stay. I thought I would try to find an inexpensive hotel until I reported to the FBI (I had a certain date and an address where I was to report for work).

The sergeant said, "You don't have a place to stay?"

I said, "No."

He said, "Okay, here's what you do. When you get to Washington, go to the YMCA ('the Y', the Young Men's Christian Association). Once you check in there you can also apply for permanent residency. You may have to be put on a waiting list for a while, but that would be the best thing for you to do, because it's safe, it's clean and it's inexpensive."

It was as if fate was looking out for me. When I got to Washington, I went straight to the YMCA, checked in and asked for permanent residency, which was very soon accepted. I stayed at the Y for a couple of years, and then I found a rooming house, which I learned about from friends. It was not expensive and a better place to stay.

I met two friends, Mark Pignone, who worked with me in the identification division of the FBI, and Al Triola - who like me - had permanent residency at the Y. One was a Jew and they were both Italian. Both were musicians and played together in a band created by Al called "Al Triola and the Knights of Rhythm." It was a Trio. Mark played the piano, Al played the saxophone and clarinet and Bob (I can't remember his last name) played a big bass. I used to go out with them when they played gigs. They were quite good. They would play at different places, usually on weekends, and we became good friends.

I had quit playing the trumpet when I went in the ROTC and never played it again. Although I was not up-to-date, nor really good enough to play with them in their band, I was interested in the music and I would go just for the enjoyment of it. That was my social life.

Mostly, I worked and then on the weekend I would go from place to place in Washington, getting to know this historic city, which has so many places to see and things to experience. Occasionally, I would take a girl with me; it was mostly casual. There was nothing serious, no long extended romances. That didn't come 'til much later.

People came from all over the world and stayed at the Y, and many became friends. We used to sit and talk in each other's rooms. Sometimes there would be as many as six or eight of us together talking about ourselves, where we were from, what we were doing, why we were there, our cultures and differences in religions.

We used to meet on the weekends, even sometimes during the week. On the weekend we sat up all night long sharing and talking philosophy. All of my friends were older than me and had a little more experience in life, but the really significant point for me was these meetings were always in a spirit of sharing; not in any manner were there attempts to condemn or suggest that one religion was any better than another, that anyone was closer to God than another. We talked about many other things besides religion, but there was always a spiritual context. I met a Jew, a Japanese Shinto and a Muslim. There was a Hindu from India who talked about Shiva, Vishnu and Brahma and Brahman, the underlining supreme god. He was also familiar with Buddhism and he spoke about Buddha. I saw Buddha to be like Jesus. Two or three others were Christians. One was Catholic and he gave me insight into the Catholic Church. In those days, I had understood Christianity only from a Protestant point of view.

These discussions were always supportive and informative. That was the beautiful thing about them and none of the people acted like they did in the various churches I had attended. In my younger years, when I was going to the Church of Christ, there used to be what they called debates between denominations. They would be heated arguments, each denomination putting down the other and saying how their religion was better and truer. But at the YMCA, we didn't have debates. We had open-minded discussions and we were truly interested in one another's religion. We just noted the differences, not judging each other because of the differences. During all of these times, I was a listener. I didn't have enough knowledge or a system of beliefs to defend; I was just open to receiving. And so that gave me a broader knowledge and understanding of spirituality without being caught up in doctrine and competitiveness. It was very freeing and helpful to me.

All of these people were staying at the YMCA, and even though it was a hotel, in the permanent residency, people respected the place as having a spiritual basis, more than just a hotel. That was a significant point to me.

Sometimes, I talked about my own my spiritual awakening in childhood and its effect upon me. Even if none of them could relate to my experience in an experiential way, they more or less had a philosophical idea or explanation about it. There were moments when I longed for that experience and I would just let go into solitude or quietude. Then events of life and situations requiring my attention pulled me back and clouded over the remembrance of that awakened state.

One year, while I was still working for the FBI and home for Christmas vacation, I met a recruiting sergeant for the Army. I don't remember how I met him, I just happened to meet him somewhere. I told him a little bit about myself and the lack of interest in the FBI and he asked, "Why don't you go into the military intelligence?"

We made an appointment for a day or two after - I dropped by his recruiting office and we had a long conversation. He built up positively the way the army worked; I would more or less be paid while I learned various things that I would not perhaps otherwise have the opportunity to learn. He could get me a position - he more or less guaranteed that if

I applied to the military I would get into the school for military intelligence because of my background in the Identification Division of the FBI. This appealed to me. And sure enough, he followed through, because I was accepted in the Counter Intelligence Corps (CIC) when I signed up.

Ramana near age twenty. *AHAM archives.*

I had to resign from the FBI and explain to my parents that my leaving the FBI was more like a transfer. That justified in their mind a change in what they considered to be such an important job.

I went to basic training in Fort Ord, California. It was very strenuous and included military tactics under combat conditions in case you were ever required to go into combat. I was in my early twenties and in perfect health and I could go into intense military training without any problem. Then following my basic training my orders came to immediately report to Fort Holabird, Maryland not far from Washington D.C. for CIC training, while my buddies in basic training didn't know where they were going.

I was much younger than most of the other people in the CIC who had been in the military for a longer period of time. The training went well and I really enjoyed it. I didn't have much worldly life experience, and I had the feeling of flexing my muscles and of freedom from being out in life and on my own.

When I finished the training, I had the choice of where I was going, as promised by the recruiting sergeant, and I thought at the time that I wanted to be close to my family. So I was re-assigned closer to home at Fort Sam Houston in San Antonio, Texas.

In Fort Sam Houston, I was in a very easy position working in the CIC. Instead of going into foreign countries as intelligence agents, the CIC located, observed and dealt with foreign agents coming into the USA. Everybody in my office wore civilian clothes. I had a uniform that I kept in my closet, and I never had to wear it. I had almost exclusive use of a black Jeep assigned to me and I was able to drive it to the motor pool, get it maintained and get gasoline. I was allowed to drive it wherever I went. It was as if I had purchased an army surplus Jeep.

Not only did I pass as a civilian, it was also perfectly okay for me to say that I was a civilian because of the work that I did. A lot of that work was secret and near the end of my time in the CIC I was cleared for even top-secret material.

I lived off the Army base in a relatively nice rooming house for men. The owner was an older woman and she had about six rooms. There was only one woman and about three guys and myself. They all appeared to be civilians too, except it turned out that two of them were student doctors in the Military. They were on a temporary training internship, because Fort Sam in Houston was also the Headquarters of the Brook General Hospital, which was a major hospital inside of Fort Sam, Houston. This hospital later became the main hospital in all of the Military receiving anyone with serious burns from battle or elsewhere.

My first jobs in the CIC were clerical. I was the assistant pretty much to everybody above me. I collected and sorted the mail and did filing. The main thing was that I was younger than everyone in my unit.

A couple of people in the unit that I didn't get along with were promoted to a higher rank. I had the lowest rank of all, Private First Class, and they were all Corporals, Sergeants and Officers. Most of the officers in my unit I got along with well, the Sergeant in particular, but he had a temper and would get upset quite easily.

I lived close enough that I could go home on weekends. I didn't have the authority to take the Jeep; I had to leave it at the motor pool. What I would do is put on my Uniform and hitchhike from San Antonio to Dallas, about a 200 miles distance. My dad would let me use the car, so I could use it to go on dates.

On a long weekend, July 4th or Labor Day, I went home. We always had weekend passes; I never had any problems and they all knew that I went home. On a weekend pass, I was only off duty Saturday and Sunday and I'd have to be back to work Monday through Friday. This particular weekend was a holiday weekend and, it just didn't dawn on me when I stayed home on Monday, and did not return to work until Tuesday morning, that it put me in a state of absence without leave or AWOL as it's called in the Military. Well, that was a big No, No!

Even though it was a simple thing, I could have easily caught up in the work I did, but a Sergeant that I didn't get along with made a real deal about it and put me on Report to my Commanding Officer. He complained that I had not been cooperative and that my attitude was not what it should be in the CIC. Another Sergeant and a young lieutenant also complained about my lack of a positive attitude and accused me of insubordination.

The Commanding Officer, who knew me well, called me into his office and indicated that the report was not good and I was going to be dismissed from the CIC. That meant I would be re-assigned to another division in the Military. He was very compassionate and told me I could apply later when I got a little older and had more experience in the Military. He said if I reapplied and gave his name, he would give me a good recommendation. At this point it looked like my lack of experience in life was my main problem. It was nothing against me personally, other than the mistake that I made and that I didn't get along well with the other people working with me.

Looking back on it now, there would have been no problem to have gone through it all quite easily. In those days, I would have been looked upon as rebellious. I had a typical ego and I didn't take criticism well. I was not giving in to them, my attitude was one of reacting to their ways of ordering me around and in the Military you had to take orders. It was difficult for me to take orders, other than in Boot Camp.

I was transferred out of the CIC and orders came for me to report to another base in Fort Chaffee, Arkansas. I was to be re-assigned to a unit of armored cavalry, a tank division. Well I did not care for that one at all. I thought of the Military as a transfer from one division of the Government to another, from one type of intelligence work to another. I had no interest whatsoever in being in some division of the Army just for the sake of being in the Army. Anyone with an overview then - and when I look back myself - would probably say that the Military training and situations I went through were a great training in discipline. But I didn't see it like that in those days.

My father worked as a Security Guard at just about any place he could get a job and he changed jobs somewhat regularly. He and my mother were pretty frugal and thrifty in their spending. They didn't spend money that they didn't have, but both of them liked to have better things occasionally, such as better furniture or appliances, so sometimes on weekends my father worked to make extra money.

One weekend he was working at an auto race as a Security Guard, holding people back from the racetrack, when one of the cars went out of control into the crowd and ran over him. He was seriously injured, breaking one of his legs and arms and several of his ribs. He was taken to the hospital where he was incapacitated for a month. The accident left him in a state of disability. Even though his work didn't require a lot of physical effort, it was going to be a long time before he could work long hours.

All of that happened about the same time I got orders to be transferred out of my unit. I attempted to get a reprieve on these orders with the intention of applying to the military for a disability discharge due to my father's inability to function. Then I could go home, get a job and help support my family. But the military wouldn't give it.

In order to try to force a delay, I spoke to my doctor friends living in the same rooming house as me, about the idea of having my appendix removed. I had gone to the doctors with pains a couple of years before and they had indicated that I had an inflamed appendix. I had been warned to be on the alert and to get any kind of pain checked, because if it was a bad appendix and burst, it would be very dangerous.

My doctor friends said it would be a good idea to have my appendix removed, but the Army would not remove it unless there was a major need. So I would have to fake the symptoms. They told me what to do so that when I went into the emergency room at the Military hospital they would assume that I was having an appendicitis attack and actually do the operation.

In those days I wanted to have my own way – I'm not proud of it – but that's the way it was, so I went into the Brook General Hospital and faked having pains in my right side. Sure enough they operated on me and removed my appendix. I was there for two weeks, and when all this was said and done, it didn't make any difference; I still had to report to Camp Chaffy, Arkansas.

I was a good typist, as I had taken a typing class in High School, and in all the jobs that I had, I used this skill as well as filing. It happened that just as I was coming into my new Unit, the First Sergeant needed an assistant. We established a good relationship, because he needed someone with my skills. He knew that I wanted my discharge out of the Military. He would assist me if I would assist him by prolonging my application for a period of time, because he was behind in his work and I could help him catch up with it. I agreed, even though I didn't want to, because I really wanted to get out as soon as I could, and this meant that I would have to stay in for another three months.

The First Sergeant walked me through the discharge application. He had contacts and knew the politics of how to move something through quickly. In fact, my discharge came in earlier than anticipated. As part of my work, I opened and read the mail and lo and behold, here it was! My discharge was approved. All it needed was the signature of my Company Commander and I was free. But there was a rule in the Military that once you received your discharge, you had a twenty-four hour period before it went into effect.

When my discharge papers came in, the Company First Sergeant, who had assisted in getting my application through, happened to be on leave. So I took the discharge papers into the office of the Company Commander who knew that I was waiting for the papers and he agreed to sign them right away. It had then to go to the Battalion Commander for his signature, but for whatever reason I couldn't go myself to get his signature. It lay there waiting and in the meantime the First Sergeant came back. He was highly pissed off that I had given it to the Company Commander for his signature to allow for my immediate release, so he modified the papers. Instead of it being an outright and total discharge, it would be a transfer into the Military Reserve. That meant that I had to go to monthly meetings - play Army for three more years.

I was in the active reserve, and I got this changed as soon as I could to the inactive reserves so that I didn't have to go to the monthly meetings or do the war drills. However, I was subject during that three year period to being recalled to an active unit in the event of a National Emergency.

Note: Later on, that turned out to be the case, as I was called back when the Korean War started (USA engagement in the Korean War was from June 27, 1950 to July 27, 1953). When the Chinese entered the Korean War, the American government said it affected our national security. President Harry Truman called up the inactive Military Reserve and I was called back into active military service.

I returned home to Dallas after getting my discharge from the CIC and there was the matter of looking for a job. My intention was to find a job so that I could assist my family, but there was a recession at that time and it wasn't easy to find work. Not only that, neither my schooling nor training did anything to get me a job that would draw significant income. There simply wasn't anything that came up that I was qualified to do, and the things that did come up, I really didn't have any interest in. I was going to make sure that whatever I did I would make good money and enjoy doing.

I applied for jobs and the time went by.

My parents were really upset with me because I had left the FBI and gotten out of the military. That I hadn't made it in the Counter-intelligence Corps was also a reflection upon me. As a result I was not getting any cooperation from them. My father would not even let me use the car to look for jobs and, in the meantime, they had moved to a house way out in the suburbs that didn't have any means of transportation to get there, not even a bus. So I was having a hell of a time getting around, until neighbors that my parents had come to know, who both worked in town, offered to give me a ride in the morning and home in the afternoon.

I had to get up very early, even though the places where I was applying for a job did not open until two or three hours later. In town I'd find a place to hang out, make phone calls and walk or ride the trolley or bus to apply for a job.

A job opened up that appealed to me, as a dancing instructor at the Arthur Murray Dance Studio. I applied and I got it, though the problem was you did not get paid until after you finished the training, which initially took six weeks and was ongoing even after that. My parents just flipped out, especially my father, at the very idea of my dancing for a living.

My girlfriend from high school, Marietta (she had found herself a boyfriend, so we were not dating anymore), and her mother, were the only people in my life who were supportive of my desire to become a dance instructor. Marietta put dancing in the category of entertainment. I occasionally went with her mother to nightclubs to hear Marietta sing and during her break, she would come back to the table to join her mother and me.

My parent's neighbors, the couple who were giving me a ride to town, took on the same attitude as my parents; they let me ride with them, but they would hardly say a word to me - just "good morning" and that was it. The neighbors started work at 8:00 o'clock. With the distance to town and the traffic, we had to leave about 6:00 in the morning to get downtown in time. If I was one minute late when they came by to pick me up, they honked the horn and I would have to run to get in the car.

We'd get into town around 7:45, the dance studio did not open until 10:00 am for the start of lessons, so I had to sit outside on the curb for about two hours. Eventually the janitor would come and open the place up, which gave me the opportunity to go upstairs early and practice what I had learned, before all the other students got there.

I was in a class with six or eight students in the training program at the Arthur Murray Dance Studio. The teacher was the dance director of the school. She was a little older than me and a very good dancer. The students danced with each other while learning, and occasionally the instructor danced with us - both the men and the women - to see how we were doing. As an instructor, you had to be able to dance both the women's and men's parts.

The teacher noticed that I picked it up quickly and she was very encouraging. The training was for six weeks, from 10:00 o'clock in the morning until six o'clock in the afternoon with about a half hour off for lunch. We learned all of the ballroom dance steps: the fox trot, waltz, tango, rumba, samba and so forth. We had to learn them all to be accepted as a fully-fledged instructor, and I had no doubt that I was going to be accepted because my teacher told me how well I was doing.

In the evening, my neighbors would get off from work at 5:00 o'clock and then pick me up at another location - they wouldn't come pick me up by the studio, even though it was close to where they worked and it wouldn't have been a problem for them. If I was not there when they came to pick me up, they wouldn't wait. So I had to leave dance class at 5:00 o'clock, missing the last hour.

Sometimes I would be late and the neighbors would leave. Then I would have to hitchhike home, which would take about three hours. My mother would fix me breakfast and a lunch that I could take to work, but she was reluctant and complaining when she was doing it. All the same, she was kind enough when I missed my ride home to at least leave my meal on the table so I could eat before I went to bed.

I was under a tremendous amount of pressure, living in disapproval from everyone who knew me: my parents were really judgmental because I had used my father's injury to get out of the military and I was supposed to be assisting them financially and I wasn't even able to do that. I would only get paid when I was an instructor and then when I first started, the pay was only a percentage of what a student paid per hour for lessons. It was going to take a long time before I made any appreciable money. And neither my parents nor neighbors thought of what I was doing as a real job. I was in training and not getting paid for it. For them, all I was doing was going into town to dance.

It was one hell of a period in my life.

I'm telling you- that was a very low period in my life, just horrendous, other than I enjoyed learning to dance. I had gone from the strict discipline of the FBI and military into dancing, which was artistic, fluid and freeing. I loved it.

When I finished the six-week training period I had to train a little longer to make up for those hours I had missed every afternoon through leaving an hour early. The training director understood my situation and technically I would not have qualified if I had not been as good a student as I was. I became a fabulous dancer back in those days.

Some nights, when I came home from the training, I would lie in bed and read the Bible. I never read any other spiritual books. I would remember my own spiritual experience, though that was not very often. I hardly talked anymore about it.

Looking back I can say this was the course of events that my life took.

In all of this, there was a lot of a typical young man's worldly involvement, which was primarily ego.

I did not complete my dance training at that time. What really was the straw that broke the camel's back happened at the end of the day coming back with the neighbors from town. It was pouring rain. My parents' house was set back a good walk from the road. I didn't have an umbrella or a raincoat, and so when I got out of the car, I made a fast run into the house.

As usual during that period my parents were not very friendly with me because they didn't approve of what I was doing, and so that day I went immediately back into my room at the back of the house. It happened that the neighbors had moved hardly ten or fifteen feet away, when they discovered they had a flat tire. Here it was, pouring rain and I had been riding for free all this time. They got very angry because, in their view, I should have come out and assisted them in changing the flat tire. But I didn't know that they had a flat tire. They told my parents and my mother and father both got very angry with me too. No one could understand - I didn't assist them simply because I didn't know that they had a flat tire.

The intensity of that event became so unreasonable that as a result of it, I just said, "OK, I give up," and chose to go back to Washington and work for the FBI. It would give me an income right away and make my parents happy doing what my dad wanted me to do to begin with. I returned to the same department in the FBI, doing the same thing I was doing before. I went immediately to the YMCA and got myself a room again because that was the place I knew was inexpensive. I knew the trolley car route that I would catch to and from work, it was all familiar. But it wasn't very long after going back to the FBI that I visited the Arthur Murray Dance Studio in Washington.

I introduced myself to the dance director and told her that I had taken the training in Dallas, although I had not completed it. In those days, there were six ballroom dances that you had to know. In Dallas, they took one dance at a time. They would spend about a week on each dance and I had gone through five weeks of training. Even though I missed an hour of training each day for those five weeks, and didn't get the full training, I danced with the dance director and a couple of students and she was impressed with my ability. They knew that I was able to dance.

I said I was working at the FBI and I could come after work to study to become a dance instructor. They said they would like very much to have me. That's really what I wanted to do more than working for the FBI.

I continued to work for the FBI, then in the afternoon I would get off from work and join the training class that was in session, which they allowed me to do at no charge. They normally would charge for the lesson, but I was there not as an ordinary student, rather continuing in training to be a dance instructor. I was able to complete the training that I had started in Dallas and they were very happy with the result and I was qualified to begin as a new teacher.

I started working part-time in the evening. I happened to be the only one doing that at Murray's, because they would not allow part-time instructors at that point. They allowed me because I was quite a good dancer. I would get off from work at the FBI, get on a trolley and rush in as fast as I could to the dance studio. It worked out because most students took their lessons at night as they had regular jobs in the day.

I don't remember now how long I continued working full time at the FBI in the day and part-time at the studio at night, but I became so distracted and finally the pull was so strong for me to quit the FBI and dance full time, that's what I finally did.

For a long time I never told my parents that I was dancing because I knew they would not approve, and they were happy I was working and I was able to send them a little money. Finally I had to tell them, because in their letters they asked me questions about my work. We didn't make any long distance telephone calls except on very special occasions; still they could more or less tell that there was something going on. That I was dancing disappointed them both, especially my father, yet finally he began to let go and realize that I was going to do what I wanted in my life. He finally gave up trying to control or influence my life that way.

As a dance instructor, I began meeting women. I met mostly older woman and I started to lie about my age. The women were okay with my youth and my age - but I wasn't so okay with it. I wanted to be older in order to try to impress them that I knew more than what I really knew. I had affairs with several - short episodes - and there was one woman in particular who was really something.

I was still living at the Y and working at Murray's and another teacher, a good friend of mine, told me about a dance student that wanted me to teach her. He had been her teacher and he told me that she was open sexually. It turned out that she wanted to have lessons with me because, as much as anything, she was attracted to me. I started teaching her to dance and she became the first woman in my life that began to teach me about sex. She was older, more experienced and daring.

She loved the daring aspect.

On one occasion we wanted to have sex and there was no place for us to go. We didn't have money to get a hotel room – there was a hotel that we used to go to, that was not too expensive, but when we went there they didn't have any rooms available. So she said, "Well, what about your room?"

I said I lived at the Young Men's Christian Association and they didn't allow any women in the rooms. It was late, about 12:30 or 1:00 o'clock at night. She said there would be nobody around.

I lived in a room on the third floor in the permanent section that was in the old building. The old building was clean but not as modern as the new section. It didn't have a lobby; there was just an entrance via the new building from which you could go up on the elevator. You would then go down some stairs and through a fire door into the old building.

I had told her about that way to my room and she said, "Why don't we do it that way?"

I said that it was pretty risky but she replied, "What difference does it make? So we get caught, we get caught. All they'll do is tell you to leave."

So that's what we did, we went up to my room. I had a roommate who was really strait-laced. I went into the room first and told him that I was going to bring in a woman and to just keep his eyes closed. She didn't mind that my roommate was there – she was real daring – and so we had sex in my room at the YMCA.

She taught me about sex and she drilled into me that I was to always consider the woman and make sure that I was satisfying her first even before myself. Ever since then I have considered the feelings, emotions and experiences of the woman. It lasted quite some time with her and we would have sex in some of the most daring places and situations you could have imagined. I learned how not to be concerned and to be risky and daring myself. You might say I had this quest for sex, because the orgasmic embrace was so blissful and it linked me back to my earlier experience of spiritual awakening.

What broke up my time in Washington was the start of the Korean War.

1951 Chevrolet Deluxe Bel Air Hardtop Coupé.
Image from Mr. Choppers, https://en.wikipedia.org/wiki/Chevrolet_Bel_Air, Creative Commons Attribution-Share Alike 3.0 Unported License (creativecommons. org/licenses/by-sa/3.0/).

The Korean War started, I was called back into the Army and had to report to Fort Campbell, Kentucky, which was the headquarters at that time of the 101st Airborne Division of the United States Army.

I had purchased an automobile in Washington while I was at Murray's - a 1950 Chevrolet, the very first Bel Air made (1950 to 1981, *ed.*). When I got my orders, anyone with a vehicle had to make arrangements for them, because we were not going to be given any opportunity to take care of anything like that once we reported for duty. Well, I didn't act upon that. Instead, I went home and then drove in it to Fort Campbell.

In the midst of the refresher training we were asked who had received their orders. For some reason, they had lost all of the orders they had sent out including mine. I said, no I hadn't had the opportunity to take leave and take care of my things. So they gave me a ten-day leave to do that. But instead of doing that, I went back to Washington and enjoyed ten days of celebration and had a hell of a good time.

I returned then to Fort Campbell. I was the only single person in my Company who had an automobile. There was a married fellow with an automobile but each time he had leave, he would just go home to see his wife.

I became popular because of my car. With a sticker on the car I just drove off and back on the base with people and was never questioned. In the evenings and on weekends I would drive. I had a business. I would take three or four guys, three in the back seat and one or two in the front seat and I charged $5.00 a person. I made $25.00 a trip and I would make three trips in an evening.

I used three different exits so that I wouldn't be seen by the Military Police. I could drive off with a vehicle full of people and then just drive back in myself. They didn't pay any attention to it.

The nearest major town from the base was across the state line in Nashville, Tennessee. I would go into Nashville for the weekend. First thing that I did in Nashville was go to the Arthur Murray Dance Studio, get acquainted, even giving a couple of lessons and dating some girls.

In military training, we went out on long marches, sleeping on the ground in pup tents. There was a lieutenant, a platoon leader, who recently had been called back into the service, just like me. He was not so conditioned by the Military. He was more of a civilian, I had a car and he was quite interested in having access to transportation in and out of the base. When it came time to go out on long marches and spend the night on the hard ground in the cold of winter, instead of marching out there, he and I would drive out, park my car, go through the maneuvers and then at night drive back and sleep in the barracks rather than sleeping out in the cold.

Not only that, as an officer the Lieutenant was a member of the Officers' Club where enlisted men were not supposed to go. But in the club civilian clothing was worn and he would just pass me in. I would meet women because I was a good dancer. I became popular because of my dancing abilities.

After completing my refresher, basic training, I was transferred to Camp Stoneman; I was trying to get back into the CIC. I put in my request and I was put into what was called the "pipeline." I didn't have any permanent orders. I was always in the pipeline and they would tell me to wait until I got to my next station.

I was older now and I realized I liked the CIC. I needed a special Military Operational Specialty (MOS) code to allow me back in the CIC rather than that of plain infantry. There was a need for Infantry in Korea and so people who had their Infantry MOS were being called. That was the MOS they had assigned to me, but I sure as hell didn't want to go into combat.

Guys were being put on airplanes and flown directly to Korea. One guy from my unit had been flown from Camp Stoneman to Korea, gone into combat and been wounded by a mortar all within seventy-two hours. He came back with both legs amputated. He was in the base hospital and we went to see him. You can understand why I did not want to go into combat and wanted my MOS changed.

They kept shipping people off, and I couldn't understand why I wasn't being shipped out like them. One day they called my name along with a group of us and we were ordered to fall out and go to the big area where you went to get ready. I went to get my pack, my metal helmet, and a rifle, but then I was given a different line number than my friends.

I stood in one line while all my other friends were over in another. I looked around and there were some old buddies of mine whom I went through CIC training with I hadn't seen in years. I had been re-classified and re-assigned to the CIC. I was absolutely elated.

We were scheduled to go out within the next two days. During that time I got a call on the loudspeaker to report to the Orderly Room. I reported to the clerk who told me to report to Battalion Headquarters and from there I was sent over to the CIC Unit.

When was the last time you had a security clearance?" I was asked at the CIC. I told the officer all I'd been doing and where I had worked. I was informed that I didn't have the up-to-date security clearance I needed now to qualify for the CIC.

I said, "Oh my God! What can I do?" I sure as hell didn't want to be in the Infantry or the Armored Cavalry, which is the next thing they had me down for.

So the officer started looking and said that I could probably qualify for the Criminal Investigation Division (CID), because I'd worked for the FBI. Then he saw that I would need clearance for that too. I asked what could be done.

He was very compassionate and wanted to help me out. He said, I could probably get into the Military Police (MP) and then, if I wanted, apply to the CID. So they changed my classification.

I was scheduled to go out on the next day on a troop ship to Japan, so they took me off of that, and I had to stay again for another month awaiting the next ship. When the time came, a similar kind of thing happened as before, I was given a different line number from most of the guys I had met. I got on the ship to Japan and when we arrived all of the guys with different line numbers got off but they told me to stay on the ship. It turned out that the ship was going to Okinawa, an island south of Japan. That's where I went.

U.S. troops are pictured on pier after debarking
from ship, somewhere in Korea, August 6, 1950.
Photo: Sgt. Dunlap (Army), Public Domain.

I was a military policeman. I stayed at Okinawa for the entire rest of the Korean War, except on one occasion I went on temporary duty to Seoul, the capital of South Korea.

In Seoul my duty was to pick up a Lieutenant who was going in for court-martial. He was a platoon leader who had refused orders. Other platoons just ahead of him had tried to take a hill and all of their men had been seriously wounded or killed. He didn't see the purpose to take a hill and be killed and your men be killed and he refused to order his men to do so. The result was he had to return for court-martial.

It was my job to get him and bring him back.

His name was Howard. He and I became very close on the trip back. He was in handcuffs and I would take them off. I turned him over to the Provost Marshal's Office and I never saw him again after that. He was a nice guy and I really hated doing that. These were my orders, but I certainly did not make it hard on him.

When I told a few of the guys in my unit that I had removed my prisoner's handcuffs and was friendly with him, they were really judgmental and critical. They all put me down pretty badly for doing that as though I had done a terrible thing, simply because they thought that he had done a terrible thing. Most of them felt that way about it.

All of that is what I was having to go through. I really wasn't enjoying the military.

After finishing my tour of duty, the return home from Okinawa was on a troop ship. The regular troops had to do much of the work in maintaining the ship. We were all assigned various work details and I got Kitchen Patrol (KP) or kitchen duty, washing pots and pans way down in the hot hole of the ship. So I thought, I've got to do something creative here.

In the upper decks of the ship there were enlisted men and officers who had their wives with them. There was not much entertainment for them.

I went to the chaplain in charge of entertainment - realizing they were having difficulties, it's not easy to come up with interesting and entertaining events for people - and told him that I was a dance instructor and would be happy to give free ballroom dancing classes to the cabin class passengers. He was delighted with the idea and that's what I did the entire trip back to the United States. So I had to have a little bit of ingenuity to get me out of that terrible KP detail that I was doing.

Although I didn't realize it at the time, I probably could have done the same thing on my trip over.

My tour of duty in the military taught me about dealing with people, getting by and making the most of a situation, but the Military and its procedures were not my cup of tea.

When I finished my tour of duty and returned to the United States, I went to Dallas and not back to Washington.

Advertisement for Arthur Murray's dance system.
Science & Invention, January 1922. Public Domain.

The Washington D.C. Arthur Murray Studio was the top ranking studio in the United States, both in dancing competitions and for the business they did. They did more volume in dancing lessons and hours of dancing instructions than any other Arthur Murray Studio in the country. I had been a full fledged instructor there, so when I returned to Dallas and saw the owner of the Arthur Murray Studio, of course he knew me and was very happy that I had returned and that I was interested in staying in Dallas rather than going to Washington D.C.

Within a year, I was promoted to assistant manager of the studio. This meant more money, but of course I had more responsibility. I was managing three supervisors and the instructors working under them. It was my job to oversee the business aspect as well as the dancing. The business system was very much like the automobile business. It was all based upon sales; you had to sell students a program of dancing instruction tailored for them. And then you would do your best to sell the student on taking as many hours of instruction as possible. In Washington D.C., my introduction into sales was selling courses in dancing instruction to students who would enroll and buy hours of dancing. I applied what I had learned there and expanded it in Dallas. I was no longer doing much instructing, I was involved in more managerial duties.

As I was in management and knew what the Arthur Murray Studio charged for lessons and the breakdown of the hourly lesson for the teacher, the supervisor, the manager and the studio, I began to get ambitious. I learned along the way that Veloz and Yolanda, a dancing team in California, were starting their own chain, a franchise of dance studios. In those days, they were a terrific dance team. The routines they taught were basically the steps in traditional dances, not much different one from the other, although they may have given different names to a particular basic step. I'd seen Veloz and Yolanda on television and they'd even been in the movies.

In the meantime, while I was working at Murray's I had a girlfriend who also became my dancing partner. Her name was Ruth Louise – I called her Ruthie – she goes by the name of Lou, now. She's still alive and lives in Dallas. I still talk to her now and then.

Our whole life was around dancing. She was my student, but she became interested in becoming an instructor as she loved to dance. She couldn't train during the day because she was working then for the telephone company, so I trained her myself at night and over time she got her basic dancing down very well and she became a member of the staff.

Being a dance instructor was not something that made you much money. The main thing was the glamour. Everybody enjoyed it. The main compensation was doing what you enjoyed.

I was interested in the possibility of a franchise as I could see the money to be made was not as an instructor. So Ruthie and I talked to Jack Stubbs - one of her students, a wealthy Texan who owned a chain of small local grocery stores - about the idea of Veloz and Yolanda. He got quite interested in it and began to talk to us about the potential of putting up the money for a franchise that Ruthie and I would operate.

We were talking about it one day but we made the mistake, a sad mistake, of talking about it in one of the small training rooms. Those rooms had been wired for sound. Whenever you were talking to a person in a training interview to sell them a package deal, there was someone listening in to the conversation; just like they used to do in automobile dealerships (They used to do that in the closed rooms of auto dealerships. I don't know whether it's against the law now, but in those days it was a definite procedure). We made the mistake of discussing it with Jack in the interview room and either the owner or his wife happened to be in, turned on the box and heard the conversation.

Well, you can imagine the result of that. Both Ruthie and I were fired immediately along with a couple of other instructors that were willing to go with us. The other instructors were later re-instated, but both Ruthie and I were completely out of a job and then Jack Stubbs reneged on the idea of financing a franchise. In the meantime Ruthie had left the telephone company and was working full time at Murray's, so both of us were momentarily completely out in the cold.

We went to the Fred Astaire Dance Studio, which had fewer students and was smaller than Arthur Murray's, and talked to the owner. We shot straight with him. Ruthie and I told him that Murray's had fired us because we were giving serious consideration to opening a franchise for Veloz and Yolanda. He knew Ruthie and I and we went to work for him barely a day after we were fired from Murray's, we really hardly lost a step.

I worked at Fred Astaire's as manager for a number of years. Jack bought a course at Fred Astaire and Ruthie continued to teach him. I was able to pull a couple of other instructors over from Arthur Murray's, which went well with the owner of Fred Astaire's. I don't remember why we left Fred Astaire. It had to do partly with Ruthie going to Houston and I followed her eventually.

Veloz and Yolanda in a scene from the 1937 film Champagne Waltz. *Paramount Films (part of an ad for the film), Modern Screen magazine. Public Domain.*

I was about twenty-four years old (1953 to 1954, *ed.*) and I wasn't really involved in any spiritual quest at the time. It just went on the back burner. I didn't go to church, I really wasn't interested in church, or in any kind of spiritual questions.

Ruthie eventually married and her husband and I became good friends. We used to spend hours talking about philosophy and spiritual matters. In those days it had to do with beliefs. He was an engineer and so he looked at everything from a scientific point of view, while I looked at everything from a philosophical point of view, and we would compare notes. What he understood and knew from science and what I knew and understood from philosophy, we would blend together. The two of us had some great conversations over time. Ruthie, she was never really interested. She would say, "Oh, that doesn't make any sense to me."

Ruthie and I still talk and visit on the phone (circa 2008, *ed.*). She's older than me, about eighty-two or eighty-three and she's got a lot of physical difficulties right now. She has bad rheumatism, a lot of pain in her back and she lives in an assisted care place in Dallas. Ruthie is still not interested in talking about spiritual matters, though we're friends and have been all these years.

.

PART 2

The Pursuit of Happiness (1953 to 1973)

Ramana late thirties. *AHAM archives.*

The movie *Giant* playing at the Majestic Theatre, Dallas, circa 1956. *Image from Wes O'Donnell, Creative Commons, Attribution-Share Alike 3.0 Unported License (creativecommons.org/licenses/by-sa/3.0/).*

CHAPTER 5

The Salesman: Pursuing the American Dream

I met my first wife, Verna, when I was still living in Dallas working as a bartender (1953 to 1954, *ed.*). I would drive from Dallas to Houston where she lived, about 200 miles, a four and a half hour drive. Finally when I moved to Houston, we got married.

I worked early evenings and nights in the University Club, one of the private clubs in Dallas. They had a monthly membership fee and you could order a mixed drink. You couldn't go into a normal bar and order a martini. In Texas, at that time, alcohol was not sold in public places. There were only package stores where you would buy a pint bottle of whiskey or a fifth (a 26 oz. or 750 ml. bottle). You carried your bottle in a bag into a bar (they called it brown-bagging), and you had to order a mixer from the waiter, pour your own alcohol and make your drink at the table.

Ruthie and I had a good party friend, David, who was a parking lot manager at a very exclusive private club in Dallas called The Cipango Club. He actually was more of an attendant, though officially he was called the manager, because he would occasionally have people work for him. David made a lot more money than we did. Wealthy people were members and some of them would give him big tips for parking and taking care of their expensive automobiles. He would get ten-dollar and twenty-dollar tips, which was a lot of money at that time.

The Cipango occasionally had big bands - names like Tommy Dorsey, Benny Goodman and Xavier Cugat. Ruthie and I used to dance to them, and people would form a circle and move back from the floor to watch and give us room to dance, because we were quite good, we were professionals.

Ruthie and I used to wait where David worked; then when he got off we would all go to after-hour clubs that stayed open all night long. That's just what we did; it was the lifestyle we were living. There was another club, the American Guild of Variety Artists (AGVA). Ruthie and I were not official members but because we were in the dancing business - and club members were in the entertainment business - we got to know the manager and many of the musicians there.

One night as I was at work at the University Club, I got a call from David. He wanted me to meet him, when I got off work, at a drive-in restaurant on the Fort Worth highway. He had been drinking, raising hell and doing some things that pissed off the manager. When I got there he had passed out in the waitress's car. She was the girl he was dating, and she was upset with him because of the way he was carrying on, but at the same time she was hung up on him and afraid of what he would do if she didn't do everything he wanted of her.

David owned a motorcycle. It was getting to be time for the place to close and we could not leave his motorcycle there. She was concerned somebody would steal it and so she asked, "Can't you ride his motorcycle to his house?" It was only about eight or ten blocks away from where he lived.

"Can't you just ride his motorcycle there because I'm afraid he'll be upset with me if we go off and leave it here?"

I kept saying we ought to leave it. It'll be fine.

No, she was afraid that he would get mad at her. So I finally said, "Okay."

I had never owned a motorcycle, although I had ridden someone else's, a brand called "Indian," when I was about eighteen or nineteen. David's was a Harley-Davidson. Well, the way these motorcycles worked was absolutely opposite of one another. If you were going to put on the brakes in one, you would get the clutch, instead, in the other. The same went for the gas. I knew they were totally opposite of one another, but out of habit, I revved it up and put it in gear when I had actually intended to turn the gas off. I went up over a parked car, down the other side and underneath another. I cut off the end of my finger all the way to the point where you could see the bone. The bone was protruding. I also knocked out my front tooth.

Here I was bleeding and this girl was more concerned about David and his motorcycle than about my being injured.

A couple of guys came in on motorcycles, and we asked them if they would do us a favor and drive David's motorcycle to where he lived about ten blocks away. At first they were going to call the police on me and file a complaint, but we were able to explain that I was trying to help out. They then helped bring the bike to his house, and by that time David, who had passed out, revived and realized what had happened and that there had been some damage to his motorcycle. He was very upset about it.

Here I was, just trying to help out, and finally I had to literally take my injured finger where you could see the bone and stick it in the girl's face and say to them, "I'm injured and you have to take me to the hospital." They finally took me to the hospital. The end of my finger was sewn back on, but they couldn't do very much for my leg. It had a hole in it, so they bandaged it, cleaned it out and I was taken home.

At that time I was staying at my folk's house. Two or three days later Bernie, Harriet and Ruthie picked me up. Bernie and Harriet lived in Houston and Ruthie ended up moving there and working for Arthur

Murray. She became a roommate with Harriet. Bernie had his own very unique kind of apartment. He had spent a number of years in Mexico City and had been involved buying things there to sell in the USA. He was quite an entrepreneur with all kinds of great ideas to make money. All of us became good friends and Bernie and Harriet later got married.

We went out clubbing that night and it made the biggest impression on them that I didn't let my condition stop me from going out with them when they happened to come into town. I still wasn't getting along too well with my parents and going out with my friends was an opportunity for me to get out of the house.

I was about twenty-four when I went to Houston in 1954.

I had met a sales professional - what we called a Sales Closer - who invited me to work with him. We sold freezer food plans. I went out with him with the idea of learning the presentation. I worked with him for a long time and the two of us became a team.

That is also the time when I started to read Napoleon Hill's books. Being in sales, I found *Think and Grow Rich* to be particularly useful. I read it many times. I studied it and it was something I used to guide my life by. I had also read about positive thinking and being assumptive in whatever it is you are doing. If you want to be successful in sales you have to have that assumptive attitude.

My partner and I would present the freezer food plan in a residential area by going directly to homeowners. We'd knock on their door or we would drive down the street, and then when we saw someone working in their yard, maybe mowing the lawn, we approached and told them we had a program that would be very beneficial to them and we'd ask them to invite us into their home to give them a presentation. We figured out how much they would spend every month for the particular type of food we had to offer. These were frozen foods including vegetables, fruits, juices and all kinds of meats. Then we would sell them the freezer food plan, so that they could have more and better quality food delivered to their home, the convenience of not having to shop for as much in the grocery store, plus they would get a home freezer. The company acted as a broker. They bought bulk quantities of frozen food and meats (in those days I was a meat eater) from wholesalers, and then they would get a distributorship for a name brand of home freezer.

Napoleon Hill, 1937.

New York World-Telegram and the Sun Newspaper Photograph Collection (Library of Congress), staff photograph, Public Domain.

I enjoyed it because it was a truly beneficial program that really worked for people. A finance company financed the whole deal, including the payment of the freezer and food. The initial purchase was for a three months supply and then the buyer usually made a monthly payment. It was financed over a two or three-year period, which included the freezer. In the long run, they actually were paying a little more for the freezer than if they bought it in a place like Sears, Roebuck &

Company, but the freezer was a higher quality than you normally could buy, one of the best made in those days, an Amana or an Admiral.

I did that for several years with various companies. Door-to-door selling was a popular method at the time. Many salesmen were doing it and working on straight commission.

I learned the profession of direct sales, communication skills and positive persuasion, being able to overcome the typical objections, skepticism and doubts that a buyer might have. My partner and I established a very good relationship with all of the people we sold to. We would go back to them often and make sure that they were satisfied with the service they were getting. Then they gave us the names of friends that we would call on. It was an enjoyable kind of work at that stage of my life.

I was selling door-to-door in Houston when Verna and I got married. I must have been twenty-four years old (circa 1954, *ed.*), but I had the tendency of not telling the truth about my age. I felt that people would look down on me if they knew how young I really was, so I always wanted to appear a bit older and more mature. I think I was telling everyone that I was two or three years older than I really was. I could pass for it, though I was sometimes told I looked young for my age. With Verna, I also added a couple of years to my age when we met. To me, she was a very beautiful woman. She had auburn hair that knocked me out. I didn't know it at the time, but she was shaving off two or three years on her age. She acknowledged that she was older than me, but neither one of us really knew our age difference. Well, when we did finally get around to telling the truth about our age, it turned out that she was fifteen years older than me. I felt at the time it was love, but of course sex had a great deal to do with it for me and for her too; we had a very compatible sexual relationship. I was also young and immature, very jealous and possessive.

Then Verna became pregnant. I was very much in love with her and so I felt perfectly okay about it, because I thought that marriage would be a sure way of stabilizing our relationship. I didn't know what the hell I was talking about. I really didn't know much about anything, even though I thought I did.

We went to a small town outside of Houston that was known as a place where it was easy to get married, like Las Vegas. We got a blood test, a marriage license, went to a Justice of the Peace and got married all in one day.

Verna had married and divorced her former husband twice and still had a relationship with him. He owned a used automobile dealership in Houston and he allowed her to drive one of the automobiles from his lot. It was the car she drove regularly. In fact, before I moved to Houston, she drove up in his car to Dallas a couple of times to see me. At the time, that didn't make too much difference to me, because we had our relationship going (and, about her relationship with her ex, she was always saying that they were just good friends). When she became pregnant, she was living in a modest home in a nice part of town, but her former husband was still the co-owner of it and because of this it was not a place that she and I could live when we got married.

I rented a small apartment for us to live in. It was not of the caliber that Verna was accustomed to. It was an impossible situation from the beginning. She was pregnant, and I was doing the honorable thing by marrying her and giving the baby a father. One day I came home from work and she was not there. She'd left a note, she'd flown the coop, she was gone.

I started looking for her. She had left her house completely vacant. It was locked. I had a key to the place, but the locks had been changed, so I couldn't get in. Then I went out to where her ex-husband worked; he was not to be found. To make a long story short, she had gone to Reno, Nevada to get a divorce.

Her mother was still living in a little town about half way between Houston and Dallas. I drove up there looking for Verna, but her mother wouldn't tell me the truth. It took me the longest time to find out where she really was. Actually, I don't think I found out until she eventually wrote me a letter. In the note she told me where she was going and that the only reason that she married me was to give the baby a name. All of this was a shocker to me because I was very much infatuated with her and it took a while for me to get over it.

She was the first woman that I became emotionally involved with. I became jealous, because I felt so insecure about the relationship. It was doomed from the very beginning because we were totally incompatible. There was not much about our relationship that really made any sense. She was thirty-nine and I was only twenty-four at that time, but I was saying to her that I was twenty-eight. She believed that I was twenty-eight and this was a justification in her mind for us to be dating. I wasn't anywhere close to being capable of providing for her in a manner to which she was accustomed. She was an executive secretary for a vice president of a major construction company in Houston. They were involved in construction in other countries; that's how big they were. So she was both in a higher income and social bracket than me and the only thing I had was the ability to dance. It was completely out of balance. I was fascinated by her and that's what it was all about, and I was just her younger lover. I had the stamina and vitality that she really got off on, but I was not able to keep up with her from a social viewpoint.

Within a relatively short period of time, she remarried her former husband, her third marriage to him. I didn't stay in regular communication with her, but I understood that her husband delighted in the role of being a father, and raised the child as his own.

After my separation from Verna, Ruthie and I got an apartment together. I remember her father came to Houston for a convention for his company and she and I had a difficult time trying to deal with that because she didn't want her family to know that she was living with me.

In those days, it was not acceptable to be living with someone if you were not married.

In Dallas, prior to my marriage to Verna, Ruthie and I had broken up our own intimate relationship and had become just dancing partners. I had a lot of girlfriends and that didn't go well for our relationship. The main thing that had really kept us together was dancing. But she was in love with me and so when I went out, that was very painful for her.

Ruthie knew what I was going through with Verna, so on one side of it she was being compassionate but on the other side she was still emotionally involved with me. I had a great fondness for her and we had many great times together, though I was not in love with her. I loved her, but was not in love with her.

After Verna left and the divorce became final, I wanted steady work that would give me a regular income. I was tired of working for straight commission as I could never make very much money. I would go some weeks without making sales and have no income. So I applied for a job in Houston that would use my background in the military intelligence and in the FBI. It was for an insurance company called Traders General, which dealt in automobile, accident and worker's compensation insurance.

It was during that period that I got interested again in my spiritual quest. I entered again into a process of coming into the awareness of my being.

I was entirely alone at that point. Occasionally, I would meet someone and we might carry on a conversation, but most of my friends thought that I was so far out and they didn't know where I was coming from. Somewhere, I got interested in spiritualism. I met a woman who was a spiritualist, a trance medium who supposedly communicated with the dead, or people on the other side. I didn't know anything about it, but I was fascinated with the idea.

I went to meet her. She conducted the séances in her home, twice a week, to a group of people. She was married to a younger man and it came up in the conversation about me having been married to an older woman. So she invited me and I went a few times, but what was significant was I met a much older lady in her sixties who, although I was still a young man in my twenties, recognized some kind of quality about me. She was herself very much spiritually oriented, a lot broader in her outlook from a spiritual point of view than the lady giving the séances. She was interested in more than just spiritualism itself.

She lived clear across town from me and from where the séances were being held. Sometimes it was late at night before they would be over and she would have to ride the bus to wherever she lived. This was not too good for her, being an older lady, but she didn't mind. It was safe enough back in those days too.

After getting acquainted we made arrangements to meet at a little coffee shop before the séances. She and I would spend time talking about spiritual things and then we would go to the séance. Other times we would go to the coffee shop after the séance. On one of these occasions, she told me about a book that she wanted me to read, as she knew it would be significant for me. So after one late night séance, I drove her to her home. She was very gracious and had a modest, not expensive little house. She invited me in and immediately started fixing a pot of coffee. While the coffee was brewing, she went to her room and brought me a book called *The Eternal Pilgrim* by Ripley Webb and then she went back to doing what she had to do.

I became enthralled reading this book. She was quiet while I read, and we talked about it a little bit, but she knew that I just didn't want to put it down. She'd already told me that it would probably affect me that way. So finally she said "Okay, I know that you really want to read it, so you can take it with you." I could hardly wait to get home, and then stayed up all night reading the book. I had to work the next day, but I was young and able to do that. So I worked at what I had to do that day;

was able to finish up quite early; got home, took a quick nap, because I'd been up all night, and went right back to reading the book.

I stayed up again, quite late, reading it and I kept reading it constantly on the weekend. The agreement was that I was to give the book back to her the next time I saw her at the séance. So I took the book with me as agreed, but as I had not yet quite finished it, she said "Well, okay, go ahead and keep it a little longer. Bring it back to me next time."

I had called various bookstores around and couldn't find the book. She had bought it some years before, in New York where she had lived, and I think she called or wrote to some places trying to get me a copy, but it was no place to be found. When it came time for me to give it back to her, she saw how disappointed I was that I couldn't find a copy.

So she looked at me and with compassion said, "You know I read this book and I've had it for a long time, it's very meaningful to me, and I can see that it's also very meaningful to you. You are really getting something out of it now, and your whole life is ahead of you and it can be beneficial to you, so I just want you to have it."

Of all the books I had in those days, that book stayed with me. I didn't have an awful lot, and that one was the most significant for me. Later, when I ended up going to Unity School to become a Unity minister, I took that book with me. It made the circuit of my friends, and even a couple of my instructors. Everybody read it and seemed to appreciate it.

I cannot remember the name of the lady who gave me *The Eternal Pilgrim*, but she was very significant to me both because of the book and the conversations we had. There were times when we met with the intention of going to the séance and rather than going we would just continue to talk in the coffee shop. Then I drove her home. She fully understood when I talked about the Awakening experience that I had as a child. She was very supportive about it and never considered it to be unusual, other than it was not a usual experience. I couldn't talk to other people about it, though I could talk to her.

I got to the point where I quit going to the séances because I was too skeptical. You couldn't find many spiritualists who were genuine and not just out to receive gratification for their egos or for the money. At the start, this medium seemed to be genuine, though things happened and I began doubting. The lady who gave me the book didn't have the same doubts at the time, so when I chose to stop attending, she was disappointed and tried to assure me that, in her view, the medium was authentic. I didn't see my friend again for a long time. When I did run into her, she herself had quit going to the meetings after she, too, started to have doubts.

She was old enough to be my mother and she was very nurturing to me in a spiritual context. She was genuinely interested, it was not just idle curiosity, and I can remember her asking me questions even though I can't remember what the subjects of the conversations themselves actually were. I can remember her support, her compassion, and the recognition that I truly had a genuine experience and that I was on a spiritual quest. She could tune in with me and she knew that my interest was far beyond the ordinary interest of a young man of my age.

The *Eternal Pilgrim* talks of life on this planet before recorded history. There were civilizations that had high levels of awareness and then destroyed themselves or were destroyed.

After reading *The Eternal Pilgrim*, I tried to find other books. A friend of mine bought True Magazine. There was a story about a woman remembering another lifetime, "The Story of Bridey Murphy." My friend was interested in it but it really triggered something in me. I went immediately to a newsstand and bought a copy. I just came alive with it; the potential, the possibility of it. So I immediately bought the book that the article was about, *The Search for Bridey Murphy*, by Morey Burnstein. It's still in print.

In fact, for a period of about four years I corresponded with Burnstein. I also wrote to Robert W. Huffman, author of *Many Wonderful Things*. It was about Irene Specht, whom he had regressed through hypnosis not only to another lifetime, but to the place in which her soul was between births. She had not yet taken on another body - and was just in a suspended consciousness - when questions were posed to her.

It was wonderful what was said about the place between lives where the true Self is able to find expression without the restraints of the personality or ego. That really made an impression on me, because I was able to come back into that awareness, the pure awareness of being, that I had awakened to when I was a child.

I also read about Edgar Cayce. I read *Many Lives, Many Loves* by Gina Cerminara, and *There is a River* by Thomas Sugrue, which is by far the best book about Cayce. I even wrote and got permission from the Edgar Cayce Foundation to copy the section called "The Philosophy" at the end of the book. Edgar Cayce had described this philosophy when he was in the transcendental state of consciousness, the sleep state that he would go into in his readings. He gave the story about the creation of man, how it came about. Cayce's account of the story of the creation and the evolution of man closely parallels that in *The Eternal Pilgrim*.

While I worked as an insurance claims adjustor with Traders General, I met my second wife. Her name was Inez, but we called her by her nickname of Sonny (Sunny spelled with an 'o'), because she was like sunshine, radiant. Her sister and mother called her by her actual name, Inez, but as she had told me her name was Sonny when I first met her, that's what I always called her.

Ruthie got married. She had been sharing an apartment with Harriet, and down the hall from their apartment lived the fellow that she married. His name was Richard Winger. She started dating him, and he and I became very good friends.

Traders General was a Texas based company, with headquarters in Dallas. I worked in Houston. If somebody insured with them wrecked their automobile in an accident, my job was to contact the insurer of the people with whom they had the accident and attempt to appease them and settle whatever claim they might have against the person insured by Traders.

I worked for Traders for a couple of years and then, wanting more money and a better position, I applied to a larger company, the Hartford Insurance Company, Hartford, Connecticut. I worked my way up starting off as an Insurance Adjustor and eventually became an Insurance Lawsuit Investigator.

The work that I had done previously in the Military Intelligence and FBI went in my favor, as I had some knowledge and the natural knack needed for an investigator. Eventually, I worked on claims that had gone into litigation, and what I was doing got pretty creative. I traveled the lower fourth of the state of Texas. I would go east to the Louisiana line, to the cities of Beaumont, Fort Arthur and Orange, Texas and then West all the way down to Bay City, El Campo and Wharton, Texas. It was quite a distance as Texas is a very big state and the area I covered was larger than some smaller states, and I eventually figured out a way to work the territory in about three days. I would leave on a Monday morning, work Tuesday and Wednesday and by Wednesday night I would be back to Houston, and then the four days from Thursday until Sunday I could be at home doing whatever I wanted to do.

Now the Company didn't know that. I never told them. I was on an expense account and I would pad my expenses a little bit, which was not ethical, but I had ways of doing that. Sometimes I would stay out of town the last two days of the week or over the weekend to interview someone for a sworn statement. Even though I could have driven back, because it wasn't that far, maybe 100 miles or sometimes 150 miles, rather than driving back and turn around and go back again, I'd spend the night down there. That was okay with the Company. But there were a number of occasions in which I said I had done that when I really hadn't.

Usually, I stayed in small motels, and I got to know the clerks on the counter. I would ask them to give me blank receipts, which I simply filled in, and then I'd turn in those receipts as though I stayed down there. In the same way, I would put restaurant meals on the expense account as though I was down there. I'm not proud now of this lack of integrity.

After Hartford Insurance, I got a job with Broyhill Furniture. There were a whole bunch of applicants, as it was really a good job and not the kind that came along often. It's amazing how many highly, competed-for jobs that I was actually able to get. It's just uncanny to me when I look back on it. But nonetheless that's what happened. I became a salesman for Broyhill and I worked for them for about two years. I really enjoyed that. I liked the company, I liked the work and I liked selling furniture to retail outlets. I set up merchandising plans with buyers from the larger department stores, the larger chain furniture stores and, as well, the smaller and privately owned furniture stores.

I was out of town sometimes for two weeks at a time. Sonny had come to accept it. I called her regularly and occasionally I took her with me back before our son Skyler was born. Randy, her older son, and my stepson, sometimes stayed with his father, which allowed Sonny to travel with me.

I enjoyed having Sonny with me, although I have to admit that I didn't let it get lonely for me. I wasn't faithful to my wife. I didn't really fully understand the significance and the importance of keeping agreements. My integrity really wasn't good in that regard. I was good though at keeping it from her and she didn't seem to suspect that I was not being faithful to her.

On one occasion, I got into a dispute with the national sales manager for Broyhill. Someone said something about me, or made some comment about something that I had said, and I was called in to account for myself. It came to the point where it was pretty scary and I had to really toe the mark. I had to sell myself back to him in order to keep my job. For the life of me, I can't remember what the dispute was about, but after that, I didn't have a very good feeling about them. My immediate supervisor, the district manager, and I still got along okay, but there was kind of a rub there. I ended up resigning; my philosophy was not to leave one horse until you could move over to another running horse, so I waited until I had another opening.

Being in the industry, I learned about an opening at another furniture company, so I contacted them, got an interview and got the job. That was with Flexsteel, an upholstered furniture manufacturer out of Texas. Broyhill manufactured all kinds of furniture including bedroom and dining room furniture, as well as upholstered furniture; Flexsteel only manufactured upholstered furniture, but it offered an even better income opportunity. Broyhill gave a base salary plus a small percentage. Flexsteel was a percentage company. You could get a draw against your commissions and I used the draw when I started but eventually I oversold my draw. I worked for Flexsteel for a number of years with much the same territory that I had with Broyhill.

I left Flexsteel to work for Silk Skin, the bra and girdle company, which was a division of a bigger company called Exquisite Form. There had been many salesmen who had applied for my job, maybe a hundred, but I got it. I went through an extensive interview with the district sales manager and national sales manager for Silk Skin, and then the sales manager for all of Exquisite Form came down from New York to give his final approval.

That job was a big step up in income and freedom. I traveled the entire southern half of the state of Texas, including San Antonio, all the way down the Rio Grande River from Laredo to Brownsville and all the way back up to the Louisiana line. I was out of town quite a bit; I would spend two weeks on the road, with weekends in Corpus Christi, then over to San Antonio, and all the way over to Laredo.

I was in the top ten salesmen with Broyhill and Flexsteel. With Silk Skin I became the top salesman in a year and a half.

I became very good friends, real buddies, with my immediate sales supervisor and often he flew down to meet me and we would ride along together as I called on accounts. We used to have a hell of a lot of fun at night. He and I did a bit of philandering; we were not very loyal to our wives. Even the national sales manager used to come to Houston with my district supervisor, and the three of us would go out and put all of it on his expense account. The next morning we'd get up and go to work with hangovers, but we did our job. We didn't let that interfere with our work.

Ramana in his late twenties or early thirties. *AHAM archives.*

So when my district supervisor and the national sales manager came into town, they looked to me for girls; to fix them up with dates to go out and enjoy ourselves. We would go out into town. I even told my wife when they were coming into town and I would give her some other excuse why I was going out on the town as well. Then the three of us would go out philandering. I'm not very happy about all this now as I look back on what I did. That's just the way it was in those days.

When an opening presented itself for a job as district manager of the southeast division of the company, as I was top salesman, I was promoted and transferred from Houston to Atlanta, Georgia. For about a month I worked and flew back home, until we found an apartment in Atlanta while we looked around for a house. At that time a new subdivision was being built in a suburb of Atlanta named Doraville and we went to the owner and bought a house before it was even built. They built it to our specifications, making some changes from their basic floor design. They had two or three floor plans that you could choose from, we picked out a tri-level. You'd walk in on one level, go down into a basement that had a sitting room with fireplace and an office, then go up to the main level, and then upstairs to the bedrooms and bathrooms on the third level. It was a beautiful home, the first of significance that I'd ever owned. I had a good income as a district sales manager. In those days you might almost say that money was my god, I was really motivated by money. I was a typically ambitious businessman progressing up in Middle America, middle class.

Sonny loved having a new house and furnishing it - and with my having been in the furniture business we were able to furnish it quite well with relatively inexpensive and good furniture. I called some of my contacts in the furniture business and bought some furniture from them and had it shipped over. Or, I contacted local furniture companies and they, knowing that I was in the business, gave me some good deals. I was always looking how to cut corners and for creative ways of making and saving money.

My wife was very happy, I was really successful in the business world and things were going very well for us. We got very friendly with our neighbor, Eddy Barker, who was a well known journalist and wrote a regular column for the two major newspapers, the Atlanta Journal and the Atlanta Constitution, which were owned by the same publishing firm. The Journal was the morning paper and the Constitution was the afternoon paper. We had BBQs in our back yards. He owned a vacation place on Jekyll Island on the coast of Georgia. He'd go there with his wife, sometimes for a couple of weeks or on weekends, and we'd oversee their house when they were gone.

One day, Eddy came to learn about something going on in Atlanta; and as a reporter he went to debunk it as a fraud. It was about a company called Nutrabio that had just begun to get big. They had a multi-level marketing plan.

In those days, multi-level marketing was not well known. Nutrabio was really the first company to come out with it and become nationally known. It was on the upsurge, and someone had told Eddy about it and had invited him to an opportunity meeting. He was going to the meeting with the intention of exposing it as a scam, but he wasn't sure. He came over and said he had something he wanted me to see. "You're in sales, in marketing," he said. "I'd like you to go with me to see this thing and tell me what you think about it and tell me if it's really legitimate." So I said okay.

The opportunity meeting was really something. There was a platform speaker from Birmingham, Alabama - and he was a whiz. He was there with other people from Birmingham, where Nutribio was already going well, but it was just getting started in Atlanta. He showed an audio-visual in two parts, one to do with the product and the other with the marketing. Nutrabio had vitamin and mineral food supplements in capsules. Two greens and one yellow taken twice a day and could supply you with all the vitamins and minerals needed to give you vitality.

A pitchman talked about the benefits of the product, how he enjoyed it and had been using it for years. He was a movie actor named Robert Cummings (1910 - 1990). He had been in many movies and on television, so he was famous and he already had a reputation for being a health nut. He had been taking literally a handful of vitamins and minerals of different kinds, fifteen or so at a time. He told how he was able to reduce the number he took to so few because of Nutrabio. He had been interviewed and had written articles for national magazines about good health and nutrition. That he was a movie star presenting and promoting Nutrabio was extremely impressive. This was in the fifties, and I had never seen or heard of multi-level marketing.

A TV actor presented the multi-level marketing plan. He had a role on a very popular show called *The Millionaire* (1955 to 1960, *ed.*). In the program, he played the role of a man named Mr. Anthony, the representative of a so-called extremely wealthy philanthropist whose purpose in life was to give away his money. He would give away a million dollars to whoever he had picked. It was his job to give a cashier's check for the money and then the TV story would be about the life of the lucky recipient. One condition was that the recipient had to sign an agreement to never disclose the philanthropist.

So, at the very beginning of each program, Mr. Anthony knocked on the door; the person would appear and see a stranger who said, "Hello, my name is Mr. Anthony, and I would like to announce something." He would walk in then and give them a check for a million dollars.

He started the Nutrabio presentation with, "If I am any judge of a million-dollar idea, this is it."

The presentation explained how the marketing plan worked and it would just blow your socks off. Then local people gave testimonials and showed Photostat copies of the checks that they had received from the company. These were huge sums of money.

The whole staging was very impressive and as soon as the program was over, Eddy Barker turned to me and said: "What do you think?

I said: "What do I think. Hell, I'm signing up!"

He said, "Wait a minute, I'm not signed in yet. You can't sign up until I sign up." So I signed up under Eddy and the way it works is, whoever signs up underneath you, how far down the line goes, you receive something from them and so by me signing under Eddy, anybody I signed up under me would be beneficial to him.

There was a columnist for Newsweek Magazine that Eddy had invited but he was very skeptical. He wouldn't sign up, but I talked him into it. Eddy knew him but had not been able to get him to sign up. He was a columnist, but I was a salesman able to influence him.

The Newsweek Magazine columnist wrote about how Nutrabio had begun growing in the South. He, Eddy and I went over to Birmingham and met the ones who got started there.

It was a whole chain. A guy from New York, who had started early in the company, ran an ad in the Wall Street Journal. It was seen by someone in Birmingham who was a comptroller for the Allis Chalmers Company, a dealer for Caterpillar Tractors. He had seen this ad running that had to do with how to make a million dollars. He was curious and answered the ad. He wanted to know what it was all about, but the guy who ran the ad wouldn't tell him.

He said, "If you really want to know, you're going to have to fly here and attend a meeting with me."

The guy said, "Tell me what it is; I'm not going to buy a ticket all the way there not knowing what it is."

The guy replied, "You're not interested in earning a million dollars, are you?"

Well, to make a long story short, he bought the ticket, feeling like he was an idiot doing so, flew to wherever it was, attended the meeting and sure enough signed up. He then went back to Birmingham, started telling his friends and one of the first people he told was his own secretary. She signed up. By the time the columnist for Newsweek went over to Birmingham to interview him, he was earning $50,000.00 a month, which comes to $600,000.00 a year. Back in the fifties, that was a tremendous amount of money. It would be about the equivalent of $300,000.00 or more a month now, it was just absolutely unbelievable, but it was a fact, that's exactly what he was earning. And his secretary was earning $10,000.00 a month.

So at the opportunity meeting in Atlanta, some of these people came over from Birmingham with photocopies of the check that they had received from the company. There was a whole string of checks; they just fanned out all the checks they had received in the past month from the company. You talk about impressive - I'm telling you, people were signing up like there was no tomorrow.

I got started right away telling people about it, but most people I knew were in Houston not Atlanta. So I eventually went back to Houston. I pretty quickly lost interest in my job in Atlanta, because as I said, in those days money was primarily what I was interested in.

One of the first things I wanted to learn was the presentation, so I got the fellow who was giving them, the facilitator of the opportunity meetings from Birmingham, a fabulous speaker, to teach me. I had to pay him to show me the nuances of the presentation. For the meetings in Atlanta, they needed someone to give the presentation. Well, of course, they got me. I lived there. I started off giving presentations in Atlanta and people were just as much moved by and impressed by my giving them as they were with this guy.

I soon was ready to go to Houston where I started calling my friends.

In Houston there was a big hotel called the Shamrock, which was constructed between 1946 and 1949 by a famous Texan wildcatter, Glenn McCarthy. McCarthy's story was the inspiration for a character in the movie *Giant* (1956), played by James Dean. Rock Hudson and Elizabeth Taylor played in the film and the Shamrock Hotel was featured in it briefly. I went across the street from the Shamrock to a very nice, but not as expensive hotel, to rent a meeting room. It didn't take long for it to catch on. I would be looking at a room of seventy-five to a hundred people. What a good feeling it was, looking out over a full room of people and knowing that everyone in that room was in the downline under me. It wasn't too long before I was making around $5,000.00 a month.

Sonny and I got an apartment in Houston. She came back to Houston leaving our house vacant. She never really liked Atlanta because she had family and friends in Houston so she was very happy to come back. We just left our house, locked it. It was about six weeks before I went back. I opened it and walked into this dead house. Sonny had left with the intention to come back. Well she didn't. So I had to empty the refrigerator, call in a maid service, clean the house, get it in order and put it on the market for sale. We had a house in Houston before we sold the house in Atlanta.

I let ambition and greed enter my life. I was doing extremely well, it was almost like the sky was the limit; we were just going up.

The person who had been up line from the one who had taught me the presentation came to Houston. His name was John. He called and told me that they had something they wanted to talk to me about. We met in his hotel room. He said it was very secret what he wanted to share with me. I said okay.

John asked me keep an open mind. That was the way of the whole presentation of Nutrabio, to keep an open mind. He opened up a slide projector and gave a presentation of another company; a competitor of Nutrabio called Vitalize. As it happened, ultimately people in Nutrabio were not making as much money as they were ballyhooing. Making the millions were the ones who started the company. Vitalize turned out to be started by a group who were making money in Nutrabio, but they were greedy and wanted to make real big money. A number of people that I knew had already gone over to Vitalize. And so, they put a strong pitch on me to bring all the people I already had over to them.

They did a good job pitching me. I was making money, but expenses and various things meant that I wasn't making as much as I had initially.

The money that could be made in Vitalize was almost double what I had been making, and they particularly wanted me because I could present the program. A couple of days later the guy who had started Vitalize flew down to Houston to pitch to me to move over and come in with them on this new deal. So I went into it.

When John F. Kennedy was debating Richard Nixon for the Presidency of the United States (1960), I watched them debate from the living room of my friends, Bernie and Harriet, in Houston. This, though, was around the time of the Cuban blockade when John Kennedy was President. He had blocked Cuba (1962) because the Russians had put in missiles and there was the threat of war. People were beginning to sell fall-out shelters and so Vitalize had come along with a survival package together with their regular vitamins and minerals. It had a broader product selection than Nutrabio and the spiel was that it was a much better deal. This survival package was promoted for people to have at home just in event of problems, a shortage of food or war.

My friend, Richard - Ruthie's husband - was part of my downline. His father was an executive vice-president of Texaco, a major oil company, and he presented to his father the idea of Texaco purchasing the survival package and selling it in their service stations as a benefit to their customers. He seemed to like the idea and asked his marketing manager what he thought about it.

Well, he thought that might have some potential, something that Texaco would go for. That meant it would be available at the Texaco service stations in America, and at that time there must have been eight or ten thousand of them.

I then made a mistake. When it came to going to New York to give the presentation to the marketing manager at Texaco, I did not go myself. Instead I let John talk me into him being the one. I knew he was a good pitchman. It would have been real simple as Texaco was sold on the idea to begin with.

Richard went with him. They flew up to New York, met Richard's father and then the marketing director. And John started his presentation this way: "Men, I've got an idea that would sell more gasoline for you then you've ever sold in the history of Texaco."

To tell the marketing director he was going to sell more gasoline then he has ever sold before was totally off. All he would have had to do was to say, "We have a wonderful idea, what would you like to know?" Or, "What ideas do you have? Let's see how it can be done; we're here to serve you in anyway we can."

John blew the deal. That could have been a million dollars because it would come under our marketing pitch. We would have been the ones who set it up.

Not only that, about two weeks after the United States Government started a major investigation of multi-level marketing. It hit the newspapers. It was a national story. We had just gotten started in Vitalize. Of course Nutrabio had been in business for a long time, they had plenty of money and so they just rolled with the punches and were able to survive all the adverse publicity, but the new company couldn't survive. Vitalize went down the tubes and I went down the tubes with it.

During the time that I was married to Sonny, my spiritual quest became rekindled and I discovered the Unity Church.

I took Sonny with me to the church, but she didn't like to go at all, she just wasn't interested, but I got very interested as I began to meet some people that I could talk to about my own spiritual experience and quest. From there the pull was very, very strong and so I eventually became a student minister and went through the ministerial training program at Unity in Missouri.

So, I had a worldly non-spiritual life and, at the same time, I had an underlying interest and compulsion to know more about the truth of being.

Back when I had that awakening as a child, I had no one that I could talk to about it, but within me I knew it was genuine. It was always in the back of my mind, prior to my mind. It never left me. I knew I had an awareness that most other people didn't have. I didn't look down upon anybody that didn't have it, because I couldn't even describe it, and any time I did, others were skeptical and non-accepting. So rather than having any kind of attitude of being better than anyone else, I looked at it as not quite up to the standard of everyone else. Still, I knew the awakening was real, and, intuitively, that no matter what happened to me in the world, it wasn't real - everything that happened would eventually pass.

I had read the Bible and what Jesus had said: "My kingdom is not of this world" (King James Version, John 18:36), stayed with me, though I never got caught up in fundamentalist Christianity. I went through it and realized they didn't know what they were talking about. I just kept looking, seeking. My whole life was a spiritual quest and the people I knew, and all my closest friends knew, there was something different about me.

Sonny and I had married in the 1950s. She had a son, Randy, from a previous marriage, who I raised as my own son. He was four years old when we got married and then we had our son Skyler.

Now Sonny's passed on and so have both of my sons. They are either floating around up there in between with no body, or perhaps they have taken on another body. I don't know which.

CHAPTER 6

Kicked Out of Heaven

During the time that I was with my second wife, Sonny, my spiritual quest became rekindled. I was in my early thirties and I discovered Unity Church (early 1960s, *ed.*). It had a non-doctrinal and open philosophy, and you could hear Jesus's message from a metaphysical rather than from a doctrinal point of view.

The Unity Church in Houston sponsored me to become a Unity minister and when I got to Unity Village in Lee Summit, a suburb of Kansas, Missouri, I thought I had arrived in heaven. It was such a beautiful place, there was a beautiful energy about it and I thought "This is my home."

In 1889, Charles and Myrtle Fillmore founded the Unity Church. They bought about 150 acres in Lee Summit. In those days it was just farmland and they used to call it Unity Farm. They had apple orchards, grew vegetables and other things, but they were known for their apples. They sold apples from a stand at an intersection of the main road. They made apple cider, apple juice and they became widely known for their apple butter. I haven't been to Unity myself in a number of years, but photographs that I've seen of it from, say, ten years ago, show the ways it has been built up and I don't think I would recognize it now.

Myrtle Fillmore, who was Charles Fillmore's wife, was the one who really started the church. It all happened out of healing. Myrtle had terminal Tuberculosis and the doctors had given her only three to six months to live. There was nothing they could do for her. She went to Kansas City to a lecture from E.B. Weeks. He had been a student of Emma Curtis Hopkins. Back in the 1800s, Emma Curtis Hopkins had been friend, co-worker and almost equal to Mary Baker Eddy, the founder of Christian Science. E.B. Weeks said that sickness is not natural; if we're sick it's because we have not recognized who we really are. As children of God we were not destined to be sick, but whole, complete and healthy. All we had to do was change our attitude about ourselves and we could heal whatever our condition happened to be.

Weeks made a tremendous impact upon Myrtle Fillmore. She took what he said to be true. She brought some literature home and started practicing the new ideas, changing her concept of herself, and, to make a long story short, she healed herself. She was expected to live only three to six months, but she lived for about another forty years before she finally passed.

Charles Fillmore had lived in Colorado. As a teenager he was skating on the ice of a frozen lake, fell and dislocated his right hip. In the early 1800s in his town, they didn't have medical technology capable of dealing with his injury. They could never get it properly re-set and he continued to live with his dislocated right hip that shriveled and did not grow like the other one.

He had to have a special shoe with a six-inch thick sole. The doctors in those days diagnosed his condition as "Tuberculosis of the hip." So his wife had terminal Tuberculosis in her lungs and he had Tuberculosis of the hip. Myrtle healed herself and he picked up the same idea, but he was more aggressive in making it his life study. Myrtle was more subdued: though she was really the base of Unity through her quiet love and stillness, while he was more active and assertive.

Charles grew his leg five inches. In his later years he wore a shoe with a sole that was only one inch thick and his limp was barely perceptible. He wrote most of the books - maybe fifty or one hundred books - on Unity Philosophy. Myrtle wrote a few, and she behaved like a Buddha. Both of them read and studied Eastern Religion, yet ended up settling back into Christianity. Charles always asserted that anything you wanted to know about God or spirituality can be found in the Holy Bible. So the Bible and Christianity were the basic teachings, but Unity was not doctrinal or fundamentalist.

Charles Fillmore himself did extensive research on the origin of words in the Bible. He wrote a Metaphysical Bible Dictionary that goes back to the metaphysical meaning of the words, including the names of people, locations, cities, regions and countries. He showed that the names really have significance.

Fundamentalist Christians believe in Jesus being the only one who was awakened and to be worshiped as God. Unity teaches that Jesus is not the only son of God; Jesus is like Buddha and all of us are sons and daughters of God. We are spiritual beings. Unity goes quite far into the spirituality of man.

My father died several months before I went to Unity and I was still dealing with my grief when I started school there. I had come to really love and appreciate him, not as much as I love and appreciate him now, but a great deal.

My father had at least three or four major situations in his life that very few people would have been able to have overcome. He lived to work as well as worked to live. And, when he was no longer able to work, as he got beyond the age of working, he didn't have anything to fill that gap, so I think he just died from the sorrow of not really having anything to do, or call his own, that was significant.

His marriage to my mother was a habit and for companionship, not that they didn't love each other in their own way as far as they could, though my father was not necessarily that happy with my mother. As they didn't have anything else, they more or less put up with each other and accepted their differences to the best of their ability. When he had to stay home all the time, I think it was more than he could handle.

I often came home for Christmas just to be with them. One Christmas, my father was working as a security guard at a fine hotel downtown in the heart of Dallas. He worked in the parking lot entranceway. People arrived in their cars and parking lot attendants would park them.

It was an easy sit down job and he made a lot of friends, as he was very personable. He met guests, bellhops, parking lot attendants, janitors and other workers. As well, many people who lived on the street came in when it was cold and he would let them stand around to get warm. He wasn't supposed to, but he was compassionate. He would just tell them that they had to go when his bosses came by.

On this particular Christmas, he came home from work and my mother noticed he did not have his overcoat.

"Where is your coat?" she asked, but he wouldn't answer and went on to bed.

The next day, when he woke up, my mother was immediately on him.

"Where's your coat?"

He finally confessed that he had given it to someone who came in from the cold and didn't have a place to stay. It was very cold in Dallas that Christmas. It was a relatively new coat, a good coat, and expensive for his income, and I think my mother had bought it for him.

My mother gave him one hell of a hard time. I interceded saying that I thought it was one of the most wonderful things I had ever heard; I gave him a big hug and he was just there, as timid as a kid and my mama just brow beating him.

Then she turned and lambasted me, because I was "defending him and taking the other side," so I just let her complain to me so that it was not directed at him.

Another time he had been in a coma for two weeks. While working as a security guard at a stock-car race, he was ushering-back people in the crowd, when one of the cars in the race went out of control and hit him, going probably 70 or 80 mph. The impact broke his leg, his arm, several of his ribs and ruptured his spleen. He was in terrible shape, though he survived it.

Later he was diagnosed with cancer of the lung. Most of his life, he had been at least a pack-a-day, sometimes two packs-a-day, smoker. In those days, before manufactured cigarettes, he smoked hand-rolled cigarettes that he made himself. He'd always smoked, even when I was a kid. My mother did too. I didn't start smoking until much later in my life.

They ended up taking out his right lung and the doctor told him that he was going to have to quit smoking because if he didn't, it would kill him. You can't do it on one lung.

Just as the doctor was telling him that, my mother and I came in. When my dad saw us, he picked up his cigarettes, handed them to my mother, and said "I quit!" And he quit. He never smoked another cigarette. Now that's the way my father was, whenever he set his mind to do something, there was nothing that would stop him.

I'm estimating that he died in 1964, so I was thirty-five. He was born, if I remember, in 1898, so that would have made him sixty-five, but I'm not absolutely sure.

I worked in the Silent Unity prayer ministry as a junior letter-writer as did other student ministers. I loved that work. We would answer the letters and say prayers requested by people from all over the world.

Unity had a very efficient and fine system. We all had Royal type-writers; about one hundred letter-writers in one huge open room. On one side of the room were senior letter-writers and on the other side junior letter-writers. There were more seniors than junior letter-writers, and every letter-writer had exactly the same kind of Royal type-writer with purple ribbon. There was a library with brochures printed by Unity. We knew those brochures and many of us had our favorites which we would pull for a particular letter.

Some people wrote to us every day, even two or three letters a day. Unity answered every letter they received. In those days they were receiving about five thousand letters a day from all over the country and the world. That's why we had so many letter-writers and one of the rules was, you never sent the same letter twice, so you would have to create the letter yourself. That was the work that I did and I loved it.

One of the requirements to work in Silent Unity was, of course, to be able to type. I had taken typing in high school; you had to type so many words a minute and I was a little bit slow. I got around that by taking a typing test at a business college. I had to have a typing score and send it in with my application. I knew the person who owned the business college. He was gay and interested in me that way, although I wasn't interested in him.

I went to him and told him that I needed to get a typing test and score about fifty words a minute and he said, "No problem." He took me to the lady in charge of typing and she gave me a test. I think I only did about forty-five words a minute, though she said that I did fifty a min-ute, and so that's how I was able to be accepted at Unity.

I could certainly type fast enough and I loved writing the letters, the communications with people, the consciousness of the place, all of the literature that had been written by ministers and instructors. It was conscious work and I read the literature every day. We were busy writ-ing letters except for the times we were in class.

When I had lived in Washington, D.C., I got a part-time job in the YMCA - where I was living - operating a telephone switchboard. I took it to make some extra money. I learned how to operate a regular switchboard where you pulled up cords and put them into a board which lit up. So when I got to Unity I needed to make some extra money because, even though they paid me for being a junior letter-writer, it was a minimum wage and hardly enough to take care of anything else than my personal toiletries, cleaning and laundry.

Unity Tower, Unity Village, Missouri, 2009. *Image from Americasroof, en.wikipedia.org/wiki/Unity_Village,_Missouri, Creative Commons, Attribution-Share Alike 3.0 Unported License (creativecommons.org/licenses/by-sa/3.0/).*

In a picture of Unity grounds, you will see the Unity Tower standing out. There was a switchboard there. On the main floor, as you came in, was the information desk and behind it was the communications room, where all the telephone calls came and the lines went to the various offices all over Unity. I think the older lady who had worked the switchboard for years had died, and they were in a bit of a bind and looking for someone.

I immediately said, "I know how to run the switchboard."

So I went to work part-time on the switchboard, earning extra money.

Everything in my life was working together and I felt compatible with everything. It felt so natural. This was my home. This whole thing was my life, my whole world was right here.

Just prior to going to Unity, my wife Sonny and I separated. We had been married for seven years, but Sonny said to me, "I'm not going to be married to a damn preacher!"

So you can see where she was coming from, as far as my spiritual life was concerned.

With Sonny, I had a daughter who we named Kyra Dee (Dee was the same as my birth name). I named her and Skyler, too. Kyra Dee drowned in our swimming pool when I was at Unity School in the ministerial training program. It was the Christmas break. There wasn't anything to do at the school and so I went home. Even though I was separated from Sonny, I still stayed there when I was off from Unity.

Kyra was just a baby, nineteen months old, just a toddler. I would be in the water, in the pool, and she would jump to me. She would jump to her mother too – and we had to be very careful, because she would even jump before we told her to jump. She'd just jump right out, she loved the water. She would jump in even if you weren't there. And that's what she did.

I was having coffee at the kitchen table and talking to the maid about philosophy and about Unity School. She was interested in knowing about it. While we were talking Kyra had been playing in the house. All of a sudden I realized that she wasn't around. So I said to the maid, "You go get her." We both looked and she was not there.

The maid went out the front door and I went out the back and as I went down the stairs, it hit me, I already knew. I knew even before I got to the pool. And sure enough, as I got to the pool her body was at the bottom. I pulled her out and did the best I could to give her artificial respiration. When I pressed on her chest, all the water in her stomach came out of her mouth. We called the Fire Department Emergency Squad - back in those days they didn't have the Ambulances like they do now - and when they came they tried a resuscitator. It didn't work, it was a hopeless situation, she was gone.

Everybody projected on me, I was responsible for it. My wife, my in-laws and some of my friends even, particularly my wife's friends, blamed me. That was really tough for me to deal with.

Then when I went back to Unity School, everyone was very compassionate, but I began to develop nervous habits, reactionary kind of emotional symptoms that I wasn't necessarily aware of, but people who observed me could see. It was somewhat unsightly. I developed a tremendous rash under my arms, down my neck and in my genital area. My penis peeled and was raw from the sweat. I would scratch, which I tried to do in private, but sometimes it would just get the better of me and I would do it inadvertently when people could observe me.

I've heard many say that a loss of a child is one of the most difficult losses to overcome. I will agree with that. When my baby daughter drowned, that was more painful than anything. After all she was my own offspring, my own flesh and blood, God's creation through me. So when my baby daughter died, it really knocked the wind out of my sails.

In those days, the grounds of Unity were very tranquil, very peaceful and I used to love to go out and sit somewhere. I had a couple of favorite spots where there were benches. I would take food, and the squirrels and rabbits would come up and eat out of my hand. I used to love to do that.

Unity was a huge school in those days with many different departments manned mostly by women, many my age and single. In those days, I was considered to be a pretty handsome man, so there were a lot of women interested in me for a husband, I could almost have had my choice, and I had a few sexual encounters that were hard to keep secret.

In the Unity organization, it became musical chairs. Husbands and wives, realizing that they may have gotten married to each other for the wrong reasons, started looking to fulfill their aspirations for a husband or a wife and looking around to other ministers and other ministers' wives. The first thing you knew, a lot of divorces and a lot of re-marriages happened. It was behind closed doors. People who knew didn't openly talk about it, but there were a lot of innuendoes, rumors, stories and gossip.

I started dating Virginia who worked in Silent Unity as a letter-writer. She had a small room in one of the main buildings, which was like a big lodge where people lived. I lived on campus too, but in a totally different building.

We would go into town dancing and have a few beers even though she was really not supposed to drink because she was in AA (Alcoholics Anonymous).

The first time I heard about AA was from another woman. We were having a sexual liaison and were in bed, when she pulled out a book that had to do with AA. She could not drink and I learned then about the St. Francis prayer (a modern Christian prayer in the spirit of Saint Francis of Assisi, *ed.*).

I had that assumptive attitude at that time. If you affirm that you are an alcoholic then your mind is going to pick up that notion and give you back that experience. So, don't affirm that you're an alcoholic, even though I know that's what they do in the AA program. I really didn't know that much about alcoholism and addiction from a medical point of view, but my belief was that you could overcome the compulsion to drink alcohol.

So I said to Virginia, "You've got to change your attitude. You cannot affirm yourself as being an alcoholic.

We saw some proof of my thoughts about this, as the grace of living in a spiritual and conscious environment helped her overcome her addiction - suppressed it you might say.

In those days, I was one of those extremely positive thinkers. I was a student of Dr. Napoleon Hill and I really believed that "Whatever the mind of man can conceive and believe, it can achieve."

One of our classmates, Nancy Davis, had contracted polio in her later childhood. She wore braces on her legs and walked with crutches that hooked around her arms, but she could still move around pretty good. So, my having been a dancing instructor, I decided I was going to teach Nancy how to dance. She loved music and she loved the idea of being able to dance. I told her she could do it. She believed that she could do it, and I believed that she could do it, so I started teaching her. She would hold on to me and I would support her weight and she began to learn the steps, which direction to move her feet. Two or three times a week we did these lessons and she learned to dance.

We'd get up on the dance floor and everybody in the school oohed and aahed over that. They couldn't believe it. Not only did she dance, she learned how to walk better too.

We had a function one night at the school, and Nancy and I got up on the floor and danced. Her mother, several of my classmates and her co-workers from Silent Unity were there. Nancy wasn't a student minister, but her mother had been in training to be a minister and later had her own church not too far from Unity School, still in Missouri. When Nancy and I were up on the floor, her mother almost sobbed from joy at seeing her daughter able to dance.

Nancy and I are still good friends and I email her every now and then.

To me, Unity was like being in heaven; in my view I had located the place, the source of my happiness. I thought my happiness came out of finding heaven on earth and to me Unity was a place that was dedicated to the spiritual life that I had chosen for myself. I could see my whole future laid out for me. There was going to be peace, love and joy from then on, because I had found it in Unity.

People at Unity were so open and supportive. I loved everybody there and the teaching itself. But with certain instructors I didn't get along, and as it ended up I was expelled.

You had to go to classes, turn in papers and write tests on the principles and teachings of Unity. In classes, I would sometimes bring up a question that teachers didn't have an answer for. A lot of my classmates also had questions, but they wouldn't ask them except outside of the classroom. We'd get together at one another's rooms or the village cafeteria and have discussions amongst ourselves.

When I asked questions and the instructor did not know the answer, they would come back with the typical, fundamentalist approach of religion - that you just had to be open and have faith. However, I was there to learn - not to bullshit anybody - I was on a spiritual quest. I wanted awakening - I was caught up in the quest for Christ consciousness as were all of the people that I met at Unity. I felt there wasn't any area that you shouldn't go into; if you had a question you should be able to get an answer for it.

From my awakening experience as a child, I was aware that we are all expressions of the One Being. That was unequivocal while I was having that experience, but whenever I was not in that experience, I was identified with the body and the mind and with the idea of being a separate individual being. I had hoped that while I was at Unity, I would be able to transcend that false notion.

I thought maybe Charles and Myrtle and some of the older people in Unity might possibly have experienced that, but I didn't meet anyone in Unity that I could sense was, in fact, living in Christ consciousness.

Now, there may have been, but I didn't meet any, and no one could truly relate experientially with the transcendental experience I had had as a child. Everyone I met was just a philosophical believer, but not an experiencer of a real transcendental state of higher consciousness.

Often, after I asked a question and didn't get an answer from the instructor, an answer would reveal itself to me. Then I would say, "Could it be this?" and I would share the answer that came to me. It would be obvious to everyone present that my answer was the closest to an answer that anyone had come up with.

My classmates were in glee that I had the gall to ask such a question, but the instructors took it that I was making a fool out of them, as though I was doing it intentionally, as if I already knew the answer before I asked a question. It seemed to them I was getting them to say they didn't know the answer and then giving my answer in order to put them in a bad light. But, as God is my witness, I never did that, it was not what I was doing. I didn't know the answer when I asked a question, but it would be revealed to me. It was just as it is right now. People ask questions that I don't know the answer to ahead of time. It's not an intellectual process, it's my being open, and in my openness, if the answer is there, it will rise to the surface into consciousness for me to see and know.

Along with my unsightly habits, my forwardness, my openness and, I guess, my ego (my need for acceptance and recognition - when you have an ego you need to have recognition) - it was considered to be a little bit too much. I can say there was also, on my part, a certain degree of arrogance, about them not having awakened to a similar experience as I had when I had been younger and, I must confess, there was also a certain disappointment that nobody there could really know what I was attempting to communicate.

In any case, they didn't feel that I would be the right image for a Unity minister and so I was expelled.

The one whose job was to tell me that I was expelled, James Dillet Freeman, was compassionate with me. He was known as the poet laureate of Unity. He wrote goodness knows how many poems published in the Daily Word, and various booklets, and he wrote the poem that the first astronauts took to the moon and later a second poem that was left in a capsule there.

It was difficult for him to expel me. He knew where I was coming from and that I was really not guilty of any of the accusations that some of the instructors were making against me. Still, he was outweighed, and he had to go along with the majority.

I was grieving at my father's death and even more so the death of my daughter, a tremendous loss. Along with that sense of loss was the feeling of responsibility that I may have contributed to her drowning, that I had not been alert, I had been involved in a conversation with the maid about religious philosophy when she drowned. All of this went together in the mind and I was really distressed. I had only been back about two or three months when I was expelled. I had been accepted into heaven and then kicked out.

There was nothing that I had done until then that would compare. Now what was my future?

I was in this tremendous depression, in so low an ebb and hurting so badly, that I was accepting any support I could get. Well, Virginia was immediately there to give me the support just in the right way that I needed it.

Unity gave me a notice that I was to vacate my room within a certain period of time and I just flatly refused. I said: "You're going to have to throw me out!"

When a new minister in Unity went out into the field, if he didn't get along well with the board of his church, they would replace him by another minister. If the minister was not able to function effectively,

Unity would not fire them, since they had already been ordained; instead they would put them back into the school as instructors to teach new ministers. Three of my instructors had not been able to make it as Unity ministers and had been brought back.

So I knew that Unity wouldn't throw me out. I said: "I'm not going to leave until I feel like it," and I stayed for about another month.

I didn't dare to go back to Houston. The church there had sponsored me going to Unity. The minister and many of the people that I knew in the congregation were so happy and gloating over sponsoring a new student minister, so my going back there in failure was more than I could handle. I had to go somewhere else.

Virginia was really looking for a husband. I wasn't looking for a wife because I hadn't even been divorced very long, but I was at a low ebb and needing support. My way of dealing with it was sexually. I used to use sex as a way to forget my concerns, but I was also looking for companionship and spiritual sustenance, and Virginia was very supportive.

Virginia had been married to a classmate of mine named Bill Cameron before she came to Unity School. He was a year ahead of me, though we had many classes together. They had come from San Francisco when Bill had been accepted into the ministerial training program.

Virginia wanted to get married again. Wherever I went she wanted to go with me as my wife. We got married in the Unity Chapel by Tom Hopper, who had been one of my instructors that I used to ask questions that he couldn't answer. I had asked the Bible instructor to marry us first, but he refused on some point of principle – I can't remember now even what it was –it was really another put down because I had been expelled. My reason for asking them though, was to demonstrate that I was not holding any hard feelings against the ones who had been responsible for my expulsion.

I always had a fascination for California. Unity had a larger concentration of churches in California than any other state in America.

Virginia and a few others suggested we go to California, so that's what we did.

We had our honeymoon on the way and we stopped at many points of interest such as the famous O.K. Corral, and places in Arizona where Bat Masterson and famous Western Marshals had been, and some of the old saloons that had been maintained for historical reasons. We went to the Grand Canyon and from there crossed over the Hoover Dam by Lake Mead and into Las Vegas, Nevada. I even won a bit at the crap tables in Vegas.

My Aunt Sally, my Uncle Henry's wife (he had died), lived in Las Vegas. The two were my favorite aunt and uncle. I looked her up – it wasn't easy to find her – and surprised her by going for a visit. It just blew her away! She was so glad to see me; she just sat and held my hand for the longest time. After I left, I never heard from her again and I don't know what happened to her.

Virginia and I were engrossed in the sightseeing, the geography, the scenery and the travel. I used it as a distraction, you might say intentionally, because of the distress I had been going through.

From Vegas we drove on to Glendale in Los Angeles County, California. Virginia had lived in both Southern California and San Francisco. She had a few friends there that she hadn't seen for a long time and there was one woman from Glendale who had been to Unity. She had become very friendly with Virginia and when Virginia called her and told her we were coming to California; she invited us to stay with her and her husband for a few days until we got settled.

We stayed in their guest room for about three or four days. Then we found an apartment in Glendale and I applied for a job as a sales-man at the Ford Dealership right there. That was my first job selling automobiles.

It had been overcast the whole time we were there; a combination of California smog and fog. You couldn't see much into the distance, but one morning I got up and looked out onto the little balcony of the apartment and I was blown away. There was a mountain range right there called Mount Baldy, with snow caps on top. I hadn't even known that it was there!

In California, I got back into the market place, the business world, because now I was married, had a wife and responsibility for a household, even though there was just the two of us.

Eventually Virginia went to work. We only had one vehicle and where we were living in the suburbs of Los Angeles, they didn't really have a transit system, so it was difficult to get around anywhere. That's why Virginia more or less stayed home all day. But as a car salesman, I eventually qualified to be assigned a car and I could drive back and forth to work. So then I could leave my car at home and that's when Virginia was able to start looking for a job herself. I don't remember what exactly she did; I know she got some kind of secretarial job.

I was involved in ordinary life as I had been before I went to Unity school. California was a different quality of consciousness. I was working and spending a lot of time talking to my fellow salesmen. Two or three of them were open, and with one in particular, I talked about philosophy. People were more open. It was not like it was in the South where most of the people were engrossed in doctrinal beliefs and their fear of going to hell.

I was still identified with the body-mind and with living in time and space and considered myself a separate and different individual, apart from everyone else and from God and from Christ. I considered Jesus as, yes, the son of God and not different from God, but I considered myself as different from God.

We moved to downtown Los Angeles because I saw greater employment opportunities there. I wasn't really the best at selling automobiles, because I didn't much like it.

I met a lady who was the buyer for the furniture department at Bullock's Department Store in the Westwood Shopping Centre, Westwood Village, a very exclusive part of Los Angeles, out Wilshire

Boulevard towards Santa Monica, not too far from Beverly Hills. She was also a member of Unity Church. I had sold furniture wholesale before, now I began working on the floor as a sales person selling retail to the ultimate consumer.

I started attending the main Unity Church in Los Angeles in Manhattan Place. At the time, it was the largest Unity Church in the United States. The building itself was quite impressive; it could hold upwards of 2,500 people and there would usually be 1,800 to 2,000 there on a Sunday morning. We lived near the church in a middle class area, though where I worked was upper middle class and wealthy.

I enjoyed going to church in Manhattan Place because of the minister who had been in Unity for many years. He was an older man by the name of Ernest C. Wilson. I got to know him. He was famous in the Unity organization because he had written three or four significant books, and to me his message was truly in line with Unity's teachings.

I was right up-front with Ernest Wilson about my being expelled from the Unity ministerial program and how sad I was; what a tremendous disappointment it was to me. He was extremely compassionate and said, not to let it bother me, and that as far as he was concerned, it made no difference whatsoever.

I was thirty-six in 1965 when Ernest Wilson left for Kansas. The minister who replaced him was not bothered at my having been expelled from the ministerial program and he gave me two posts of importance and responsibility. I functioned like an assistant minister, although I didn't have an official title or designation; and, it was unpaid and I didn't receive compensation.

I was the director of both Young Adults of Unity (YAU) and the teenagers or Youth of Unity (YOU). Every Sunday morning I worked at the two services. At the nine o'clock service, I would give a talk at the YAU, on average, to fifteen or maybe twenty young adults, and at eleven o'clock I would teach at the YOU. During the main service there would be a ritualistic process; everybody would come together in an assembly and then the youth would leave in a group. I did that for a couple years.

I knew the ministers of ten to fifteen churches in that area and I was assistant minister on a number of occasions. I had also come to know many of the ministers in Southern California, most of whom knew my story, but it didn't make any difference to them. As far as they were concerned, I had had more actual time in training than many of the ministers. They knew of my capability, my knowledge of the Unity teachings, and my teaching the youth and young adults. I was called upon to fill in for ministers needing time off to go somewhere, have a vacation or go back to Unity school during Unity conferences. I became pretty popular as a substitute minister and the head office there knew about it.

When I gave a talk or a sermon, I would call on my knowledge, insights and what I had come to believe. What I believed then, I don't believe anymore, but in those days I was still just a believer. Things were working well for me, which gave me a sense of acceptance, and finally I was getting over the shock and the sorrow of being expelled from the Unity residential ministerial training program.

Unity offered two ways to become a minister: a resident program living on campus and taking the classes, and, as far more ministers didn't have the ability to go live on campus, they could take crash courses during the summer as their schedules allowed. After I had settled in California, I wrote a letter of application to be accepted in the non-resident ministerial training just like many of the other ministers, but I was not approved.

The same instructor involved in my being expelled had somehow, in the interim, moved up to being in charge of training applications. His justification for refusing me was that the ministers who came once a year for one or two months needed less training than those who were in the school full-time and therefore I needed more training than practicing ministers. What he really meant was, that I wouldn't get conditioned by their way of thinking.

Many ministers knew the politics of Unity and how it all worked. They were out in the field and had their own churches and did whatever they wanted to do the way they wanted to do it. The school couldn't necessarily do anything about it. And since the school couldn't do anything about it, if there was someone like me that was contrary to the way the school wanted things to be done, they were able to nip that in the bud right away.

That rejection was the end of my ever considering being an official Unity minister, even though I was actually being called upon as a substitute minister.

It was extremely painful when I was expelled from the residential ministerial training program. It was also very disappointing to be rejected when I applied again to be able to go on through Unity in their non-resident program, because, up to that point, I didn't have a basis other than Christianity and the basis of Christianity that I had studied up to this time, was the Unity philosophy.

Another disappointment was that I had not met anyone that could really, truly relate experientially with the awakening experience I had had as a child. Even though I talked to people about it, no experiential exchanges took place with anyone that I could tell. The sorrow from being expelled even gave rise to a quality of arrogance as a justification. I was being expelled, but what difference did it make? Nobody here had awakened to what I had awakened to. When I had talked to fellow students about my own experience, some listened, but they hadn't had the same experience, and to them it was just more or less my belief.

So, I had no one who was high enough on the ladder spiritually to even recognize that I had any kind of awakening, yet it would bleed through, shine through in classes when I asked questions of the instructor they could not answer, and I then came out with the answer. That had been my problem; I did not accept the Unity fundamentals and way of doing things. I was always taken as being a trouble maker, trying to show up the instructor. I called them on stuff, which was unwise of me.

If I had been quiet, gone along with the policies, smiled and acquiesced, I could have probably finished the training and gone out into the field and done whatever I wanted to do, the way I wanted to do it. But it would not have been true to me. I couldn't do that because I was genuine, I was sincere in my questioning.

I couldn't do it. It was not my destiny.

Ramana, circa 1965. *AHAM archives.*

CHAPTER 7

The World Is Not the Cause of Happiness

I was selling furniture to support myself and Virginia, though I really didn't enjoy what I was doing. I was doing it just for the money. My own quest was expanding during that period and I found the job to be very limiting.

Many opportunities came up to meet someone or go to a lecture that interested me, and one occasion came up that I was really looking forward to. There was an ad in the Los Angeles Times for a job as a trainer to teach Napoleon Hill's *Think and Grow Rich.* I had already taken off from work as much time as I could and I couldn't get off to go for the interview. So I just resigned, without another job to go to.

Allan, a business man living in Arizona, ran the ad. He and a group of chiropractors had put up money and purchased the Los Angeles County franchise for the Napoleon Hill Academy and they were going to open eight sub-franchises in the area. They were looking for someone to be the training coordinator. The job paid a stipend but the main money would be from commissions. The person hired would be working with Allan in developing the other eight sub-franchises, giving training and teaching sales representatives to sell the Napoleon Hill Science of Personal Achievement Philosophy as a course.

There were 250 people who had applied for the job and they had narrowed it down to about fifty, then to fifteen. I was one of the fifteen who were to take a seminar for the final selection, and I'm the one that got the job!

In bringing this up, I don't want to give the wrong impression that I'm trying to enhance my ego or any sense of ego, but it just so happened to me a number of times in my life that I was interviewed for a position in a highly competitive process with many applicants - a relatively significant job, not just a fly-by-night, but one that offered great benefits - and I was the one that got the job.

I was able to operate with a high degree of efficiency. For example, in the insurance company as a claims adjustor I would actually complete my entire work schedule quickly allowing me three to four days of free time. I didn't always tell my employers I had completed my workload in such a short interval, because they would have given me that much more work to do above and beyond the load of other fellow employees. I just didn't see any reason to spend time doing more work when I wasn't being compensated accordingly. Practically, in every case, I was either the top salesman or in the top five percent or ten percent of the sales force, as I always directed consciousness to a successful conclusion once it was determined what it was that I wished to achieve.

Allan and the conglomerate of people who had put up the money for the franchise had talked Napoleon Hill (1883 to 1970) into the deal. The course manuals they printed were very poor in quality, they didn't proofread them properly and they were in plastic binders though the material was very significant. It was really an edited version of an original work called *Laws of Success* that Dr. Hill had written in 1928 under the tutelage of Andrew Carnegie. Then in 1937, he published the book *Think and Grow Rich.* I heard him tell it from his own mouth that *Think and Grow Rich* was so popular that it sold second only to the Bible and it had been translated into something like ten languages at that time. I'm telling you, he was very famous in those days; people knew about him by reading his books.

I got the opportunity to meet Dr. Hill. He was paid to come and do a seminar for the investors in the franchise. He gave a lecture at the Grand Ballroom of the Biltmore Hotel and, bless his heart, he was a tremendous speaker.

During that time I also met Neville Goddard (1905 to 1972). He was giving lectures at the Wilshire Ebell Theatre out on Wilshire Boulevard and a friend of mine had invited me along to hear him. Well, all of the time in Unity I'd been looking for someone who had had a spiritual awakening and, lo and behold, here was someone who obviously had.

After his lecture, I went up to talk to Neville and he was very gracious, very open. I told him about my involvement in Unity and he invited me to come back again. He was doing talks on a weekly basis, but occasionally he would do it more than once a week. I started reading his books and listening to him.

Neville was occasionally interviewed on television, and the TV talk show called *The Joe Pyne Show* (which ran from 1965 to 1967), had Neville on quite often. Joe Pyne would put people on the "hot seat," but he didn't do that with Neville, because Neville had proven his knowledge and his understanding about the Bible, and Joe Pyne would have Neville on to see if someone knew what they were talking about with the Bible. On one show, I watched Neville with three fundamentalist Christians who all had their Bibles out. Neville was without a Bible, but he had it in his head. As they debated, they would open their bible and start reading from it. Neville would say, "Oh that's the King James, that's the Revised Standard or that's the New English, whatever it happened to be. He knew the Bible like no one I have ever met before or since.

Neville would explain the nuances of differences between the various translations of the Bible. You would ask, which translation is correct?

How do you know that this one is not the way it should be? Neville was not arrogant, though he knew not only the nuances of the Bible, but the actual Greek words in the New Testament and the Hebrew words used in many of the most famous biblical verses of the Old Testament.

I didn't get to know Neville intimately, but I was able to go with him a time or two with a group out in Los Angeles.

One of Neville's students owned a piece of business property and wanted to put a building up on it, but didn't have the funds to do it. He wanted Neville to see this property and to be with him, to do whatever he could do to lend consciousness and energy to his being able to build on this property, because Neville had this ability, a real knack for awakening the feeling that something would be yours, whatever it was you wanted to have, do or be. It was already a fact - a manifested fact.

So he invited Neville and asked him to come out and look. It was not easily accessible. It was inconveniently located and that was one of the reasons he was having difficulty finding people to go along with him. He wanted to borrow the money from the bank, but it was not being supportive.

I was invited to go along and two carloads of us went to see the property. We pulled up, got out of the car, Neville walked out and we all went with him into the middle. There was all kinds of trash - paper, rusty beer cans, bottles and broken glass - and it wasn't very appealing to the sight, it was just a vacant lot, but Neville stood there looking around and said to the guy who owned it: "I can remember when this was a vacant lot. Well, this is certainly a nice building you've built here. Can't you remember when that was a vacant lot? I can remember it."

It was to get everybody into a false feeling of what it would be like for there to already be a building standing. Within a month, they were breaking land on that property and started building.

Neville's depth and insight and the quality or feeling of his consciousness was so direct and immediate. He was the first being that I ever met who I knew and could feel was coming from awakened awareness, from a quality or state of consciousness that was higher than my own state of consciousness at that time. That was very significant to me then.

Neville Goddard
as a young man.
Image Public Domain.

Santa Monica was one of the areas where there was going to be a Napoleon Hill Academy sub-franchise and I was very much interested in it myself, but I didn't have any money. Marty Schwartz, who was a great guy, a Jewish fellow, put up the money, and he and I bought the sub-franchise. Our agreement was more just a handshake based upon principles of integrity, as we both trusted one another. The deal was I would give the teaching and he and I both would develop the sales and establish the sub-franchise. I also continued to work for Allan in the overview of the other schools.

The main franchise's offices were in an impressive space with an amphitheater for the talks I gave. In my view it was not the best way to teach it, but that's the way Allan envisioned it and what he had put his money into. In the courses, I would incorporate a lot of spirituality, with Unity-like teachings that were not in the course itself. Most people really liked the spiritual part of it - except for two or three fundamentalists.

However, the sub-franchise in Santa Monica didn't really last very long as we were having to pay a huge amount of royalties. The whole thing was out of balance. It was all money oriented and there was greed, you couldn't make anything off of it. The people that you were trying to sell to couldn't afford the course and the ones who could afford it felt they didn't need it and were not interested. It was a losing proposition to begin with. I was in it for quite a while but I never did do anything really big. I was just holding my head above water.

The eight sub-franchise academies didn't come to fruition. Dr. Hill was really being used for his name. I don't think he made that much out of it.

One of the things that I learned through all of these occurrences is that there is nothing that is dependable in this world and certainly there is no happiness from the world itself. Freedom and joy are all qualities of the higher nature of the Self.

Dr. Hill had separated and divorced twice; his second wife had gotten all the royalties – and, bless his heart, the end of his life was really unfortunate. He died broke and an unhappy man, despite all that he had experienced and all the people that he had known who were wealthy and famous.

This was the case of most of the one hundred men that he had interviewed when he wrote the *Laws of Success* and the book *Think and Grow Rich*. Most had died unhappy proving that wealth and success in the world were not the cause of happiness, were not the location of happiness. I began to see this during that period of time.

CHAPTER 8

Flashes of Success

It was in 1968, after I had resigned from my job with the Napoleon Hill Academy franchise, that I saw a newspaper ad looking for people who had public speaking ability.

I applied in the evening and went up on a stage around eight o'clock to give a presentation. They had words you were to read to whoever was out there listening. Al Young, who turned out to be my very dear friend from that point on, and business partner for a number of years, his friend and associate Ed Hand, and a third person whose name I can't remember, were involved in the interview process. When they heard me their eyes all went up, all three shook their heads and unanimously agreed that I was the one - and I got the job right on the spot.

They were going to say to the people ahead of me, and all the other people that would have been after me: "We'll get back in touch with you," but I think they just cancelled it right then and sent everyone home.

We all went out for coffee after that and met again the next day, and then it turned out that I became a partner in the very enterprise itself that I was being hired for. I told Al that I wasn't in it to build his business for him, and what was needed was someone who was capable of not only speaking but selling, motivating, and merchandising. Well hell, I had it all at that time. I had earned it the hard way. I went in to deal with him, with the intention of being part owner of the actual business as it was just getting started, and so he and I became friends and business associates for years and years. Our friendship went on until he died.

It was called 777 Marketing. Al, Ed and this other guy had come up with the name and then I got involved with them right away in masterminding it. I even designed the logo, which was a coat of arms.

We leased a building for headquarters, with a huge meeting room, out in Paramount, California. The business grew so rapidly that we had to knock out the walls inside of our offices and move our offices into different locations to utilize that space for holding our meetings.

The company had formulated household cleaning and skin care products under a private label. Al was in the process of getting a manufacturer to put these together in a package form and we came up together with a new multi-level marketing concept. You would buy a seven-week supply of seven products and when you became a distributor you would earn a commission override, on everyone that you recruited seven levels down the line from you. That was how 777 Marketing worked. There were other multi-level companies in operation, but we had come up with an innovation; it was fresh and different.

I started giving the presentations, but as we grew I was needed in other activities and duties and we hired a fellow by the name of Peter Riggs who became our primary platform speaker. He was highly professional. Al and I had met him at another multi-level marketing company that had got into difficulties, and he ended up leaving. We grabbed him right away because he was a hot commodity and quite a guy. There was also one other fellow that I had trained myself who became another one of our speakers, but I don't remember his name.

I wasn't a good letter writer in those days but I had stayed in communication with an occasional letter and phone call to a friend of mine from

Houston, Jim Collins. We went back before Unity College, although we also had been in Unity together.

I had gone into the student minister training program at Unity school and shortly thereafter, Jim Collins and another man, John, both from Houston, applied to Unity. They were both older men than me, and John was older than both of us.

John was a chain smoker and couldn't quit, Jim also smoked, and I had smoked but had given it up. Unity preferred everybody to be non-smokers and put it to them to quit smoking. Eventually they graciously let John go. Jim continued, and when I was expelled he was just as surprised as I was, really he was flabbergasted by the whole thing. Still he continued on. However, he was having a hard time trying to quit smoking - and that was a big factor - and there were other things as well he didn't quite agree with. He eventually got to the point where he was dissatisfied with what was going on in the student ministry program. It didn't seem to suit him well.

Meanwhile, he heard from me about doing very well in California, and knowing that he was a good salesman, I offered him the opportunity to join us and ultimately that's what he did. He came out to California and contributed considerably to our business; he became a sort of comptroller overlooking the accounting aspect of our business.

Jim was also what you would call a "closer" and he was a whiz at signing people up when they were on the fence or when people brought someone to a meeting but they were not very good themselves at closing. He had been a car salesman, so he knew how to do that. John and Al got along very well because they had both been in the car business, and Al was really happy to have John because he was both a closer and understood accounting. Al had been a car dealer. He and two brothers had large used car dealerships outside of Los Angeles in various parts of Southern California. He had been quite well known himself as he used to advertise on TV. Al was one of the people who started using comedy on television, hollering at people, to get their attention to buy cars.

Other people who knew him from before I knew him called him Sandy. On TV, he went by the name Sandy Young.

As the business grew, we opened another office in San Fernando Valley clear across town. We also opened in San Bernardino, and so we had three areas operating simultaneously (the main office was in Paramount, sixty-four miles West of San Bernardino; and thirty-one miles south of the San Fernando Valley).

When we had opened up a center in the San Fernando Valley, Jim Collins went over with me and helped me to manage and operate it. I was giving the meetings over there and Peter Riggs was giving the meetings in the main office which were drawing a larger crowd because it was longer established. I was beginning to draw some good crowds myself. Then, along the way, we hired another fellah to give the presentations in San Fernando.

Our company grew very fast and we were making big money, in gross sales we made a million dollars in about six months (about 6.7 million dollars in 2014 terms, *ed.*). That was really an accomplishment. It was uncanny.

This was a real flash of success and it happened all by word of mouth - people telling their friends - there was no advertising at all. People of course were drawn to it because of the opportunity to make money and we had so many people making so much money in such a short period of time - really it was very motivational. It was easy enough for people.

I also began traveling twice a week to meetings in San Bernardino. Jim sometimes traveled with me and then somewhere along the way, we hired a black fellow who used to drive over with me because he had a lot of contacts in San Bernardino and he became instrumental in getting the branch going over there. He was married to a white woman and being a black man married to a white woman, back in those days, was not very popular. His wife was from San Bernardino and her parents lived there, so we would go over and when we finished, it would be late at night and too late to drive all the way back to Los Angeles, so we would often spend the night.

Virginia and I were still married, of course, and I was heavily involved in the business and spent a lot of time there. I can't remember the dates exactly, the chronological sequence of events, but along there, Virginia became pregnant with our daughter, Devi.

I'm not happy to say - I was unfaithful to her during that period of time. I had so many opportunities with so many single women who were looking for husbands or lovers. I had two or three women including one that used to ride over with me to San Bernardino. We would stay together in a motel for the night after the meetings in the Valley. Many times after having sex, I'd talk to them about spiritual matters. That happened during much of my life. If a lady friend didn't show an interest in spiritual matters then the relationship was always very short lived. But when there was an interest in spiritual matters, more than the mundane worldliness of daily life, and an interest in understanding the purpose of life, our relationship with life and with God, we would have talks and exchanges that appealed to me. The relationship might then be long lasting. Yes, they were sexual relationships, but it wasn't just sex for only sex, it had to be more than that.

Al and I worked very well together because he had a consciousness of big things - expansiveness - and I had ability as a platform speaker and knowledge of positive thinking and self-improvement. It was really a good combination.

Based on the principles from Napoleon Hill and Neville Goddard, I taught regular seminars to people who came in as distributors or used our products. Al's interest in these philosophies was mostly intellectual, but as a professional - a salesman - he understood the importance of positive thinking. I was teaching courses regularly on how to succeed, how to think with a positive mental attitude and to live spiritually. I brought into it, as well, Neville's teaching about how to awaken the feeling of what would be yours if you were succeeding, having what you wanted to have, doing what you wanted to do, and being what you wanted to be.

People were coming in, learning; buying into a distributorship. They all got training, which I gave. That's what made us grow. From the course, people understood the principles of how to function, how to approach their friends, how to live their own lives in a positive mode so that they could feel success consciousness. We built our business on that basis.

One time, a guy in a class made a statement that it didn't make any difference what was in the products, that you could just as well have straw in them and still succeed at it. When remarks like that were made, I was on it like a hen on a June bug. "How dare you make such a statement that we're just here to sell something that has no benefit! That is absolutely inappropriate. What we are selling is one of the finest products that you can purchase and we have a very effective marketing plan." That was why we were growing so well.

We would quickly cut short people who had such an attitude, who did not understand the principles upon which we operated, but this sort of attitude turned out to be our undoing.

A guy came out and tape recorded one of my presentations in our San Fernando Valley Centre. I was very innocent about what I was saying, but the way I was saying it and the way it was presented made it, according to their concept and idea of the City code, a scam and a con. All three of our places were immediately told to cease and desist during investigation. It made the headlines right on the front page of the Los Angeles Herald-Examiner: "Million Dollar Lottery Ring Busted." It was one of the main newspapers of Los Angeles and you can imagine what it did writing about us as being a lottery, which was against the law.

We had then to prove that we were neither a lottery nor against the law, but a legitimate business. No lottery was involved whatsoever. The programs we gave and the products we sold, along with the marketing structure, were, in my and Al's mind, sincerely adding to people's lives. People felt the benefits themselves and that's the reason they were drawn into it. A lot were drawn to it for money, but there were as many drawn to it because it was elevating their consciousness, elevating their standard of living; everything about it was upward, progressive and beneficial.

We had to hire an attorney to represent us and Al picked one who charged high costs, because he felt we needed to quickly get through the situation, but the attorney just ripped us off something terrible. We were making big money and he was charging us a big fee.

Even though we went to court and proved our case, it shot us down because we could not overcome the public image and the impression it had made. It was in the newspaper and on the television news, so everybody had heard about it and nobody would come to a meeting because they thought it was a lottery and against the law. The news never says: "Well, we're sorry folks about the way it turned out." You can't get that kind of coverage. No way, they never publish the positive side of it; if they do, it's just a tiny little article hidden away on the inner pages.

That was the end of 777 Marketing. We ended up closing down in California. We'd lost a tremendous amount of money, but we still had some.

After 777 closed, we went for an interval of time in which Al and I didn't have anything going on together. But while 777 was still operating, Al had met a fellow named James Breckenridge Jones who became my good friend. James was living in Santa Monica and Al took me over and introduced me to him. Well, it turned out that James, himself, was really one of the grand-daddies, one of the originators, of multi-level marketing in the country.

James had his own problems, but he was on the rebound and getting back into the flow of things. He was always on the lookout himself for something good and he had learned about us. When 777 ended up closing its offices and operation, I got involved with him. He was setting up his own business again, this time in the brassiere business. When he and I got together, he had already started, but then we began working and masterminding together and his business began to build. It all sort of dovetailed together as I had earlier on worked in sales for Silk Skin, another bra and girdle company.

The bras were firm fitting, custom made and uplifting and James had a lady up in Northern California who made them. They would sell for two or three times more than what a brassiere would cost in a regular department store.

In the bra business, we literally sold ourselves out of business. Because they were custom fitted brassieres, it took time to make them, and they couldn't be made quickly because you had to take the measurements and so forth. It was a great product and the women loved

James Breckenridge Jones

had been a distributor for Nutrilife and he was the one that saw how you could use the system of network marketing to put more emphasis upon developing and recruiting distributors to go out and increase your sales. Nutrilife was the first company to sell vitamin and mineral food supplements through multi-level marketing. It is still in business today and owned by Amway. But at the time of James, the marketing was done in a non-big-splash manner. An individual would sell a product and then if one of their customers was interested, they could also become a distributor and sell the product to their own customers.

James created AbundaVita - "The AbundaVita Corporation of America," - with the notion of outreaching with multi-level marketing and at one point it became one of the largest network marketing companies with something like 3,500 distributors.

them. Ladies would come into the business, become distributors themselves, and then start selling their friends on the product and it was growing so fast that we couldn't manufacture them as fast as they were being sold. That became the problem. Basically, we were too successful.

After we had gone out of business, I went out on an occasion to see James at his house in Santa Monica. He was moving out and I don't remember where he was going. I don't remember what happened to him at that time.

I never knew about the history of these network marketing companies until I met James. AbundaVita was a knock-off, if you will, of Nutrilife and its competitor. It became very big but then some of those that started off as distributors, or who James had hired, left AbundaVita to start The Nutribio Corporation and went into competition with him.

James himself was a self-improvement trainer. He had known Napoleon Hill, as I had, and he had written a book (*If You Can Count to Four*, 1957) that had become very popular, particularly when AbundaVita was operating. It was out of print during that time. I had heard of it, but I hadn't read it, then I found a copy.

James had started out with nothing, as a plow boy, a farmer in Southern Tennessee and had gone on to be very wealthy at one time and Dr. Hill had told him that he was a living example of his *The Laws of Success* and *The Science of Personal Achievement.*

I learned about a fellow in Northern California who actually owned the patent for the bras that we had been selling. Technically, it seemed that we were in violation of his patent, because we were manufacturing them as our own brand - which we supposedly had the authorization to do from a lady who said she owned it, but evidently didn't. I got acquainted with him and started working with him. He had more sewers and seamstresses and more machines than anybody in that field.

I took along the people that I had recruited in the organization that I had built with James Breckenridge Jones and along with my wife, Virginia, we started selling the bras. We sold in the multi-level marketing program and, as well, Virginia and I sold them from a little shop we rented two doors down from a local movie theater in the area that we lived.

Virginia became involved because with these bras a woman had to be measured. You had to try on samples, which gave the general idea of the fit and then feel where to tuck it in or expand it. You had to be in a fitting room and it took a lady to be able to fit you, so Virginia and I worked together. She did the fitting and I did the selling, which worked out really well.

I was working as the national sales manager and being paid a salary as well as a commission. I went to a sales convention in New Orleans. I was there for about one week, met a girl and got on with her - a little sexual episode. Virginia didn't go because she had to stay home with Devi.

As sales manager I was to have a kick-off meeting, give prizes to the top producers, pump up sales and expand the company. I met a lady there named Esther (I can't remember her last name), who was married to a much older man in Mississippi. She was the top distributor in the company and I worked with her and some of her ideas at the sales meeting.

I was living in Los Angeles and the owner of the bra business, who lived in northern California, would fly down quite often and I would fly up to where he was. He had an operation but it wasn't really big enough and I kept telling him: "It's not big enough, it's not going to work. If we have the big blast of increased sales, this is not going to work." He had never done the kind of volume that we were capable of doing by then.

Esther came from Mississippi and told him the same thing: "You're going to have to get more seamstresses, you are going to have to increase your production." But he felt kind of complacent because he was making good money and he couldn't see the forest for the trees. Sure enough, to make a long story short, the same thing happened as before with James Breckenridge Jones and we sold ourselves out of business.

Esther and I had become friends and we went to do the same thing on our own. We called it the Bosom Buddy Bra but it hardly got off the ground, not with me. I started out with her but I didn't stay with it. She continued on with it for a while and she was making a lot of money. Her husband had the money to invest in doing something with it in a big way. As it turned out, they didn't get along too well together. She was not suited to him. She had married more or less for his money and he began to get that. Of course she was traveling all the time, not at home, and he was more or less somewhat like a shut-in. She had two sons that were twins by her former marriage. And that's another story...

We ended our relationship and here I was without anything going.

Mankind First Lands on the Moon, July 20, 1969. Photo by Astronaut Neil Armstrong of Astronaut Buzz Aldin, 1969. The Mission Control Center for the Apollo flights was in Houston, Texas.

NASA. Public Domain.

CHAPTER 9

History Repeating Itself

My Mom passed when I was still in California. It was now around 1969, Al and I were from Texas, so we thought, why not go back and start again? We went to Houston. We changed the name of the company from 777 Marketing to Century 21, back before the real estate company called Century 21 was in business (the real estate company was founded in 1971, Orange County, California ed.). We sold house-hold cleaning and skin care products.

My contribution to the business was mainly in sales and marketing and in the presentation and training of new people. Al was in the administrative and the executive aspect of running the business.

Al wasn't married but he was living with his girlfriend at that time. Virginia and I with our daughter, Devi, were together and we started actively attending Unity church. We got acquainted with the people there, many that I had known before, and new people. A new minister had taken over and he and I became good friends and, as well, his wife became a very good friend to Virginia and to myself.

During that same time, my friend in California, James Breckenridge Jones, also moved to Texas with his wife and baby. James went to work for Al and me in our business. I went to Murfreesboro, Tennessee, where James was from, and we had a couple of meetings there at the start-off of Century 21.

James had been a fundamentalist preacher in the early days. Then he gave that up and went into religious science and then from there to Unity. He was in search of Christ consciousness and into spirituality, as I was. That's why we were such good friends in California. We had so many things in common.

Century 21 rented a pretty impressive building, and various people who had been involved with us in California told their friends in Houston and area about us. It was slow in the beginning, but boy, once we got started, it moved very quickly and we did very well for a short period of time.

But history more or less repeated itself and the same kind of problem we had with 777 Marketing approached us from a different perspective. Another so-called legal reason was found to shoot us down.

Century 21 had the same principles and ideas as 777 Marketing, but we had enhanced it a little bit and we put in safeguards to keep things from happening the way they had happened in California, where we had been accused of being a lottery.

In those days, when companies that sold their product under a simple, old traditional way of selling to grocery or drug stores, saw you come in with a successful multi-level business, they didn't want that competition. You began to make a splash, people began to buy your product and there was a dent in their sales; then they started complaining about what you were doing because you were hurting their business. They used politics, went to the powers that be and their bureaucrats, and looked at anything they could come up with to shoot you down. That's what was happening with us all along the way. Even though we would change and conform to what they wanted, they would come up with something else, because all they really wanted was to keep you out of business. That's what we were dealing with.

In Texas, we were said to be in violation of the Security laws, and even though we were able to prove that we were not – and we were not – we got publicity in the papers and on television and it didn't take long for the word to spread that we were in violation of those laws. The newspapers never retract the stories and once you got the adverse publicity going against you the damage was already done and it was difficult to get people to listen to what you really were about.

There was nothing different to do because what we had done was not against the law. We had won our case.

What really killed us though was money. Our comptroller made a big boo-boo. In his calculations he had overlooked some major factors, how much money we actually had as opposed to our expenses, and he had told us that we were better off financially than we were. When push came to shove, Al had made decisions based upon us having money that we didn't have.

We had been holding meetings with twenty or thirty tables sitting four to six people on upholstered chairs, but we ended up having to close the offices that we were leasing and renting a warehouse space to put all of our office belongings (the furniture, desks, dining room tables, and products we had left) into storage. When the time came that we needed to generate capital, some operating money, we'd have people come out there and the best we could do was to sell things at about ten to fifteen cents on the dollar cost, which was a tremendous loss.

We were now out of business and this time out of money. Both Al and I had some money ourselves, but as far as our business was concerned, it was down and both of us were on our own.

I was again out in the cold, so to speak, and I had the responsibility of Virginia and Devi, so I started looking for a job and saw an ad in the paper: "Business Tax Service, looking for a representative."

It was called the Gulf Coast Business Tax Services. I applied for the job and got it. One of the things they were concerned with was that I would be under-employed if I went to work for the company. I was over-qualified because of my history and what I had been. I let them know that that didn't make any difference. The main thing was, I had the responsibility to maintain a home and to take care of my family. It was the sales manager who gave me the job and the two of us became good friends.

The owner of the business was likeable enough. While there, I had an affair with his sister. He turned out to be a con artist in his own way and he ripped me off. I took him out to show him the warehouse, as he needed a desk and chairs and various things that we had in our Century 21 office, and I agreed to let him use things we had there, but he never paid me for them.

During that time, I had really begun to see my shortcomings from a business point of view. I didn't really know the accounting principles needed to maintain a business: where the money was going, where it was coming from, what it was being spent on, the percentages of expenses to income, all of that kind of stuff. I had not been involved in this type of thing so I didn't know much about it, and I began to realize that it was ultimately what did us in at Century 21. We were not keeping good business records, and so we did not know the facts and figures - the truth about where we actually stood financially.

We thought we had money we didn't have. That was the major thing - the big problem. I didn't know that before.

Gulf Coast Business Tax Services sold a service that would let a small business owner know how much they had coming in and their expenses on a daily, weekly, monthly basis, the percentages of expenses to income, whether a particular expense was a wise one for the amount of money they had coming in and the amount of money they were spending overall. It was a complete service and at the end of the year we would file their income tax with the government.

I would meet with business owners. They might say, "No, I'm not interested, bye," but if they didn't have the kind of record keeping, a comparable service to what we offered, I wouldn't take no for an answer.

I was thrown out of many offices because I would say, "You don't know what you're doing. I'm the best friend that you've got. How is it that you don't have a service like this? You don't know what your expenses are, related to your income. How in the world could you be operating like this?"

I sold the daylights out of that company. I became a whiz, its top producer to the extent that they put on three or four new accountants and bookkeepers just to handle the increased business that I started bringing in. I presented a positive philosophy and I even began to train additional salesmen.

As well, the owner had a friend in Atlanta who had the same kind of business and we ended up taking a few salesmen and developing a sales force for this friend. While in Atlanta, I saw my old friends, Bernie and Harriet Corpin, who had in the meantime moved there from Houston.

Somewhere along there, though, the Tax Service business went down and on this occasion Virginia and I separated. She got herself an apartment elsewhere in town. I found out where she was and would go by occasionally to see Devi. When all this began, Virginia started drinking again and to go to AA Meetings, and she started dating a guy named Harold Graham. He was a member of a family in Houston who were quite well-to-do. They owned three or four stores in Houston called Graham's Men Shop and he had ability to generate money but he was on a low ebb at that time.

I wasn't making a great deal of money, though I had a little money of my own - just enough to live on. I got a small, old, one-bedroom apartment in Westwood. Right outside of my door was a swimming pool. I was a bachelor, separated, kind of living free and enjoying myself.

Generally speaking, I was personally satisfied during that time, except at Christmas it was pretty tough. I was still identified with a body and a mind and I remember one particular Christmas, I couldn't see my daughter, Devi. It was an emotional time, boy I was low.

During that low ebb, I needed to do something to get a positive attitude, something that I could enjoy. I was very much still involved in my spiritual quest, I had all this knowledge from all that I had done up to that time in speaking, training and motivating people and I knew so many people who were in sales, marketing, and working for small organizations that didn't actually give sales training. They were entirely on their own to motivate themselves. So, I came up with the idea of starting a motivational program for salesmen, calling it "The Early Bird Gets the Worm - Training and Motivation."

With this idea I went to see the Phoenix Bookstore where I knew the owner, Jackie, who also went to Unity. I had bought many books there. It was a nice old mansion that had been converted into a bookstore. Upstairs they had a kitchenette and a room that could easily handle fifteen or twenty people. I made a deal to use the place for early morning workshops, seminars, so that a person could start the day off motivated and inspired.

I'd stop and get a couple of dozen donuts and orange juice and in the little kitchenette I would make a pot of coffee, set up and be ready when people came in. I advertised in the local publication, printed up flyers, and handed them out around the various places of business and told sales people that I knew about it. It didn't take long for it to begin to catch on.

The seminar started one morning a week, then two and three mornings a week, from 6 o'clock in the morning until about 8:00 am or 9:00 am. Some people would have to leave to go to work at 8:00 am, others not until 8:30 or 9:00 am, so I would stay there until 9 in the morning. Because the bookstore didn't have an adequate parking place, people parked up and down the street. They did have a few places to park in the back. There was a yard and a driveway with room for four or five cars, but the rest had to park on the street.

We were doing well until the city changed the parking rules and you couldn't park on the street in the morning before a certain time of the day. That eliminated the ability to park, so I had to move the seminars to another spot. The first turned out to be inadequate, without a good room. Then I talked to the owner of a huge cafeteria who had various banquet rooms as well. I made a deal that I could use a banquet room, even their public address system, as I could foresee the time that the meetings could grow, to fill up the whole place one day. It started off three mornings a week, on Monday, Wednesday and Friday.

I'd done a little bit of advertising but not much, mainly it spread by word of mouth, one person telling another. A flow pattern was occurring and soon, to my surprise, it had reached a level of about twenty-five or thirty people on a regular basis. Then one morning I arrived a little later than I would usually - barely in time to give the program - and as I came into the parking lot, the place was filled with cars. My first thought was that there must be something else happening here this morning, but as I walked in, to my surprise, there were about a hundred people in the room for the program that I was giving. I was very surprised, overwhelmed.

What had happened was that one of the people attending told a friend, who happened to be the head of a large sales organization, about the seminars and they had told their organization to come that morning, as this was when they normally had their own sales meeting. The sales manager himself came and then encouraged them to continue coming as they found the meetings to be more inspirational and beneficial than what they were doing in their own company. People shared with their friends around the city and it grew to the point that I had visions of filling the main meeting facility of the cafeteria every morning. I could see that the growth potential was there.

The themes of the training were both personal self-improvement and motivation and company effectiveness. I was sharing in the teaching - how to bring about whatever it was that you wanted to have, do or be in your life. It was going quite well and I had all kinds of testimonials from the people based upon what they were getting from attending the meetings, how beneficial it was to them, how it was helpful to them to attain a positive attitude, and how they felt it increased their efficiency and effectiveness in their jobs. People would stand up in their place or come up to the front of the room and share how they had used what they had learned, how it was working for them and what they had achieved or accomplished. They were confirming that what I was sharing was in fact working for them in their lives.

Leads came as owners, sales or personnel managers at different companies came to know about the meetings. When there was a group of people interested at a company, I would make an appointment, present testimonials and sell them on the idea of coming to the seminars. I would sign them up and their entire sales force, or however many on their sales force wanted to come.

The growth was consistent and it reached the point where I was drawing about 100 to 150 people regularly. The cafeteria would allow me to hold the meetings there for nothing, and I would pay them a dollar a person to provide a continental breakfast with sweet rolls, orange juice and coffee for each person.

A lady assisted me at the door when people came in. She had been my girlfriend at one time - I can see her clearly, but frankly I can't remember her name. I had tickets printed which we'd sell for $3.00 a person. Of the $3.00, after I paid a dollar to the cafeteria, I was left with two dollars a person and with 100 people coming on an average, that was $200.00 three times a week or $600.00 a week. For 150 people it was even more than that. I was only working twenty hours a week, so I was making some very good money.

When the door to my apartment opened up, immediately to the right was the swimming pool and very often I sat out beside it. I knew all my neighbors, the people who swam in the pool and some of their guests - and I would have my own guests, friends who would come - and we would sit out at the pool and talk with one another. It was a nice atmosphere and I used to watch my own mind and how it would bring up various judgments, criticisms, and uncomplimentary thoughts. I would tune in and watch what was happening.

I can recall one time in particular. Sitting out by the pool was a fellow I knew who lived in the project and would come to the pool with his friends; I couldn't put my finger on it, but there was something about him I just didn't like. He was a nice enough fellow, he always came across as friendly, but I noticed my own reaction to him. In my mind and my thoughts I caught my criticism of him. I watched it over a period of time to see to what extent I could do something about changing this pattern of thoughts about him. I'm just mentioning him because that is what triggered it off for me to start looking at when those kind of thoughts came up with regard to other people I knew or met.

I started trying to eliminate these kinds of thoughts because I knew it was not good for me, even though it may not bother the person against whom I was thinking. I was not happy with myself having these kinds of thoughts. I noticed to what degree I would tell myself the truth about them, and attempt to change them. That worked to some extent, nonetheless, it was not an easy thing to overcome and these thoughts would keep coming up.

I prayed to God to help me not to think this way, using my own form of simple prayer. That was the main thing that I did in those days.

Later on, I came to learn about a revision process that replays thoughts and awakens the feelings that could be yours if you thought differently about a situation; to have good thoughts instead of bad thoughts. In this process, you would look at the mind as though it was a cassette tape recorder and thoughts were tape recordings that you could erase by playing over them; like an old cassette tape that had a message on it that was not important, you would record something new over it.

That's what I taught during that period of time. I was very strong about having to live what you taught. You couldn't be saying one thing and doing something else and so I was being very truthful with myself in that regard. Otherwise I would be a fraud.

The first photograph taken by humans of Earthrise during Apollo 8. Space Flight, December 24, 2008.

Photo: Astronaut Frank Borman, NASA. Public Domain.

I was still looking to reawaken to the experience of awakening that I had had as a child. I had glimpses from time to time, a feeling that would come upon me. I was using marijuana fairly often. It gave me a quality of something like transcendental awareness, a higher state of openness. I had also occasionally tried forms of prescriptions. Benzedrine, an 'upper', is one that I had used. I had even used Peyote and LSD. LSD gave me an experience very similar to the experiences that I had had earlier in my childhood - it was very close to it. You could get high, but you couldn't be high, and I was still interested in trying to be high rather than simply get high.

The morning talks were growing; more people were attending, giving me more income. All of this was happening in parallel with my spiritual quest. I had not become ultra-rich, though I had become affluent enough to recognize that no matter how much money I made, that was not going to be it. I knew many people who had already made large amounts of money, and still had a compulsion to try to make more - and who were not capable of seeing that making more was not going to bring about true and lasting happiness or contentment. The mind will always be there with the desire for more, better and different situations, circumstances and experiences.

With more income, you have the ability to do more things, to have more things, to experience more things, but now I had started looking at WHY; why all of this, what is this doing? Where is this going to end up? Just MORE, more stuff! A larger place to live…, if I got a larger place to live, that was going to require more responsibility, more expense, more people to have to come in, to pay – a maid, more assistance… Did I really need that? Was that going to make me feel any better?

It came to me one morning out of the blue, I thought, "Why not apply the same principles that I've been using for financial or worldly achievement to awakening?" It had not dawned on me before to use the same processes that I had already learned and taught others for my spiritual quest.

I thought about, "How can this work?"

It was Neville Goddard who gave me the way and the means to have this happen. He was the first person that I had met that I recognized was coming from a much higher state of consciousness than me. I considered him to be an awakened being and he was far more significant in my life than anyone else had been up to that point. I knew from Neville that all one had to do was awaken the feeling within oneself of what it would feel like to already have, do or be whatever it was that you wanted. When you awakened it in consciousness, and held on to that feeling, it would naturally manifest in the world.

My relationship with Jesus was then predominant and primary in my life. Neville's books had made Jesus come alive even more for me. In particular *Your Faith is Your Fortune, The Power of Awareness, Seedtime and Harvest* and, *The Law and the Promise* were absolutely captivating.

In the Bible, Jesus's words are: "Whoever has seen me has seen the Father." (John 14:9, New Revised Standard Version); and, "The Father and I are one." (John 10:30). Would I be able to be in the state of consciousness that Jesus must have been in all the time?

So I started to go to sleep every night asking myself "How would it be to feel as Jesus felt knowing - not believing - that I am the son of God and I and the father are one?" I would ask that question and enter into the sleep state.

PART 3

Self-Realization
(1973 to 1978)

Bhagavan Sri Ramana Maharshi (December 30, 1879
to April 13 1950), circa 1949. Bhagavan, one of India's
great sages, was instrumental in A. Ramana's awakening
and future path. *Portrait known as the "Tilted Welling Bust," taken by
G.G. Welling, used by permission of Sri Ramanasramam.*

141

Portrait of Arunachala Ramana in
Meditation, Pencil on Watercolor Paper.
Saroja 2008.

CHAPTER 10

Awakening

It was about one to two months after I had begun asking the question at the time of sleep that I had an appointment with a sales manager in his office in downtown Houston. I had given the morning seminar and then had started out and gone quite a distance toward the area of Katy Road when I saw that I had left the exact address of the fellow at home. I had to rush back to my apartment to get the address and I couldn't even call him because I didn't have his telephone number.

Along my way home, when I was passing very close to the Phoenix Bookstore where I had started the first morning seminars, a tremendous urge came upon me to stop by the bookstore. I really didn't have the time to stop, because the distance that I had to go to my apartment and the distance that I had to go to get to that appointment, really didn't leave me enough time to make any stops on the way. I could not overcome this urge.

I was driving on the street going towards my apartment. As I came to the cross street Elgin - which became at a certain point Westheimer Road where the bookstore was - an impulse, like a need, came up to turn in the direction of Westheimer.

I had been to the bookstore on my own many times as a customer. I had bought most of my spiritual books there, and that's where I started giving the morning workshop, so I knew all the people that worked there. My first impression was that maybe someone had been trying to reach me there, because occasionally people would come by knowing that I had given programs, or for whatever reason. My mind was telling me that was the logical reason for this urge. So, I could put off going to the bookstore for another time. I could simply call them later, because I had an appointment and it was not the time to stop there.

As I got closer, I had to stop for the red light and I sat there thinking that this was a silly thing for me to do and that I should just turn around and go home, so I got over to a lane with that intention. I sat there impatiently waiting for the light to turn, because I really needed to get home, I had a distance to go if I was going to make my appointment. When the light changed again to green, I started to turn into the convenience store in order to turn around and this urge would not let me. It was so strong - it's difficult to try to explain other than the urge was stronger than my ability to overcome it.

What was I doing? It was a battle within myself. I was now really feeling kind of odd; a little upset with myself and embarrassed about this crazy feeling.

I went on and pulled up to the first parking place closest to the entrance of the bookstore. I got out of my car and even then, I was saying, "Why am I doing this?" I was trying not to even get out of my car but I couldn't stop myself.

So I got out of my car, went on into the bookstore. The clerk there was a young man that I knew and I asked him if anybody had been trying to get in touch with me? He said, "No," and he went to the back to see if anybody else knew." (The Phoenix Bookstore is no longer in business. It's been closed many years. A friend of mine, Jackie Pound, was the owner, and she had a partner who I didn't know as well as I knew her.) Then the other owner, it wasn't Jackie, came out and she said, "No, not that I know anything about."

She suggested that perhaps I just came by to buy a book. I said "no," and that I didn't have time to do any shopping now, but she replied that there were some new books in and that maybe there was something that I've been looking for.

I turned to leave and I couldn't. The way the counter was set up was, you walked around it to go to the back where the office was, over on the left there was a stairway that went up to the little room where I had given morning seminars, and to the right there were aisles of books. All the way down one aisle was a window seat opposite the wall and facing the street. I used to sit there and peruse a book that I was thinking about buying.

I walked to the aisles with the rows of books, as that seemed to be the only thing to do. There were three or four aisles. I went down the first aisle looking at books and then down the second aisle. About half way along – feeling I had not far to go as I felt an urge was guiding me – I stopped and looked to the left. There was a purple colored book that had no printing on the spine that I can recall; it was just a purple color, which in itself did not attract me. It was the book itself that attracted me.

I picked it out of the shelf, turned it over with my hand and opened it to a page. There was a black and white picture of a man and under the picture was his name, Bhagavan Sri Ramana Maharshi.

I just stood there and looked at the picture. I became weak in my knees and I went to the window seat and sat down just looking at the picture.

In those moments I "re-merged" with the Allness of Being. Every item that I saw, everything in that room, in that bookstore, all the books, the shelves, the chandelier hanging there, the curtains, the floor, everything that I could see was one with me and I was one with it. It was that picture that did it.

There was only an apparent separation between all of the items, the objects, the situation, the people - I think there would have been maybe one or two people in the bookstore besides myself, I don't even remember - but they were no different from me and I was no different from them. There was just Oneness that cannot be put into words. Words can be used, but words don't do anything about it, they can't touch it.

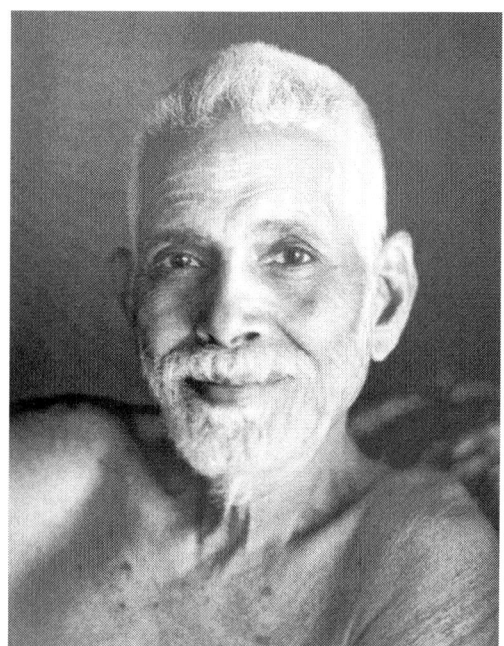

Bhagavan Sri Ramana Maharshi, circa 1949.
The portrait known as the "Welling Bust" by G. G. Welling,
used by permission of Sri Ramanasramam.

The quality of non-difference, not two (non-duality, *ed.*), pure being, I am-ness, the very essence: I guess the best way it could be described is like being on an acid trip, but it was totally and absolutely natural.

Seeing the picture of Bhagavan and the title of the opening chapter "Who am I" just knocked the wind out of me. In those moments the re-awakening happened fully, I was back to the awareness of being, the same state that I had been in when I was a child.

I knew without any question or doubt, absolutely and truly, that here was the answer to all the questions that I had ever had.

I just sat there in a state of indescribable joy. I was totally overcome. I laughed and I cried simultaneously, tears rolling down my cheeks.

About the Book by Bhagavan Sri Ramana Maharshi

I had a little dog that got angry one time, pulled the book off the table, and ripped it up, but I was able to save the photograph of Bhagavan. I've read a copy of the same book many times and I don't recall it necessarily ever opening up again to Bhagavan's picture.

The portrait of Bhagavan called the "Welling Bust" is the same image that I saw on the day of my awakening on June 4, 1973.

I really didn't care for the clerk to know what I was going through so I just went to the counter and paid for the book. I didn't say anymore and left, got in my car and drove home.

By then, it was already right at the time that I needed to be at my appointment with the sales manager, and I was able to call him and apologize. I told him that something had come up and I would call him later to re-schedule the appointment.

I also called the young lady who assisted me as she had the list of the names and telephone numbers of all the people who were coming to my program. I asked her if she would do me a kind favor and call them all and tell them that something very significant had occurred, and that I must apologize but I was not going to be giving a talk for a period. I didn't know exactly how long it was going to be, I'd have to contact them and let them know. I asked her if she would also ask them to pass this on to their friends and if she had enough time to go to the cafeteria and cancel the meetings.

That's all I did for the rest of that day. I just remained in my room and read that book. The day of my awakening was June 4, 1973.

Dialogue on Awakening 1
Our Higher Nature

Saroja: Jesus has always been present in your life - especially after your initial awakening when you were a child. How did you relate to Jesus after your second awakening?

Ramana: Prior to the awakening that occurred in June of 1973, I was, of course, a devotee of Jesus, and I had not, as far as I knew, ever known about Bhagavan Sri Ramana Maharshi. I'd seen photographs of different awakened eastern gurus, so there was the possibility that I may have at one time seen his picture; if I had, I didn't remember it and I had not considered any eastern guru in my own spiritual quest.

I was really involved just with Jesus, and even with my disappointment at not finishing Unity Ministerial School, I still went to Unity Church and I was grateful for Unity's teaching.

I had met Neville Goddard, who in fact was as Jesus oriented as I was, and reading his books made Jesus come alive even more for me. Neville was very much a factor in my own awakening. His writings confirmed what I intuitively knew to be true from the awakening experience that happened when I was a child - and that I was trying to rekindle.

After the awakening on June 4, 1973, there was direct understanding, a direct knowing of what I had intuitively already known. I had no doubt about it before, and when I had the awakening, I then knew for myself what Jesus had felt. He was living in a body but awakened to being one with God, to being the Son of God. It was not his being the Son of God that was unique about him; rather, what was unique was that he was awake and aware that he was the Son of God. That's what I now knew for sure in myself. I had intuitively known this before, and I knew it directly now after the awakening.

Ramana greeting people at a Satsang with the gesture of Namaste, circa 2008. *AHAM archives.*

That's what I have been sharing and teaching to those who have been open and receptive and willing to hear. What is unique about Jesus is his awakened awareness of his "Son-ship," his "Oneness with," his "non-difference from" and the pure awareness of being that "I am that, which is God." My relationship with Him has not changed. If anything, you would say it has just settled down to be more functional, practical, understandable - and in a way, livable. I'm not able to perform miracles; I understand that the real miracle, the most important miracle, is the awakened awareness of being. In Jesus's story, Lazarus, metaphysically speaking, is everyone who is dead to their own higher nature, and when you awaken to your own higher nature, you're raising Lazarus from the dead. When you awaken, if you are capable of bringing people into the same awakening themselves, that's far more significant than having Siddhis (or powers), being able to miraculously cure illnesses.

Jesus was the one primary influence in my life prior to my awakening, but when I say "my" awakening, when I look at these words, there is no "my" that is awakening. The awakening is the freedom from the sense of "my," from the *sense of I* and the sense of "me." Awakening is just awakening. "My" and "yours" divide consciousness into "I" and the "other than I" - and that is the problem.

I'm just pointing this out, making distinctions. We have to use words in order to try to communicate in duality, words are necessary, but remember that words are only pointers to the qualities and states of consciousness. Awareness itself is prior to any qualities or states of consciousness.

CHAPTER 11

Giving It All Away

After my awakening, there was nothing needing, nothing wanting. I was happy and fulfilled as I was, without doing anything or going anywhere. Nothing came up, except, I went back after a week to the bookstore, taking the book by Bhagavan Sri Ramana Maharshi with me and looking for more books by him. I first looked on the shelves, but I didn't see any books by him at all.

To my surprise, they didn't even know about the book by Bhagavan that I showed them and they said, "Well, where did you get this book?" They had not ordered it and they had no record of it even coming in. In the front pages, as you opened the cover, it had been marked, penciled in with its price, so all they could logically assume was that the book had been inadvertently sent to them from their supplier and they had just added it to the shelf.

I went to other bookstores in the city and called the ones that were inconvenient to go to, and not one of them had any book by or about Bhagavan. In fact, none of them had even heard of him, though after that a couple of them started carrying his books.

I've told this story a number of times to people. That's how it happened. Why, I have no way of saying. It brings in the factor of a phenomenon that is very significant, as other people have shared stories of

Bhagavan that are of a similar nature. In some accounts, he has appeared to people at their door or elsewhere, even though he had never ever left his own Ashram, yet they had no doubt that it was Bhagavan appearing to them.

A year or so later, a friend of mine, who's an attorney, Bob Howingburg, went to New York. I had told him about the book. He was a follower of Gurdjieff and although he couldn't fully understand about my awakening, to some degree he knew, intellectually, something about it. He was in New York on some business matter as well as going to visit the Gurdjieff group. While there, he went into a bookstore, looked in the spiritual section, saw a copy of *Talks with Sri Ramana Maharshi,* and as a surprise, bought it and gave it to me. I was just delighted.

I still have that same book, it used to be my bible and now it is falling apart. I had that very book with me when I later stayed in the desert in Arizona. I wrote comments in the margins.

My girlfriend at the time of my awakening, Frances, whom I later married, came around occasionally to bring me food. Other friends came around as well. I didn't leave the apartment for anything. I lost weight (which in those days I didn't need to lose), because I didn't go out and didn't eat, I didn't feel like it, I didn't want to. I just stayed in and remained in a state of awareness - I was really in Samadhi (a transcendental state *ed.*).

I was at peace, I was free and I saw the absolute craziness, insanity and compulsiveness that people were caught up in. There was no way that I could describe that peace to people when they were caught up in the world and thinking that's where happiness and joy actually are. What I was saying would have been an affront to them.

The awakening brought insight and understanding experientially rather than intellectually, or as a belief. I wasn't going to have the seminars for a while, although there were individuals who were interested in knowing more about where I was now coming from, so that's when I started giving seminars again - I had to do something.

I called a number of people myself, who were themselves centers of influence and had friends who were sales managers, to let them know that I was going to resume my early morning talks - and the person helping me with the seminars called up a number of people as well. This was roughly seven weeks to two months after the awakening,

There was a tripod that could be set up in the lobby at the entrance-way to the cafeteria. I had made the easel in order to put up a flyer or poster, so I got it out of the closet, and put it up for people to know that I was coming back again.

The cafeteria didn't mind my doing that, because it was more business for them when people came for the seminars. Oh, there weren't as many people as before, because we couldn't get hold of everybody, but there were probably close to seventy-five people. They were all really glad to see me and I was glad to see them; they were anxious to know what had happened that made me quit giving the talks and what was going on, so I started telling them what had happened, where I was going, and what I had to share.

My statements presenting where I was coming from, were probably not very wise. I was able to see as ludicrous, as empty, as going nowhere, and as totally meaningless, how people were living their lives. What I, myself, had been doing - and what I had been teaching people to do - was contrary to what was really significant and meaningful. You see, before awakening, I had only an intellectual belief that we were all one awareness and sons and daughters of God, and afterwards, I was no lon-ger coming from strong faith or belief - I knew it as a fact. People were not yet ready to accept all of this as a fact, because their belief systems got in the way.

With our minds, we can fashion and form consciousness to mani-fest life in the way we want. That's what I had been teaching - and I still continued to teach - but I was able now to teach it with conviction that came from awakened awareness. I pointedly said that the power of awareness is the power of the mind. When you awaken in yourself the thought and the feeling of whatever you want to be, or to have, or to do, as if it is already happening - keeping that feeling alive at the forefront of your consciousness - it will ultimately come about as a physical experience in your life. I used to caution people to be very sure about what they wanted, because that's what they were going to get.

Most people could not grasp when I was sharing the awakened awareness. I guess it had become too incredible, incredulous and unbelievable. I had been drawing large numbers of people - when I was teaching an intellectual process. People could accept it that way - receive it - and they were doing the processes gladly, but when I began to share coming from awakening, I guess it scared people.

From 100 to 150 people on an average, it dropped down to only five to seven people, that's all. Those who remained though, were those that were into awakening for themselves, so I continued the seminars for a while, and then I gave up teaching in that fashion. That was the end of that.

After ending the morning seminars, I started giving everything away and then for a while I lived out of my car.

After my awakening, I just lost involvement and interest in everything of a monetary, financial, worldly basis. I had no further interest in worldly things and in seeking to accomplish, to succeed, to acquire, to accumulate or to own anything. I gave away everything that I owned.

If I had been living in India then, I would have been like the Sadhus you see living around the hills. I would have been in that category because I literally gave away everything.

The mind can still enter in even after awakening. My understanding and conclusions about what had happened to me in my awakening were based upon what I had studied. I had read the works of a number of Eastern teachers about renunciation, giving things up, leaving the world and going to the mountains or forest to live. Although I did not necessarily draw on my childhood memory of Uncle Billy, a hermit living in the woods - I remembered that he was living in the grace of being. So, I didn't feel that there was anything at all inappropriate in my no longer having interest in worldly things.

I just felt like unloading everything that I felt attached to, ownership of, or that was not a necessity. That included my clothes.

There was a period in my life when I would only wear the very best of clothes - shoes, ties, all of that. I had white on white - shirts, silk ties, lizard and alligator shoes - and Hickey Freeman and Lowe suits, name brands that I used to have attachment to. I had an affinity for the best, very good and expensive stuff.

After my awakening, I just saw the vanity of all of it. In the Bible's *Book of Ecclesiastes* - which I read during that period of time - there was a great deal about vanity. I saw how much I was attached to and identified with things, all simply to do with vanity. So, when I saw I had an attachment to something because of vanity, I just gave it away. That included a relatively new television set, a stereo system, an electric skillet, a toaster, all of that, I gave them away. I gave Frances my chest of drawers where I had kept all of my shirts, my clothing. She knew I was giving everything away. I gave someone else my sofa and living room furniture.

I called all of my friends and told them they could come and have anything that they liked. If nobody came, I would give things to strangers, just to anybody; the main thing was to alleviate myself of owning it, just to clear the space. Someone came, I gave them my bed.

There can be tendencies that you still have to work through after awakening. In my case, the tendencies were about my relationship with Frances and getting rid of all my personal belongings, which I completed at that time. I saw my identification with personal things, and took action in the form of releasing everything. I eliminated everything but the necessities for the body's physical survival and some books. At one time, when I was still married to Virginia, I had three thousand books. I had given many to her when she and I separated, but I still had about a thousand books that I sorted out. There were about two boxes of books that I wanted to keep and all the rest I invited my friends to take. What was left over, I gave to the library.

I kept a couple of stew pots and small pans for cooking, in the event that I needed to cook something. It was just a small box. I left my apartment clean, except for a pile on the floor of a few things that nobody wanted; otherwise the apartment was totally vacant. I had kept my car, and I just drove off and lived out of it for about six weeks.

What I misunderstood at that time was that it wasn't necessary to give up things themselves; what is important is to give up the attachment to things. Today, I guide people in giving up their attachment to material things, but it's not necessary to give up material things themselves. Back in those days, I didn't make that distinction.

I lived under the stars – it was in the summer – and it was a delightful period, so freeing. I took showers in truck stops and in people's homes when they invited me. Sometimes I'd spend the night on their sofa but many nights I slept in my car or on the ground, on a blanket under a tree. One spot in particular that I used to go - my favorite place - was an old deserted mansion, near where Frances lived. I used to go down the drive - not very many people knew about it –an isolated and private drive back into an area with apartments around it. It was closed in by a group of cedar trees that had grown together; so you could hardly see it. I used to go there, park, put my blanket under a big oak tree, and sleep on the ground.

While I was living out of my car, I ran into a very nice lady at Unity - Caroline Hirsch was her name. I'd stopped to go to a meditation in the Pyramid church. I'd met her before when she had attended my morning seminars and although she was not one of the five to seven people who had remained at the end, she was on the spiritual path.

Caroline had heard about what had happened to me. Rumors were going around that I had fallen "out of my tree" - I'd lost my mind. People were mourning that something awful had happened to me. She had thought that I would be despondent, in a state of worry and upset, but she saw that, to her surprise, my God, it was just the opposite, I was doing very well: I was happy. I was in a state of delight!

She told me that she had rented an office on Hillcroft Street, which was the same street as the church. It was only a few blocks away from Unity and on the same side of the road. She had started giving programs there, mainly to housewives. She herself was married and she was teaching a number of homemaker or housewife friends who didn't have anything to do. She had started out in her home, but her husband was not very supportive and he only passively accepted what she was doing. She recognized that, and as they were relatively affluent, she went into an office.

A number of people were following her teaching, which was a form of positive thinking. She wanted me to come by, and so I went. It was actually a nice suite of three rooms, in a small office building. She invited me to participate with her in her talks.

She asked me where I was living and I said I didn't live anywhere.

"What do you mean you don't live anywhere?"

"I don't live anywhere. I live in my car. I just live wherever I am," I said.

She couldn't believe it, but yet she could also recognize that I was genuine and that I was truly living happily - not unhappy - in what I was doing.

It was starting to get cooler; the weather was changing, so she invited me - if I wished - to use the office. I would take a bedroll, put it in the closet and pull it out at night. Since I was already sleeping on the ground, I could sleep on the floor in the office, and wash up in the bathroom down the hall - and I did that for a while.

Here I was, living in her office and joining her in what she was doing, beginning to give talks to the people that she was bringing there. It went on for a while and then, eventually, her husband began to be less supportive of her involvement and the time that she was putting into it, so she was required more or less to withdraw from it, and left it with me. So here I was, with an office.

Caroline left the office with all the furniture for me. It was mainly seats for people to sit on around the room, tables and a small desk, but it meant I was now getting active again. I needed a place to stay that was more appropriate than living in the office, so that's when I got another apartment.

The Sadhu with One Loin Cloth

There is a story of a Sadhu who had one loin cloth. His guru left him sitting under a tree meditating, and said he would be back later to see him. The Sadhu had only the loin cloth and a towel. One time he left his loin cloth out to dry and while he was covering himself with his towel, rats came and chewed on his loin cloth. Devotees came and one of them offered him another loin cloth, which he accepted, along with another towel. So now he had two loin cloths, one he could wear while another was being washed, but the rats kept eating his loin cloths.

In order to do something about the rats, someone suggested that he get himself a cat and so he got himself a cat to chase the rats away. Now the cat was hungry, so someone suggested that he get a cow in order to give milk to the cat. So he did. They got him a cow and he accepted the cow and then the cow was hungry and someone said you need hay for the cow. So they started bringing him hay, but pretty soon they quit bringing it and now the cow was still hungry and he was feeling compassion for the cow, so he started planting grass to make hay for the cow.

In planting the grass for the cow, he needed oxen to pull the plow and so someone gave him oxen. Then he needed a shed and he had to build a shed for his cow, oxen and all of the equipment. Soon he needed assistance, because it was more than he could handle by himself, and the first thing you knew he was a householder.

A few years later his guru came back and started asking people what had happened to his disciple, the Sadhu.

"Well, he lives over there in that house."

He went over to the house, and sure enough, there was his disciple.

"What's happened to you?" asked the Guru.

"All for the want of another loin cloth!" replied his disciple.

A. Ramana

Dialogue on Awakening 2
Getting Your Sea Legs

Saroja: How do you function when things are required of you, while you're abiding in awareness?

Ramana: Back in those days I went through a phase in which I had to kind of get my sea legs, so to speak. Have you ever walked in a boat, a small boat or a canoe?

Saroja: Yes.

Ramana: Try standing in a small row boat or a canoe and then walking from one end to the other - it's not easy to do. But if someone stands or walks in a boat or canoe all the time, they don't have any problem with it, do they? Until you learn how, it takes effort. Once you learn, it doesn't take any special effort. It is the same way in awakening. Once you have awakened, there will be an adjustment that you have to go through for a period of time, when you are required to be involved in actions or activities in which you learn how to keep your balance between being in awareness and being in your mind. It's a matter of making the distinction between the awareness of what you are, and the mind which is what you may think you are.

Baba Muktananda, whom I met a few years after my awakening, says the real problem is that we identify the "Self" that we actually are, with the "Not Self" that we think we are.

If we stop identifying with the "Not Self" we think we are, we really don't have to do anything to be the Self that we really are. So it's about making the adjustment and moving our identification from the "Not Self" to the "Self."

Do you have a vanity, a tall mirror that you sit in front of, in the bathroom or somewhere else?

Saroja: I have a huge mirror.

Ramana: Okay. Here's another way of looking at it. Do this for yourself: While sitting in front of your vanity, get another mirror, let's say 8"x 10" or a larger mirror and hold it up perpendicular to the mirror you're looking in.

If I am giving a talk and watch myself on a TV monitor, I then see myself as other people see me. You can create the same kind of a thing when using two mirrors and you have a reflection of your reflection. If you have a reflection of your reflection then you are seeing yourself as other people see you. Are you with me?

Saroja: Yes.

Ramana and Saroja greeting with Namaste, Ottawa, Canada, 2001. *Photo: Elizabeth.*

Ramana: Normally, when you're looking in the mirror, you never see yourself as other people see you. Do this right now.

Looking at your reflection of your reflection right now you're looking at yourself as I'm seeing you, not as you would be seeing yourself in the normal mirror.

Saroja: I'm looking at my normal mirror image now.

Ramana: Now, touch your left ear. Looking in at your own reflection, is it on your left or is it on your right?

You've been doing this for so long that out of a habit you know how to part your hair or put on your makeup.

However, if you put one mirror up next to another mirror and see the reflection of your reflection, you will see yourself in the opposite way that you're normally seeing yourself in the mirror. Now when you're seeing yourself in the opposite way to what you normally see yourself in the mirror, looking at the reflection of your reflection, you're going to have trouble doing your makeup because everything will be in reverse. It's very difficult to find out which way to do something when it's all reversed.

Before awakening, we've been seeing things upside down and backwards to the way they really are and so because of this, after awakening - for you to be able to see things as they really are, you have to learn how to see right side up. For a period of time you go through an adjustment. Is that helping?

Saroja: Yes, thank you, Ramana.

CHAPTER 12

Teaching Meditation

I was not bringing in enough money to take care of everything, to pay the rent, buy my food and gasoline and all of that, so I needed to find a way to start making a little more money. I was looking around for something that would be easy enough to do and didn't take a lot of responsibility and a lot of time, but paid relatively well for the time put into it. The main thing was I didn't want to put in a lot of time and my son, Randy, came up with the idea. "Why don't you drive a school bus?"

"Hey, that's a pretty good idea."

So, I started driving the school bus. It all fit together. In fact, I ended up driving a school bus in two different periods, first when I lived in my own apartment and then later when I lived with Frances.

Randy knew the owner of a bus company that had a contract with the school board in Houston to provide a bus service in areas of the city and out into the county where they didn't have regular school bus runs. This fellow purchased used school buses that had been traded in for new school buses in High Point, North Carolina, where most of the school buses were built. He had bought a fleet of used school buses that were still in good condition. Randy knew him through a friend who worked at a service station where the bus fleet owner stored or parked the school buses and bought gasoline for them. So, Randy made arrangements for me to meet him.

For years, I had a commercial driver's license that I never ever needed, because I only drove a car. I had got the commercial driver's license when I had learned how to drive a truck. That already put me in good stead for driving a school bus, because when I was asked what kind of driver's license I had and I said, "commercial," the owner said it would be easy enough to get a chauffeur driver's license, though I'd have to be tested for it.

I had to be able to drive a bus for the test, so he just gave me a key for a bus and told me to drive it around to get familiar with it. I drove it, backing it up and all of that. Driving a bus you have to be a lot more alert about what you're doing, especially going around corners at intersections. You can't of course cut across the corner. You have to make a wide swing, and if there is someone over on your right side lane or similar lane, you cut him off. You also had to be careful backing it up, looking out through the rear view mirrors, and there was a big mirror inside the bus from which you could see all the kids in the back. It was important to watch that the kids were all sitting down. It took me only one day to get comfortable and understand how to drive the bus.

After that, I went to the driver's license agency and got checked out in a bus by the State Police, who issued me my chauffeur license immediately. It took a while for the official one to be sent to me from the State Capital, but I was able to use the certificate that they handwrote for me. The owner of the bus company needed someone right away - he had a route that either was opening up or one on which a driver quit, I can't remember which - and so I went to work right away. I worked for him for a couple of years. That was very enjoyable.

I had moved from the office I was using as my residence to an apartment, and then started inviting people to come there who were interested in what had happened in my awakening. I quit teaching in the traditional fashion at seminars and I began giving the teachings in Satsang. On weekdays, I drove the school bus in the day and at night a group of us began to meditate in my apartment. On weekends, we went to a lady's home by a lake in an area North of Liberty. The whole thing began to escalate. From about five people, it grew to fifteen or twenty people who met in my apartment five nights a week.

It got to the point where the apartment management didn't want me to have the groups, because they thought I was conducting a business, and I was asked to move. They didn't understand meditation was a spiritual work. At the second apartment, it was more convenient, I had a little more space, but it was the same thing. I was trying to do something to get more people to come, which would give an income to pay my rent, and the management saw that as my being involved in a commercial endeavor that I was practicing out of my apartment, which went contrary, they said, to the lease. So I had to move from there, too.

Then I found another place, but on that occasion I talked to the manager first and explained to him exactly what I was doing, where I was coming from, how it all worked, that people might be coming to see me. I told him that I taught meditation and that these people would come and that we would be quiet; you would not hear a sound out of us, there would be no problem, no difficulties, and no concern about people coming and going, because they were coming to a spiritual endeavor. There was nothing that anybody would have to worry about. They understood and agreed to allow me to do that - and that was the apartment that I ended up moving into. So I had it all set up in advance. It was a small, one-bedroom apartment, but it was situated in such a way that it was convenient, well located so people could easily find it, and there was adequate parking.

Before my awakening, while I was teaching the early morning seminars, I was established and operating under the auspices or umbrella of the "Academy for Self Knowledge." I called it ASK. It was based upon

Jesus's statement: "Ask, and it will be given you; seek, and ye shall find; knock, and it shall be opened unto you:" (Matthew 7:7, King James Version). I had registered it as a non-profit organization under the full name, but I never did get the non-profit charter. Those seminars dwindled away, until five to seven people remained interested. I printed up a brochure and gave it to people to give to their friends and we gradually began to grow.

It was primarily a Satsang meditation group. We meditated in stillness and silence for an hour, a quiet time, followed by two hours of talk and discussion, and then if there were any questions, I answered them. During one period, on Friday nights, the entire room would circle around me. Friday night has always been significant to me, first in ASK and then a few years later in AHAM (Association of Happiness for All Mankind).

In the meditations, some people were able to sit up straight and unsupported, while others sat leaning against the wall, and I sat on a spot that was raised about six inches. I had bought a piece of carpet that was the same color as the rest of the carpet in the apartment, and laid it a little higher. It was wide enough to sit cross-legged on and tapered on the sides and I could easily see people who sat in front of me.

Four people moved to that apartment project to be close to me. Gradually we were influencing the whole apartment project - it wasn't a large one, it was a small one – but myself and four others were living there, then eventually there were four apartments with six people living there, and we were all meditating five nights a week from about seven until ten, three hours a night.

The group became known by a number of people at Unity, and we occasionally went to Unity Church, however, we became a little controversial because we were considered to be radical in our approach. We had very strong convictions that Jesus was not the only Son of God - which was in fact actually no different than Unity teachings - and that awakening to Christ consciousness was the primary thing. For many people going to the church, this was just their religious philosophy. It was something you believed in, and it was not that important if you lived it twenty-four hours a day.

There weren't many people in a group relationship as we were, living in conscious company, in Satsang, and following the teachings of Bhagavan Sri Ramana Maharshi. In fact, it was rare to have a group in the city that was so involved and dedicated to an intense practicing of spiritual teachings, practicing disciplined meditation.

One Indian group in town was involved in Kundalini Yoga. It was very Eastern oriented. During that time, I was studying Vedanta and Bhagavan's writings and other Eastern teachers, though we were not living a life style of an Easterner. The Kundalini Yoga group wore white uniforms, which they had chosen instead of ochre. They were as equally dedicated to their own teaching as we were to ours. We visited with them on one occasion, and we had a friendly relationship with one another, but we were different. We were in our own teaching, we were doing our thing and they were doing their thing.

About a year later, on Friday nights, we began to meditate in the nude to see who was really into what we were talking about. It was entirely platonic. The point was to stand naked in front of God and the world. It had nothing to do with sex. It was to be free and to be open. We didn't do that for very long, it might have happened for three or four months, but it was a matter of a person making their commitment, seeing if they were going to let go and be in the pure awareness of being.

We set it up with the curtains and Venetian blinds drawn closed, so there was no way that anybody could see in. My car was parked immediately outside my back door in the parking lot. People would arrive, walk in the back door entrance, remove their clothes in my bedroom, and then walk into the front room where we sat and meditated.

Everyone in my group - I called it my group as I was their teacher and leading the group for three hours a night, five nights a week - worked in the summer except for me. As soon as they got off from work, they'd go home and take care of whatever they needed to take care of, and come at seven o'clock. We would all be there and if there was anyone missing, then the question was, "Where is so and so?" and "Why are they not here?" Someone would know where each person was, and if they were not there, whether they had something to do or there was something wrong.

I hooked a big tin can, a coffee can, on a nail inside the door as you walked in my apartment. People in my group would drop money in it, a donation of cash or checks or whatever, and that's what I lived on. My rent, everything came out of it. I never asked for anything. They gave willingly because they knew that I was totally dependent on the donations to pay my rent, the food I ate, gasoline for my automobile, and clothing.

Names are not easy for me to recall any more; one lady who was a member of our group owned a house on a nice lake outside the little town of Liberty, Texas, about fifty miles away. The lot itself was right on the lake, so the house was hardly any distance at all to the lake itself. It was a little two bedroom house with a living room, kitchen and dining area, a large back porch that extended the full length of the back house and then a pier into the water of the lake within easy walking distance.

We used to swim in the lake or go fishing, and occasionally a guest would be invited to come, but mostly it was the people in our group. We were there every weekend without fail. We would all go to the lake to meditate, swim or lay about, and be there in conscious company. Usually, we would be there on Saturday and on Sunday mornings, waking up and meditating together. Everybody would bring food and it was like a picnic, eating on the back porch. It was just a joyous time that we would all have together. It was less formal on the weekend than on week nights, and we would do whatever came up, but we would still have our quiet times together. If questions came up, we would deal with them and people shared their experiences or what was going on with them.

You might see us as radical, because it became not just the five nights a week, but the entire weekends at the lake house. It would vary from time to time, as some could not always go and others could, but most of the time all of us would spend the weekend there together in meditation, enjoyment of one another's company, swimming and relaxation. It was a very delightful time for all involved, even though people didn't have much free time because everyone had a responsible and time consuming job. We did that for the longest period of time - goodness knows how long - at least a year, I'm sure. It was a very spiritual and intense period.

The lady who owned the lake house died and that ended the weekend lake house gatherings. This was in 1974. I then went to stay in the desert of Arizona for a while, and on my return I was involved in preparations for Baba Muktananda to come to Houston.

Dialogue on Awakening 3
Seeing "Others"

Saroja: Once you awakened in June 1973, how then did you perceive what we call "others?" How did Papaji (an awakened spiritual teacher in the lineage of Bhagavan Sri Ramana Maharshi, ed.) see us? You mentioned a great compassion is present. You must see us hanging on to things that don't exist.

Ramana: As expressions of your own being... There is only one consciousness and I am that consciousness and you are that consciousness. We're all that consciousness. We all are actually expressions of the one consciousness, expressed as different appearances or forms.

So how do you see others? You see them as an expression of yourself; they're the same thing that you are. They're formed by their minds. What makes them different is their minds are formed in different configurations of beliefs, notions, ideas, than maybe your mind is, but still they are the same as you. They're not different in truth than you; they're only different in form than you. They're not different in essence than you. Now the patterns of their mind and the tendencies from those patterns might make them act and behave totally differently than you.

Saroja: Do you see the patterns and latent tendencies in people, or is this coming to you more as a feeling?

Ramana: All the patterns of consciousness, the patterns of your mind, your questions, your doubts, your fears, your concerns that you have when you are with me, those are states of consciousness that are still active in you. I can feel them when you are with me, or when I'm with people who have those states of consciousness, which are active and alive and coming forth to the surface of their being, to be expressed.

I feel these as states of consciousness that at one time had been alive in me, even if they may now be no longer active, but they are potentially there for me to know and understand and feel their expression. It's more of a feeling. I can tell when I'm in the presence of someone, for example, who is a meditator rather than someone who is quite worldly. And it doesn't take long for me to tell the difference. It is as soon as when they open their mouth and start to speak. You can tell that yourself, can't you?

Saroja: Yes.

Ramana: That's the way it is. It's not a big deal, but I might be a little more sensitive to that than most people.

I can feel someone's compassion if they're a compassionate person. I can feel their potential. That's the way it works with me.

Ramana and friends, "conscious company," in dialogue at AHAM, Asheboro, USA, circa 2007. *Photo: Jim Dillinger.*

Now with someone like Baba, they may have Siddhis (paranormal powers) based upon their degree of pure consciousness. You might call it the quality of omniscience. When in the presence of someone, Baba literally could read their thoughts. Now I can't normally read people's thoughts but occasionally I do. Occasionally I know if someone is thinking or feeling a particular way. They may deny it, but I know that they are.

Sometimes I also know what a person is capable of even when they may indicate that they are not capable of something. I see that mostly on the positive side. In your case, I can tell - on the positive side - what you're capable of, your potential, if you just let go and let yourself see and be. For example, when just a while ago,

I said to you to be still, be quiet - pretty soon you were back in the pure awareness. Right?

Do you understand what I'm saying?

Saroja: Yes.

Ramana singing during a Christmas celebration at the Arunachala Village School in Tiruvannamalai, India. December, 2008. *Photo: Saroja.*

Ramana: If someone is open, if they're genuine and true in their receptivity, the thing of significance is that I can tune in to them and act as a catalyst for them to have their own insight and their own "deepening."

But you see, it's not deep, it's right here, present. It's not any deeper than just saying "I." When you're saying "I," you're right there saying "I." How deep do you have to go to say "I?"

Do you get what I'm saying?

This is where people misunderstand words and they take the words to mean you have to go real deep in order to get something. Well, it's not real deep, it's what's covering it up that seems to be deep and you've got to cut through all of the ramifications, all of the entanglements, all of the patterns that are woven together. It's almost like a knot, which when you loosen it comes apart.

Are you with me?

Saroja: Yes, absolutely...

I want to ask if people's behavior affects you in the way I have seen, for example, with Papaji, doing some things to his body. One of his disciples, a woman, kept breaking her arm and at one point Papaji broke his arm too and some people said that he somehow was just absorbing the whole energy to help this woman stop breaking her bones. I don't know if am clear, but do you absorb things like that or does it go right through you? Does it affect your own body or your own health somehow?

Ramana: Yes, that happens sometimes. I do have the tendency to take on what other people are going through in a manner to help them to clear it in themselves. That function traditionally has been called the guru function. The guru sometimes takes on some of the karma of his or her devotees.

Now, when we say that the guru takes on, it's not an "I "taking on this for a "you," for, in the awakened being, there is no "I" and "you," there is no "I" and "other," only the one being expressing itself in form, in the apparent forms of "I" and "other."

It's like when an awakened being who has Siddhis is apparently demonstrating these powers; it's not, "Well, I'm going to demonstrate power and I'm going to show them."

If that were the case then the one demonstrating those powers would not be an awakened, liberated being. It would be ego. The awakened one has dissolved the sense of "I," as an individual, back into the pureness of being; a liberated one has done that.

Now I can't speak for all the phases. We're talking here about the unlimited number of potential possibilities, so I can't speak for all of the possibilities or all of the probabilities; I can only speak in principle. Am I making myself clear?

Saroja: Hmm… clarify it a little more please.

Ramana: There are cases of people who devote an entire stage of their life just to helping people. Take Mother Teresa as an example. It has been recently discovered through people close to her, and I think from her own writings, that she was living in a place of despair. She was in a state of despair because she saw so much suffering in the world, so much so that she even had come to doubt God. Why would there be so much suffering in the world? She had seen so much and she had given her life to helping others overcome suffering that it had overcome her to the extent that she had actually fallen into a state of despair. Can you hear me?

Saroja: Yes.

Ramana: We can't doubt Mother Teresa's intentions. We can't doubt her compassion and her love and all of her good works. She created an order of nuns that had branches all over the world. She's a saint in a Catholic Church tradition. She's a saintly being.

I don't question Mother Teresa's sincerity, her dedication and her compassion to humanity, even though she may have come to the place of actually experiencing despair because she saw so much suffering. She saw so much poverty, so much depravity in the world, in Calcutta where she lived and throughout her entire life.

That doesn't take away whatever from the fact that she was a saint in my view.

Saroja: But she was still coming from an "I."

Ramana: Yes, she was still coming from an "I."

Saroja: So that's a bit different from you, or other awakened beings, as you do absorb from people sometimes, but there is no "I" there.

Ramana: When there is a seeing of whatever is going on and a quality of concern for someone is felt - like Papaji who broke his arm because his devotee was always breaking her arm - the *sense of I* can rise up and be felt.

But that doesn't take away from Papaji's being awakened, that doesn't take away the fact that Papaji was liberated. It shows, rather, the depth of compassion that a saintly being has for his or her followers who are going through times of trials and tribulations.

Bhagavan, for example, had devotees. There was one lady devotee - I don't remember her name - who had lost every member of her family. Her daughters, husband, sons, every member of her family had died before her and had suffered tremendously and she had suffered tremendously. She would come to Bhagavan and while telling him of her sorrow, tears would stream down Bhagavan's face as he listened to her. Could you say that Bhagavan was not liberated because he had tears, because he felt the sorrow? You could not say that. No one could say that.

So in a similar sense, yes, there are times that I feel sorrow and have compassion; there are times that I feel anger.

Saroja: I've seen that (laughter).

Ramana: But while I'm feeling anger, while it's going on, it's being felt without there being a "me" here that is feeling it, meaning a separate individual "me." It's an appropriate emotion because the events themselves have brought it up in the moment, just like sorrow can be an appropriate emotion in the moment, because of the situation that has brought it about.

The main thing is, as Bhagavan would say: "Don't be the doer of your actions, of your feelings; don't identify with them as a "me." They are just the feelings, the emotions that are occurring in the moment. Stay prior to them."

Yes, there will still be the feeling of them, but you don't lose yourself. Awareness is there while engaged in such thoughts and feelings. Are you with it?

Saroja: Yes. What you're saying is very important because we assume a lot about awakened beings and we project a lot on them, so you are mentioning and clarifying things that are important for everyone to know.

Ramana: Yes. And the statement that you are making right there - should appear in the book as well.

Have you ever read *Talks with Sri Ramana Maharshi* or *Day by Day with Bhagavan*?

Saroja: Yes, I have those books.

Ramana: Or, *Maharishi's Gospel*? Someone is asking the questions and then he's answering, and then the person who's asking the questions makes their own comments about their understanding of what Bhagavan was saying. Well, you'll want that to appear the same way in this book: these statements you are making as part of our conversation itself need to be in this book.

CHAPTER 13

Gurus

I think it was a year after having the awakening experience in June, 1973, that I went to Arizona and stayed in a tepee.

My friend Al bought access or control over something like five thousand acres of excellent land outside of the little town of Wilcox, Arizona - with the intention of developing it or selling it. He had ways that I knew nothing about, he would come upon a good deal and he had one there. First he purchased a double-wide motor home and set it up where he lived and he invited me to come out.

The tepee was set up in walking distance and in sight of his house, but it was isolated. I lived in that tepee just enjoying nature out in the desert. The climate was ideal, cool at night, and warm, even hot in the daytime.

Al had been to Houston a time or two visiting and I had traveled out that way with him, and then I'd gone there on a bus and stayed for a while. After my awakening, nobody could relate to me. I was coming from a totally different place, living in the awareness of being and I had no concern about the mundane, financial aspect of worldly life, worldly activity. I didn't have any interest in it at all.

Al thought he could understand where I was coming from. I tried to explain it to him. He had read a lot of books and there was much that he and I could talk about and explain to each other, but not this. He couldn't quite grasp it. It was beyond him. I described it, in a sense, as like being on an ongoing acid trip. He could relate to that, because he and I had taken acid together a number of times. He said: "Hell, you still want to come down and you don't want to stay up there all the time."

"I'm trying to explain to you that's where I am; it's a natural place and it's like that all the time."

"That means you don't want to do anything."

"There's not anyone here to do anything for. Whatever is going on is whatever is going on, and I'm not directing the show, I'm watching the show."

His wife Nell could somewhat understand the awakening, but I couldn't get Al to understand. It was beyond him and most of the people that I talked to.

When I returned to Houston from Arizona, I heard that Baba Muktananda was to come on his second world tour to America (1974 to 1976). It was posted on the bulletin board in the Phoenix Bookstore (the same book store where my awakening occurred), with the name of Matt Walford, a devotee of Baba, to contact. I called him, we met, got acquainted, and I got involved with him in bringing Baba to Houston.

Up to that point, my understanding was that it was necessary to have access to a guru to confirm a transformed awareness or state of being as genuine. That's what I had heard, but I didn't have a guru, so thinking this was important (although I didn't fully understand it), I was really looking forward to having contact with Baba Muktananda, who was living as a Siddha (one who has attained spiritual perfection, ed.).

I shared with Matt where I was coming from, that I was living in awareness, and being a devotee of Baba he could somewhat understand it, and he was interested, as well, because he had the need to try to get his mind to calm down.

Many people understood I was dedicated to spiritual work from my background in self-improvement, motivation, and personal and company effectiveness. Because of my history, people knew I wasn't bullshitting when I spoke about awakening, although I think it appeared to them that I was simply advancing further in a progressive process. Except, my awakening wasn't part of a progressive state, because I was no longer seeking: there wasn't anything else to seek, I was just abiding.

At that point there were about fifteen or twenty in my Self-Inquiry group. Being in the awareness, I was teaching people the Self-Inquiry as I knew it to be from reading Bhagavan's teaching and from what I myself had experienced. I knew that it worked to bring the mind back into the pure awareness of being.

Matt was in communication with Baba's headquarters, and he told them we would like Baba to come to Houston. We wanted anybody interested in experiencing Satsang with him, helping to influence him to come. At that point I had no income, so I was not in a position to spend money to go to the nearest place he was going to be, probably in New York, Atlanta, California or Michigan. The headquarters also was very much in favor of Baba visiting as many places that they could find devotees or new people interested - and there were devotees wanting him to come to Houston.

Matt and I went to look at a retreat center about ninety miles south of a town called Bayport, southwest of Houston on the Gulf Coast. I can't remember the little town, but there was a non-profit organization run by Baptists who had a retreat center there. Matt and I met the owners and operators and made arrangements to have a retreat there when Baba came. We had the dates and everything set up and got confirmation from the main Baba group in the New Jersey/New York area.

Then lo and behold, shortly thereafter, the Baptist Retreat Center heard about Baba being an Indian guru, a Hindu, and cancelled the deal.

We had already started notifying people that Baba was going to be there; we had printed literature and gone ahead organizing. I wasn't involved in paying for any of this; I was just involved in setting it up with Matt. We even discussed the potential of suing the retreat center, but Baba said no, not to sue them. Baba was now in California and he was coming across the country.

At the time, I could understand when many people got upset about the cancellation by the Baptist Center, but it turned out to be a good thing because we found a location in Houston - and again I was involved in it.

A lady invited my Self-Inquiry group over one evening for meditation. She was relatively affluent, in a nice part of town. When we went to her home, we saw that she had her house set up for Baba. There was a whole room with pictures of him and a special chair designated as Baba's chair. She was a Jewish lady, wholly dedicated to Baba and had been to India two or three times. She had a group of people in Houston, about eight or ten friends, many who had also been to India to see Baba in his ashram in Ganeshpuri.

A couple of people in my group had long beards and long hair and looked hippie-like and she didn't like that. After we had all gone in, one fellow named Tom, who didn't know the difference, inadvertently sat in Baba's chair. Boy oh boy, that really upset her.

It was humorous for me to watch this whole process play out in front of me, how people got triggered off, how there was so much importance put on bullshit that had nothing to do with anything. It was upsetting to people in my group because they were still caught in the identification with the mind and with their attachments and so we finally left early because our group was uncomfortable being there. We went back to my place and I listened to them going on and on about what was happening that they didn't like.

I said to them, "Can you see all this? Are you watching this? Do you see what is taking place?"

I saw the humor of it and I was just laughing, but it was a beneficial process at the time to point out to everyone to what extent they were identified. Finally, before it was over, I got everybody to look at it and laugh at the humor of it.

In the end, we stayed with the process of getting Baba to come to Houston.

I was involved in all the pre-planning stages before Baba came to Houston. There was an advance group from Baba that would go a week or so ahead to prepare everything for his coming. My Self-Inquiry group played as big a part as the advance group.

Ramana in his mid to late forties, with friends.
AHAM archives.

One of the main devotees in the advance group, whose spiritual name was Purnima, was from Paris, France and spoke very good English, but of course with a French accent. She and two or three of the others, hung out at my apartment because they could feel the energy there. She used the term Shaktipat to describe the presence she experienced and she really got off being in my apartment during that time. The people in the advance group used to come there to lie around on the floor and to cool down.

My place had a great quality of energy, as do our AHAM Ashram centers. Of course, I was living and meditating there - as well as hosting my Self-Inquiry group. I sat on a chair by the window for my own meditations, and I sat on the floor to meditate when people came. The large front window was at sidewalk level. You'd pass it as you walked in front of the apartment to the apartment next to me and people would see me sitting there meditating. The front room in my apartment had just mats and cushions to sit on. In my bedroom, I had a bed and a chair to sit on to meditate; an altar with Bhagavan's and Jesus' pictures and a table with a stereo to play soft music.

I'd already set all of this up with the owner, so having people coming and going to my apartment was okay with him, and, as I said, Purnima and the others really enjoyed hanging out there.

They began using my apartment and my telephone to communicate with the main office in New Jersey, to make arrangements for Baba's arrival, etc. and so they asked for permission and I agreed that they use my telephone number the whole time that Baba was in Houston.

Baba's devotee moved out of her house and lent it for his use and there was also a Yoga Center at which we had made arrangements to have what they called an "advance," the term they used instead of "retreat." They had my telephone number transferred over there, which they agreed to pay for, and my telephone line was disconnected (although the phone was still there) – so, for the whole time that Baba was there, I didn't have a telephone.

I had access to Baba, which wasn't easy to get in those days. I was one of the inner circle and the people in my Self-Inquiry group had easier access to him than many others, because we were all involved in the arrangements for his visit. Baba was very popular and he traveled with an entourage of fifty people and then they would draw people from all over. It was not easy to see him as there would be two to three hundred people around him at any one time.

It was during that time that I had the opportunity to be with Baba, and met his translator, Yohindra Jain, whose spiritual name was Swami Yogananda. We became good friends. He fell off the wagon - lost his swami-hood - after he met a young lady in New Jersey, a devotee of Baba, and they had struck up a relationship, had a tête-à-tête and a little sexual encounter. He invited her or she just came to Houston while Baba was there.

Baba shaved his own head and covered himself with ashes, which were qualities of mourning, at the loss of Yogananda who had to take back his civilian name, Yohindra. He was then taken off his duty as translator. He didn't even have civilian clothes. Other people had to give him clothes to wear.

A young woman became Baba's interpreter, his translator, right there in Houston. I knew her as Malti but she became known later as Swami Chidvilasananda. She was only about nineteen then, but she spoke very good English, and so she became Baba's translator from that point onward.

He would say things sometimes that were a little off color, using profanity, and she was required to translate what Baba said. So if he said shit, she'd have to say it. Whatever it was that he said, she would have to say it, and he would watch her, as he, as well as others, knew enough English to know if she was translating exactly (Baba addressed his audiences primarily in Hindi, with words and expressions in Marathi and in his native language, Kannada. He frequently quoted from the scriptures in Sanskrit. Source: The SYDA Foundation Questions and Comments Team, ed.)

Malti became the head after Baba dropped the body. She and her brother had a conflict as to who was going to succeed Baba. It became quite a conflict, not too nice, but she's the head now and she's pretty famous.

While we were in Houston, Yogananda and I used to walk quite a bit up and down the sidewalk, just talking and visiting the house where Baba stayed. I had access to Baba and one day we walked up to the house, to the porch on which Baba was sitting. People could sit on the side of the landing with their feet on the steps, and on the floor it was wide enough to sit comfortably. There must have been fifteen or twenty people sitting around on either side of the stairway; and others on the floor at the feet of Baba. He was sitting on the chair when we walked up to him. He looked at me and Yogananda and announced to everyone present:

"Here is a Yogi, a great Yogi, a Sage, many life times he has been a Sage."

His acknowledgment of me at that moment was very significant, because it was giving me the confirmation of my state of awareness. He made that statement and also said that I was a Siddha, living in awareness, and complete. He said this in front of everyone in Houston and then again on the trip to Dallas.

Baba used to come and put his hand on my head or hit me on the head when he'd say things to me. One day in Dallas, I was sitting on the floor next to him and he put his hand on my head and said: "You're Ramana, that's your name. You're playing in God, reveling in God." He told me that's what Ramana means and it was my name from then on.

I was very moved by his giving me the name of Ramana, but I didn't feel worthy of using Bhagavan's name, God's name. I didn't understand all of it, so I accepted the name, but not fully, because I didn't feel it was appropriate for me to actually take the name of my own guru, Ramana Maharshi.

After he gave me the name, I used it, but I left off the last "a" so I said, "Raman," but I didn't even know how to properly pronounce it.

I thought it was Ra<u>ma</u>na instead of <u>Ra</u>mana and when I left off the "a" I thought it was Ra<u>man</u> instead of <u>Ra</u>man. So after that time I started using the name of Ra<u>man</u> without the "a," and it was that way until I went to India.

Baba wanted me to turn my group over to a Siddha Yoga Center and start initiating people into Siddha Yoga and I did that for a while, but I didn't feel that was appropriate because, although I had great honor and respect for Baba, I didn't see him as my guru. I didn't feel I was in his lineage, so I quit doing that. A couple of others in Houston did start giving initiation in Siddha Yoga, and turned their centers, what they were doing, over to him. Baba caused quite a stir.

Baba was in Houston a whole week doing his advance group and then he went to Dallas for another week. I was able to get to know and be close to him, and Baba himself invited me as his guest to go to Dallas. It was to reciprocate for all I had done, it didn't cost me anything. In those days it cost about $700 or $800. They charged a lot of money. They charged for everything in a big way. They had set up there at a Salvation Army Retreat Center, which is where he gave his advance group.

I rode up with Matt in a convoy of people; a whole entourage of people went along with Baba from Houston up to Dallas. It was two hundred miles and we stopped, at the half way mark, to have a meal at a Holiday Inn, which is a motor lodge. We all went into the restaurant, but Baba stayed in his car, which in those days I didn't fully understand. Now I do, because I don't care for such things, I'd be the same way now.

The time with Baba was bringing to an end another era for me. I had followers who considered me as their teacher, the ones in the Self-Inquiry group that met five nights a week. When Baba came, I took the group along with me, and those who were able to get off work had Satsang with him the whole week he was there. Some could not get off work and they could only come to the evening functions that Baba would have occasionally. During this period, some of them went over to Baba, as they had begun to see him as their teacher. That was fine with me.

Several of my friends met Baba. John an astrologer, Carole a psychic who gave psychic readings, as well as a number of my acquaintances - all got involved with Baba. Carole even went to India and saw him in his ashram there.

My friend Al was also very interested when I told him about Baba and he decided he wanted to experience him. So Al and Nell and one of Nell's three daughters from a previous marriage, his step-daughter, whose nickname was Sunshine, drove to Dallas from Arizona to meet Baba. Sunshine, who was a young girl, even got to sit on Baba's lap, which was a big deal for people in those days.

I was still relatively new in my awakening and there was a lot that I was adjusting to and beginning to understand. Nell and Al getting to meet Baba meant they could better understand where I was coming from, though it was still hard for them to fully accept and acknowledge I was anywhere close to being the same category spiritually because they knew me as just an ordinary guy from our long relationship.

Here was Baba sitting on a pedestal with an entourage and hundreds of people coming, and fame all around the country and world. Baba himself had even said that I was spiritually complete, a Siddha. He had said this to the people around us, but Al wasn't around when that was said, so it was hard for Al and Nell to recognize what actually had really taken place. They knew I was different but they didn't understand it. Al could never quite grasp it in the early days after my awakening; he knew I had gone through something in the way of a radical change, though he didn't know what it was.

After Dallas, Baba continued on his tour. I don't recall where else he went, but he ended up in Oakland, California.

Then it came up for me to go to California, so I went with two of the people who were interested in seeing Baba: Chuck, his girlfriend and me, the three of us went in his van.

It was kind of an open van without any seats in the back where we put a mattress, so we lived somewhat rustically on our drive from Houston to San Francisco. On the way we stopped in Wilcox, Arizona at Al's. By that time Al was living in a house he had purchased in town rather than in the mobile home that he had out on the land.

Bhagavan Sri Ramana Maharshi was still primary to me. Because of this, in California I wanted to meet Bubba Free John, as he had indicated, in his earlier days, that Bhagavan was his lineage. He had been to the Ashram in Tiruvannamalai in South India and he had written several books about that time. His last book from that period showed a picture of Bhagavan, declaring Bhagavan to be his guru.

Bubba Free John was getting to be well known. He had also seen Baba Muktananda at his ashram in India. Baba had even given him a spiritual name, though he didn't use it, as well as the authorization to initiate people into Siddha Yoga.

After being at Baba's ashram, Bubba Free John had spun off and started teaching on his own with his own devotees. Baba's devotees had reacted to that and Bubba's devotees had reacted in turn and they had gotten into a controversy and conflict that was written about in their mutual magazines, particularly Bubba's own harsh press.

We stayed a day or two in Arizona and went on to San Francisco. We saw Baba but we weren't allowed to see Bubba Free John. We went to his center, which if I remember was on Polk Street in San Francisco upstairs in a book store. To see him, you had to have read, I think, three of his books and attended some kind of special introductory program and the only one of us who was given permission to be able to see him was the girl that was with us. She didn't go, so none of us saw him.

On the way back we spent a day with Al and returned again to Houston. Then I moved out of my apartment, did another give-away. I gave away everything that I had accumulated up to that time, and with Chuck, and my sons Skyler and Randy, went back to Arizona with the intention of possibly staying out there for an indefinite period. It was school time and Skyler started school there.

After my awakening I went through a period of making adjustments with regard to what was going on in my life. One thing was my deeply entrenched relationship with Frances. That was not over yet.

When I was in Arizona I was living out in the desert, it was bliss. I was in a blissful state. It was delightful to be there living in the tepee and to look out in the distance. It was very rustic and I wasn't looking for anything from a material, monetary, or ordinary mundane point of view. Pulling on me was the incompletion of my attachment to Frances and her attachment to me; which I would pretty well get over when I stayed with the Self-Inquiry and didn't communicate with anyone.

I told them, if I'm out there – unless it's some real major emergency like a life-threatening situation – I don't even want to be bothered. I don't want to be disturbed by anybody. I would come in after being out sometimes three of four days or a week. Occasionally Al would drive out to see me, to see how I was doing and even Nell would come from time to time and bring me some food, but they would be the only people that I would see. I had all the food available that I needed. I didn't eat that much and I really wasn't wanting or needing anything.

I could go out there and not see anybody, not a soul. I was happy there, but then I would walk back the distance to where my friends lived, 'civilization,' and they would sometimes tell me that Frances had called and left a message wanting me to call her whenever I came in. She kept working on me and finally I would call her to see what was going on with her and then she would ask me something like:

"Well, are you finished with what you are doing? When are you coming back? When are you going to be back?"

And I would say: "I don't know!"

Then she would say something that would stimulate within me some kind of a spark of wanting to come back, or maybe she'd even indicate what she had been doing, where she had gone, and maybe who she had gone out with. Due to my attachment to her, that would start my mind working and wondering what she was doing, who she was with and all that kind of stuff.

I had told Baba, speaking through Yogananda when he was Baba's interpreter, that I was complete in all areas of my life except one.

Baba said: "What is that?"

I said that everything was perfect in my life at that point other than the relationship that I was in with Frances, that I was very much at the effect of that relationship.

Baba laughed and said: "Haven't you got it yet?"

I just shook my head.

At that time, I didn't fully know what he meant, but I have got it now. The point being that I was looking for happiness in a relationship and there's no happiness there. Not only was it not happy, it was miserable. It was pleasure, pain all wrapped up into one. It was so pleasant and so unpleasant, because I was so attached to her, and there was so much pain in that, it was not meant to be a spiritual relationship. Frances was in the world and I was in the spirit.

That period had to come to an end and it got to the point where I had to do something and I think Al was getting a little tired of me. He wasn't requiring anything from me to be there, but I decided to go back to Houston.

Dialogue on Awakening 4

Freeing Ourselves from Entanglement

Saroja: I think acceptance is really the key to relaxing and being with what is - it's a very important part of the teaching.

Ramana: Acceptance is the basis of freeing oneself from entanglements. It's like the analogy of walking through a forest wearing a knitted sweater and you snag yourself and try to pull loose.

Rather than pulling and putting pressure against where you stopped, relax, back up and wait a minute and notice where your sweater is caught. Then you'll free yourself by accepting the fact that you've caught a snag. You can relax and disengage the snag from where it's caught and free yourself. So acceptance is allowing yourself the space and the way to free yourself from wherever it is that you are caught or stuck on.

Whatever it is that you're caught up against, acknowledge and accept that you are, let it be okay. The moment you let it be okay, it will, in turn, let you be okay. Not pulling against or fighting against whatever it is that you're finding difficult, it will ease up, allowing you to disengage or free yourself from it, whatever it happens to be.

That even includes a disagreement you might have with some individual. If you don't pull against that individual, and instead give them the space to be right, you are giving them the opportunity to free themselves from you, which gives you the opportunity to free yourself from them. It's just a way of working and releasing yourself from areas or situations in which you find yourself entangled. Okay?

Ramana at dinner in Gatineau, Quebec, Canada with Elizabeth (left), Hafiz (opposite), Gulabo (right), 2001. *Photo: Saroja.*

Saroja: I heard you often say what you resist, persists. There is another part to it, the part of responsibility, taking full responsibility for your life, whatever your background or what has happened to you. Somehow, I see that as full acceptance. Could you talk more on that subject?

Ramana: When we talk in terms of acceptance for what is occurring in our life and in our experiences, what makes it difficult for people is not recognizing that we are in fact the source and cause of all that we find ourselves in. Every situation we find ourselves in and reacting to - the experience and upset about the experience - is occurring, in fact, in the consciousness that we are. It's not going on outside of our consciousness, otherwise we wouldn't even know that it was going on, period. We'd have no way to even know that it was happening.

That which is going on in our consciousness is going on in us. When we're upset with regard to our situation, who is it that is upset? The only answer is "Me." I am upset. It's not someone else and there is no one else inside of our head being upset for us. So, we're the actual cause and the source of the upset that is occurring in us.

Ramana in dialogue with Jason, age 11,
sharing with Jason about Self-Inquiry, 2001,
Gatineau, Quebec, Canada. *Photo: Saroja.*

We may say: "Well, someone else is making me upset."

That might be what we believe to be true, but if we stop and look at it and accept the fact that the upset is actually my upset going on in me, we can stop it - cease from thinking "upset." In other words, stop calling it "upset," just call it an event.

We don't have to name it as an upsetting event, we don't have to qualify it and classify it as "upset," rather it is just what's occurring. And if we don't call it "upset," how can it be "upset?" Our calling it "upset" is what makes it so. Otherwise it's not.

So, we're the source that causes the upset; our naming it as "upset," and thereby seeing it as being that, is the creation in us of it as "upset." That is so simple and so profound once we really get it and that is how we can free ourselves in the moment from whatever that is upsetting to us, thereby being totally free!

But we don't recognize this usually. There are very few people who know this and yet this is such a simple process, the key for anyone willing to be free of upset.

It is me that is the source and cause of all of the inner feelings that I'm having. I am the creator of my own feelings and I can free myself from my own feelings simply by ceasing to name them and feel them that way. You get that?

Saroja: What you said reminds me of my own experience. Even as a small kid, I often knew for a split second that I had a choice of how I would feel about something happening. A few years ago, my partner told me he had slept with another woman, and I could see I had a choice between having a tantrum or of not reacting.

We talked about upset, but isn't it the same thing for so-called good thoughts? It's the same principle for everything in life, right?

Ramana: Everything. We are always the only source of our own thoughts and feelings. No one else thinks our thoughts and feels our feelings for us. We always do it ourselves to ourselves and for ourselves no matter what the thought is, no matter what the feeling is - good, bad or otherwise.

We are the pure being of the Self operating through the *sense of I* and as the *sense of I*. Being that we're the source of the *sense of I*, we're the source of our own faults and our own feelings, since no one else is thinking our faults and feeling our thoughts except us.

That being the case, all we have to do is stop, look and know in the moment what it is we're thinking, what it is we're feeling and then choose to modify or change that thought or not have that thought, withhold that thought or not identify with a particular thought that might be just happening in the universal mind.

It's like fishing, we just don't grab that fish, but let it swim on by. Or, a cloud passing over - maybe a thunder cloud - it passes on over and we don't identify with it. We don't make it ours. Then we don't have to do anything about it.

Now a situation may occur and problems may happen. We don't call them a problem, we just see them and say they're situations, which is what they are. Someone else can see that same experience, and very well may call it something else. If they can call it something else why can't we?

It's entirely up to us to choose what we call a situation, what we say what a situation is. If we say it's bad, then to us it's bad. If we say it's okay, then to us it's okay.

Just yesterday, out in the portico, an older gentleman was saying to me that it was going to take a long time for a person to get free.

I said to him: "Yes, if a person thinks and feels that it takes a long time then to him it takes a long time. If you don't think and feel that it's going to take a long time, then to you it's not going to take a long time."

That's because it's not a matter of time, it's a matter of change of consciousness.

Now it may appear to take time, it may appear for some to take more time than others. That's an appearance because - when you ask yourself the questions: "What is time and how long is a long time?" - it's always relative, there is no absolute answer.

CHAPTER 14

Will You Marry Me?

I had given up my apartment when I went to Arizona with my sons Randy and Skylar. I had a good relationship with both of them, but something happened that they ended up going back to Houston. Skyler returned on the bus and moved back with his mother. I stayed out there in the tepee.

The bug really had me with Frances. I left Arizona to go back to Houston as much as anything because of her. I didn't have an apartment; I had no place to stay, so I called Frances, then moved in with her.

Frances was in her later thirties yet she still couldn't do anything without her mother's approval. Her mother lived in Jacksonville, Florida.

We lived together for quite a long time - I don't remember how long – and the entire time Frances kept it a secret. Frances wanted to keep it from her mother in particular. Her mother was the primary person, though there were a few others that she didn't want to know either. This was back during the time when living together was still a thing you kept secret. It was humorous to see. Frances had been married before, she was a divorcee and still she didn't want her mother to know; that was her wish and I respected her wish in that regard.

Frances was a receptionist and secretary to the Unity minister and she didn't want the word to get out about us, although everybody in the church knew about our relationship and many at the church knew that we were living together. Today, people don't even pay any attention to it, but in those days, you didn't speak openly about living with someone you were not married to. It certainly was not something that you let be known if you happened to be working in a church.

Once her mother came to Houston for a couple of days and I had stayed elsewhere and I had already been living with Frances for a few months.

Whenever the telephone rang, I couldn't answer it because we couldn't let it be known that I was a man living in her apartment. When Frances called me, it was the only time I could answer the phone. We had a signal set up. She would call, let the phone ring once, then hang up and call back again. That was her signal that she was calling me. Or, if anyone else I had told about the signal was calling me, they knew that they would have to let the phone ring once, hang up and call again before I would answer it.

That was the way we operated until we got married.

During that time I got a job - again, driving a school bus. It was not for a city or county operated school bus line; it was a private school bus company. I did that for something to do and to earn enough to pay my part of Frances's rent, since I was living with her. I didn't want her to have to pay for me.

The kids were of different ages and school grades and I was like a teacher getting acquainted with the new kids when they came in the classroom. It took me a while to get familiar with them all, along with learning the route that I was driving; all the bus stops along the way, and where each kid lived.

We could set up wherever it was we wanted the kids to get together, to pick them up in a neighborhood or on a city block. My route though was not in the city. The kids outside a residential area, I would stop and pick up right in front of their house. In residential areas the kids would congregate on a corner. I would pick them up there, and if it was raining I would let them off right in front of their house so that they wouldn't get wet.

I got to know all the kids and where they lived. I knew their names, even when they graduated from one year to another level.

I taught my young passengers who rode the school bus how to meditate. That was quite the deal because I probably had the quietest school bus in Houston.

I would have a contest to see who could stay quiet the longest. I'd get the children sitting in their seats, quietly and being still. There would be no movement, they were not doing anything, and they were not going anywhere, just sitting on a seat. They would look up and see the world coming to them as they were just sitting there. Then I would say:

"Okay now, the world is coming to you, to us and we're just sitting here. So we're not going anywhere, it's the world that is going as it moves by us, as it moves past us."

I'd get them into that state where they could actually feel that they were still and quiet and not going anywhere. They could do it pretty easily. It became a game and all of them enjoyed it. The first thing that some of them wanted to do when they got on the bus was to play the game.

Some parents wanted to meet me; they'd say that they were amazed at what they had heard and what their kids had told them. Kids would come up to me in the shopping center with their parents and say: "Here's our bus driver."

At Christmas time, we'd sing Christmas songs. We would ride singing Jingle Bells or something like that. The parents couldn't get over how the kids really enjoyed it and they were happy to have me as the bus driver.

That was a great period. I had a great time driving the school bus; I tremendously enjoyed teaching the kids how to meditate and do Self-Inquiry.

I had been living with Frances and driving the school bus for about a year, when one day I got a call from Mark Pope. I had come to know him well, as he had been into my teaching during the time that I had given the morning seminars, and at a few other times that I was invited to give a talk at nighttime.

He knew about my Self-Inquiry group. It had become widely known that I led a group of people who were all meditating. I no longer had followers, but I was invited from time to time to go and speak to various groups of people who wanted to know more about spirituality.

Mark knocked on the door of the apartment where I was staying with Frances. He came to talk to me about a longtime friend of his, and his father's (Mark had known him as a teenage boy). His name was Frank Cameron and he was a business man living in Greensboro, North Carolina. He was the director of a chain of physical fitness centers – health spas –throughout North Carolina and Southern Virginia, and he wanted someone to do seminars for his managers and staff.

Mark had said he was going to do the seminars, and he was looking for some assistance from me, because he didn't feel that he was fully qualified to do them. I was candid with him, that I really wasn't interested in getting involved in assisting anybody to do anything, though I would be very supportive of him. If there was anything that he needed, if he wanted me to be with him, I would be happy to assist, in the sense of what he needed to know, or to give him encouragement.

It turned out that the fitness centers were part of a group of franchises, and the main money people and owners actually were in Houston.

Frank was not actually the owner; he was the general manager in process of becoming an owner of the group in North Carolina and South Virginia. He had individual managers that he himself had hired and trained and his wife, Samantha, who we called Sam, was also involved.

Mark talked by phone to Frank about me. Frank was coming to Houston and Mark wanted to introduce us. I agreed and they came by one day. It turned out that Frank wanted someone to do a seminar that was the equivalent of the Erhart Seminars Training (*est*), which was founded by Werner Erhart and very popular back in those days.

When Mark finally introduced Frank and I to each other, Frank asked me: "Can you give, or is what you give, equivalent to *est*?"

"I don't know," I said. I had to answer him honestly. I had been told by some of the people who had attended some of my programs and training, as well as *est*, that it was comparable. They seem to come into the same or similar state of consciousness by attending *est* that they went into at my seminars. But, I couldn't honestly say that what I was about was the equivalent or the same as *est*.

"Well, is there any way to know?" Frank said.

"The only way to know would be for me to experience an *est* seminar and frankly, I am not really interested, as I don't need it," I told him.

"Would you be interested in experiencing it, just to find out?" Frank asked me.

That created a little curiosity in me and as Frank was willing to pay my tuition, I agreed. So he gave me the money to take the *est* seminar, which I did.

The training in those days was conducted over two successive weekends in a hotel banquet room. Two to three hundred people came for the seminar. As I remember it, they were charging, $350.00 a person to attend. So $350.00 x 250 was $87,500.00 a pop they were making. Werner Erhart made a few million dollars because they were having them in four or five major cities across the country almost simultaneously. It was quite a whirlwind in its day. It was intense, very intense.

Est was about awareness. It was not meditation; it was transformation, an awakening to the process of how the mind works, getting prior to the mind, having the ability to see the conditioned patterns and getting free of them. What we teach now at AHAM is inclusive of all of that.

When it was over, I could say honestly it was good, a very fine program that brought a person into the awareness of being. The only problem was you couldn't stay there. It would be a whirlwind trip into awakened awareness that very quickly people would fall out of and lose. You'd stay there for a while - for some people the awareness would stay longer than others, and there might have been a few that it stayed with continuously, but I never really knew.

I was now able to say to Frank, "Yes, what I do is very similar, and could produce nearly the same results." So I came to Greensboro, did a seminar with Frank's managers that went quite well, and then returned to Houston. Frank and I stayed in communication. Then he wanted me to come back and do another program. I did that and then he came over with the idea for me to consider relocating to Greensboro.

Frances and I had to look at our relationship. I was living with her when I made my choice to go to Greensboro, and it was not time for a permanent separation.

"What are we going to do with our relationship?" we asked ourselves. We had been through highs and lows and it had been on again and off again.

"Are we going to get married?" we asked. That was the incompletion and it wasn't going to be complete until we got married, and Frances was not going with me if we were just living together - it had to be marriage.

"If we're going to get married, then it's got to be your idea," I told her. "I mean, it has to be coming from you. I'm in agreement with it, but to be sure that's it's coming from you, you have to ask me."

We were in love - there was no hatred, no resentment - but we were together, then we were not together. There were tremendous emotional highs and lows. We would be as hot as can be and then it would turn cold. We hardly knew from one day to the next, or one month to the next, whether it was on or whether it was off. It was one of those things, we were having a hard time living with one another and it was equally hard to live without one another. That had gone on for a long extended period, a few years. My relationship with her was going on before my awakening, and it was going on during my awakening.

When I brought it up with Baba Muktananda, I said to Baba that everything was wonderful and complete in my life except this one thing. I was involved in a relationship with this lady that I had been in for a few years now and it was just eating me up. It was still going on, I was still at the effect of it and I didn't know quite how to deal with it.

Baba had laughed, I mean he really laughed. What he said was: "Haven't you got it yet?"

He was saying that there's no happiness in a relationship as such. You have got to recognize that happiness is in the Self, it's not in a relationship.

Baba had personally invited me to come to Dallas, and Frances had even gone with me. I didn't have quite as much access to Baba there as in Houston - even though I still had access to him - because there were so many more people that had come in from other cities. Even so, I certainly enjoyed the time there.

I knew already that happiness is in the Self, not in a relationship, but I was still caught. I was hung; the knot was not loose, not broken. There was attachment. It was a karmic situation I had going in my relationship with women. It had been going on my whole life, I had been in love and then not. I was in love with Verna and then after that I was not in love. My marriages to my other wives were not ones of love, but I had fallen in love again with Frances, just as I had originally been in love with Verna.

Here I was, caught in this attachment, and it was really a pull, a strong identification that I was very aware of and working on attempting to free myself from, but I wasn't doing too good a job.

I said to Frances, "Okay, I'm going to Greensboro and that can be the end of our relationship."

'Maybe that can be the release,' I thought, although I didn't say that to her.

She was not ready for it to be the end of our relationship, so I said: "Well, if you're not ready, then it's up to you, because I'm going to Greensboro - and the only way that we can remain in a relationship is for you to go with me and for us to be married. Then you're going to have to ask me to marry you, instead of me asking you to marry me; and me being the one that initiates and keeps the relationship tied together. It's got to be you."

I kept after her to ask me. I said, "You've got to ask me."

She said, "Okay, will you marry me?"

"Okay, I will." I said (laughter).

So we got married. It was on Easter Sunday of 1978.

We got married in Houston by Sig Paulsen, who had taken over as the minister of the Unity Church there, a short period before then to handle a transition when something had happened in the church. I had even met him way back before Unity school, when I first started out in Houston in the Unity teaching.

There were one or two people in Unity who I could tell were in a high state of consciousness, as high as me or perhaps higher. Sig Paulsen was one. He was in charge of the field department in Unity in those days. He was very significant and I had a high regard for him. He had written several books, and he was the one that performed the marriage ceremony when my wife Frances and I got married before we moved to North Carolina.

Another person was James Dillet Freeman, known as Unity's Poet Laureate. He was in a high state of consciousness as a poet, mixed a great deal with the intellect. Still, poems would just flow out of him. He was a great one.

Both of these great men have passed on now, though many in Unity who knew them are still living.

The first time that I came to Greensboro before I moved there, I got off the plane wearing blue jeans and a blue denim shirt. I had just a few clothes that I had purchased before coming and I didn't have any dressy clothes. Frank Cameron's group was really into clothing. Frank was a clothes horse and seeing me get off the plane dressed as I was - I did bring a suitcase and I did have nicer clothes - they didn't know what the hell they had gotten themselves into.

Frank had a chain of about six or eight centers in different cities in North Carolina and in Southern Virginia with approximately five thousand members - meaning clients who had paid for his services - who came on a somewhat regular basis to his various fitness centers.

In those days, his managers earned far more, I would say two to maybe three times more, than the average person might earn in the area. All his managers were women, though he had other employees that attended the seminar I gave, and one of them was Claude Phillips, who at the time was Frank's comptroller, chief accountant, kind of an overseer, his administrative director.

Frank had agreed to pay for a moving company to move all of Frances's furniture (it wasn't mine, I didn't own any), then I bought some clothes and moved with Frances and we got a nice two-bedroom apartment off of Lawndale Drive in Greensboro. Frank supplied me with a car, a used Lincoln Continental.

It wasn't long after we got here, that two of the people who had been in my meditation Self-Inquiry group also moved to Greensboro; they came here to be close to me. Frank had invited them to come and he gave them both jobs, one of them, a lady, to babysit his boy who was eight or ten at the time.

Mark Pope also came back for a while; he was living and dating a manager of Frank's fitness studio in Greensboro.

Frank and his wife Sam quite often invited all of us in his organization to get together for dinners and special events. This was to keep everybody motivated. Frances came as well. I didn't always care to go to them, but they were enjoyable enough.

Sam was a gourmet cook and we had some of the most fabulous meals that you could ever imagine at their house. Frank was always inviting his managers over and in those days there was a lot of booze, a lot of drinking. I would have wine with them occasionally, although I wasn't into the drinking aspect of it; I was into the food. Frank was always looking for a new place to eat; experimenting in new things, new and more and better and different - a constant escalation.

There was an amiable quality between Frank and me, and we started off totally on a hand shake - no written contracts. We both agreed eye to eye with one another that if you're men of integrity, a contract is not necessary. The verbal agreement was for a year. Frank was going to pay me X numbers of dollars a month for a year, expenses, plus an automobile. That was enough to take care of necessities and needs, not other desires. I would move from Houston to Greensboro and develop seminar programs for his employees and members.

We really got along together as friends. I mean, I liked Frank very much and Sam. They were all positive, really up, upwardly progressive in consciousness - and they were really delightful to be around. It was always a party, constant fun. Everything he did was just to add more fun and delight to all of his employees. I was just going along enjoying it, and, at the same time, I could see that they were entrenched in that way of life.

Frank already had trainers offering different kinds of things, mostly of a motivational nature, positive thinking, health improvement or on increasing sales, doing a better job and thereby bringing more people to buy more time in his fitness centers.

Regarding my seminars, one of Frank's ideas was to promote them to the members of his fitness clubs, who would purchase a seminar program. The purpose was entirely financial, to make more money for himself and his wife. I didn't see anything wrong with it, except I had already ended all of that in my life and it was incompatible with my intent and purpose. I wasn't looking to make more money. I had already discovered that, for me, there really was no happiness in that.

Frank was presenting the seminars to his managers and assistant managers and the people who worked for him, as more and better and different ways to be "so-called happy" from all situations, from all the objects and events in the world. I warned Frank that the seminars might not work out the way he wanted. When his managers really began to get what it was that I was teaching - that there really wasn't any happiness in more, better and different, no absolute peace or sense of completion in just continually living it up in the world - they might not be so easy to manipulate.

The whole thing just backfired, almost immediately. It came about rapidly with a friendly disagreement that was not quite as friendly as we got further into it. We worked on the seminars for only a short time and realized we weren't compatible and it was not going to work. There was a conflict of interest. Frank and I had come to a verbal agreement, each taking the other at his word. Sam, though, was not part of the agreement and she began to be very resistant to what was happening. We still got along amiably but the time came that we could see that it was not going to work out.

I was interested in introducing people - who were open, receptive and ready - to what I had seen and what had been awakened in me. That was entirely my mission and purpose. I intuitively knew that Frank and I were going in different directions, yet it was a situation where Frank thought he could turn me around to his way of thinking and I thought I could bring him around to my way of 'no thinking.'

When I came to Greensboro originally, I fooled myself into believing that I would have direct access to the five thousand members in Frank's organization, and that I would have been able very easily to convince them to be open, receptive and willing to hear what was being shared from a spiritual point of view. I was a novice as to what had awakened in me and still spiritually immature as far as dealing with people in the world; so when Baba laughed at me and said, "You haven't got it yet," he was really laughing at me for that, more so than my attachment to my relationship with Frances. I hadn't gotten it. I should have known, but I didn't have the vision to see it. I still had a lot of disappointments to experience with regard to really believing that people were just going to be ready, willing and able, right away, to hear the message of truth that I had to share with them.

I had been waiting for something to reveal itself, something to come up in my life, and moving to Greensboro from Houston was the opportunity that presented itself. I made the choice, yet it was a paradox. It wasn't easy to explain at the time, because intuitively, I already knew that what I was coming here for, in the form it was being presented, was almost destined to fail.

My working relationship with Frank ended rapidly, within three or four months, and then Frances and I also separated.

I was on my own.

Claude Phillips, as the comptroller of Frank's company, knew what the situation was and about the agreement, and why I had moved to

Greensboro. He was familiar with all the financial matters and our particular agreement.

Claude really liked me, he was a nice guy, and we got along very well. He understood the situation and he could see it both ways and he always voiced to me that I was left out in the cold. He felt I had gotten a raw deal and yet he understood Frank's point of view. It was not that there was any bad blood between Frank and myself; we got along pretty well even after that.

I was without an income and without a place to live and Claude Phillips offered me a place to stay. He felt good about hanging around me; he recognized the energy around me, he was sensitive to it.

Claude was a bachelor. He lived in a two-bedroom apartment with a delightful poodle dog and a bedroom he wasn't using, other than to store a few personal things, so he cleaned the room out, putting his personal things into another storage facility and I moved into that bedroom.

During those three first months in Greensboro, I was in meditation every morning, and I would be in the darndest place. I could feel good going into the meditation, yet I was still praying for something more to be revealed as to what was going to happen to me, because really I was so miserable otherwise in my relationship with Frances.

I thought, *What is going to happen, what's got to happen?*

With Frances, the emotion of our relationship was still there, though it was obvious that we were not meant to be together in an ongoing relationship. My life had taken a totally different turn.

Frances moved to Florida to her parents home. Her stepfather sent her money and a moving company came and packed up all of her things. I went to the airport to see her off, still having an annoying feeling in the pit of my stomach, seeing her go.

Almost a year after that, I ended up going to Jacksonville to see her and it was the funniest thing, it was the same situation, because she was afraid that her mother would know about me.

She was staying in her own apartment – we had been married, we were still married, we hadn't had a divorce –and I was there for about two days. She had a job then. Her stepfather had bought her a sports car she always wanted, a Chevrolet Thunderbird, which was a very expensive automobile. All the things her family bought her turned out to be so that she would give me up and agree not to come back with me. They were absolutely afraid of me, because I was going to corrupt her mind. Here, Frances and I were grown adults and still married (she was working on getting the divorce) and while I was staying at her apartment and she was at work, I could not answer the telephone.

I continued to communicate by telephone occasionally with her. We still had a friendship.

It happened during that time that I went to a conference. I met a woman there; we hit it off pretty good right away and ended up playing hooky. We went to a motel and had a little playfulness.

In those days, I was living in impeccable integrity with regard to telling the truth, and so the next time that I talked with Frances, I had to tell her the truth about what had happened. Two days after that, I received a little package, a little box in the mail in which she had returned my wedding ring. That was truly the end of our marriage relationship.

I saw Frances about three times afterwards. She came to Greensboro some years later. I was doing a seminar after AHAM had gotten started at our facility there and she came out. It was time for a break and she went outside, I thought to have a cigarette because she smoked, but she didn't return to the seminar. She drove off and I think another person left too. She was really having a time dealing with where I was coming from.

I don't think the person who saw her knew who she was and I thought he was kidding me when he said she had left.

"No, I'm not kidding you," he said. "She left. She drove off."

So that was the end of the situation and I don't know if I ever saw Frances again after that. I have no idea where she is now and I have no idea how to even get in touch with her if I wanted to.

Dialogue on Awakening 5
Liberation

Saroja: Ramana, I have a question, something to clarify for me and for those who will read the book. You said earlier that you felt miserable because of the ending of your relationship with Frances and you were not in the right place even in meditation. It is very much of a surprise to hear that from a realized being. Can you explain from your perspective more of how you felt - being realized for me, means that you're not attached to all these things, they may happen but you still are in the awareness of being.

Ramana: You see, after the 'awakening to the awareness of being' occurred in 1973, I went through a period of adjustment with regard to what was going on in my life. One thing that was still going on, as I've already shared, had to do with this deeply entrenched relationship with Frances. Well, that was not over yet.

Saroja: One question that comes to me when you were talking about Frances earlier is, living from the wholeness of being and seeing, I mean the whole joke of her behavior, the way she was behaving, how did you put up with that?

Ramana: How did I put up with you? (laughter....)

Saroja: (laughter...) *I see the humor of the whole thing, but we imagine that beings that are realized all of a sudden are very different and they will not react to things. So, if you can clarify some things like that it will be for the benefit of everyone.*

Ramana: When you have awakened into the awareness of being that doesn't mean you die. You're still alive. You still experience everything that is going on but you're not identified with it.

You see everything in the same way that you have seen everything all along. The way you see and feel things happening is not different. You still have a body and a mind, it's just that you're not identified with your body and you're not identified with mind. You're seeing everything the way it really is, from and as the awareness of being.

As well, the things that Frances used to do and the way she did them, didn't change just because I was awake. She still did everything the same way she was always doing it. What mainly happens to the one who is awakened is compassion. There's a deeper and broader and all-inclusive sense of compassion in which you understand that people are identified with their bodies, they're identified with their mind and they live as though the world has reality and that the world is real on its own.

They believe that the world has always been here. They have read and learned the history of the world when they were in school; there are text books, which as a child and a student, you're required to learn. Learning world history, you take it to be the truth; and, you really believe that the world exists as its own reality, quite independent of you. That's not the truth!

The world exists in the awareness or in the mind of the one who is aware of it. When you go to sleep at night you're no longer aware of the world and while you're asleep, the world doesn't exist. Yet we don't see that, we don't recognize that, because we are so conditioned by the mind - by the false notion that the body is who and what we are - we don't get it that when we're sleeping we are totally withdrawing from the holistic consciousness that is inclusive of the world. You're back into the pure being of the Self while in dreamless sleep.

Ramana in dialogue with a student at mealtime, AHAM, Asheboro, North Carolina. *Photo: Jim Dillinger.*

Saroja: Is that apparent as soon as one awakens? So for you everything was just okay?

Ramana: It may not be absolutely apparent even to one who has awakened into the Self, but it begins to become real or known or seen the longer one remains in the pure awareness of being, as the pure awareness of being, and it becomes fully known with liberation when there is no longer identification with the body and the mind as the Self.

For a while you can be, while awakened, still partly asleep, half asleep and half awake. You're knowing that what you're seeing and what you're experiencing is more like a dream and you see it and recognize it like a dream or like something you're doing while half asleep.

Saroja: Like, for example, when I am in a conversation with someone from my work and in some moments it becomes as if I'm watching a movie.

Ramana: Yes, that's it.

Saroja: I have some moments like that – all of a sudden it's like I'm watching a movie.

Ramana: Exactly. That's it.

Everyone has those moments but they don't quite know how to relate to them. It's just something they're seeing for a moment and it quickly leaves their mind and they don't question it, they don't look into it, they don't inquire in those moments. And so, they quickly forget those moments and they are quick to regain the normal ordinary experience of still being identified with the body living in time and space.

Saroja: After the moment of awakening in June 1973, did you have to do anything to remain in the awareness? Or, was there no going back?

Ramana: It was continuous, a constant seeing and knowing of what is as it is; a non-forgetting, no longer forgetting.

Saroja: And is there a deepening in that, something that has evolved or is still evolving?

Ramana: Sometimes we use words like "deepening" and "broadening" or "widening "and so forth; because there are no other words you can use to describe or to state what it's like to live in just the simple, pure here and now awareness that is always present. You don't have to go deep into it, as it's always here and now present. It's just covered up, it's just hidden by the mind and by the beliefs that you have, and by the habit of thinking that the body and the mind are the Self – when, in fact, the body and the mind are not the Self.

Once you get it, it is like (as an analogy) a person who has amnesia and forgotten their identity. They've forgotten who they are, their name, their family and their personal history. They don't know anything about themselves. Then all of a sudden, they remember who they are or they gradually remember who they are, and now they begin again to recognize the members of their family, their name, the school they went to, all those kind of things that they had forgotten. Well, they didn't change, the people that they're remembering have not changed; nothing has actually changed other than now they can remember who they are. In a similar sense, when you have awakened, nothing changes about you, it's just that now you're remembering the true Self that you are when before, you were incorrectly thinking that you were who or what you were not. Are you with me?

Saroja: Yes, I am.

Ramana: The analogy, the explanation that I'm giving right now, would be good to have in the book.

Saroja: It will be in the book, Ramana. You'll see it. You have to stay long enough here in this body to proof this book.

Ramana: I can't promise if it's not my destiny, but as far as I'm willing.

Saroja: *You can't leave before that.*

Ramana: I'll attempt to stay around.

Saroja: *All these attachments and various reactions that you had, were you aware of them, and not just being pulled unconsciously, as it happens for most of us?*

Ramana: I was able to see them; I was able to know that they were there, but they didn't go away. In other words, when you move into the state of awareness, it doesn't mean that things in the world go away.

Bhagavan Sri Ramana Maharshi said to his devotees, "I'm not telling you to close your eyes to what's going on, you're going to see what's going on, you're going to know what's going on, but eventually you're not going to be affected by it like you would ordinarily be."

I went through a phase in which I was beginning to let go, although it didn't happen overnight. I would stay with Self-Inquiry. Each time something would come up, one of these pulls on my mind and attachments, I would watch it. I could see it happening. Over time, it did not affect me as much as it once had. It took a while; it was a gradual thing before it was finally gone.

Saroja: *That's one thing I always had been assuming, that after realization everything is finished, from that moment on you are liberated. It doesn't seem to be this way at all.*

Ramana: Look at what you just said. To 'realize' is one thing, being 'liberated' is something else.

They're two different things. Being realized is when you are living and abiding in the awareness of being and as the awareness of being. You are able to observe and see the patterns that are still active in the mind. You're not forgetful of the awareness of being, you function as and from the awareness of being, but the patterns are still there. Some of the patterns may still be pulling on you to the point that you have to deal with them. Situations still can be coming up at you that you have to deal with.

In people's lives, it comes into three categories, basically: money, food and sex - and you might say a fourth one is power, the need for control. The areas in which you attempt to have control are money, food and sex. With the need for control with your money, there is how much money you're making, and your ability to earn money and to no longer be at its effect.

Sex has to do with more than just sex. Sex has a lot to do with the relationship of your chosen sexual preference. So if you're a heterosexual than it would be your mate of the opposite sex. If you're a homosexual it would be your mate of the same sex. When these patterns come up in consciousness you have to deal with them. You have to work yourself free from these patterns.

The first phase then, or the first thing after awakening, is that you recognize and are able to make the distinction between you as awareness and you as the body, the mind or the ego. So once the awakening happens you're not just immediately free, you have your patterns that you now have to deal with; but you're dealing with them from the level of awakened consciousness - rather than from unconsciousness, where you don't know rhyme or reason about them, and where you're totally at the effect of them (Being at the effect of is believing in outside causes for the problems or things you find disagreeable or upsetting in your life, ed.)

After realization, you may still be at the effect of them, although you're not at the effect of them to the same extent that you previously were. There's no way to know how long the process of dissolving your identification and attachments to all the patterns of body-mind is going to take: it could last days, weeks, months or years. Then, after you've been in that phase, for however long it takes, when all of these patterns are finally dissolved - that's Liberation!

PART 4

A Vision of Happiness (1978 to 1984)

The logo of AHAM (Association of Happiness for All Mankind), is a butterfly symbolizing transformation, Founded by Arunachala Ramana in 1978, AHAM teaches the method of Self-Inquiry given by Ramana Maharshi and principles of conscious living.

Ramana, 2005. *AHAM archives.*

CHAPTER 15

AHAM (Association of Happiness for All Mankind): A Wonderful Vision

It was 1978, Greensboro, North Carolina, that was the beginning of the current era in my life.

I was wondering what I was going to do to make some money - which I had to - even though Claude was not asking for anything. He wasn't asking me for any rent and just said move in. He knew that I didn't have any income. I had nothing, I had to eat and for a while he was willing to share his meals with me. He would bring things in and stock the refrigerator and the pantry with food, telling me I could eat anything I wanted. I didn't want to overdo it, so I would eat frugally.

I was looking for something to do and I fell back upon the days that I used to be a dancing instructor.

Both Fred Astaire and Arthur Murray had dance studios. Fred Astaire had a bigger one and was working on expanding it and so one day I went by, just out of curiosity, to meet the owners. I told them about my history, the days that I used to be a dancing instructor. The manager of the Fred Astaire Dance Studio was from Dallas and right away they offered me a job.

A lot of water had passed under the bridge and I didn't even think they would have an interest in me in that regard. It turned out, though, that they had a lot of older ladies who were taking dancing lessons and they felt that my being somewhat of an older man would have an appeal to them. I needed the money so I took the studio up on the deal. I can't even now remember for how long I did it; it gave me an income, some money coming in.

I had to go through refresher training for the current dances with the dance director, because I hadn't been involved in dance for a long time. We're talking about thirty something years ago, so it wouldn't be that modern now - back then, though, they were the up–to–date dances.

There was a popular movie that John Travolta had played in. It wasn't *Saturday Night Fever* (1977), but another movie, *Grease* (1978). The music in it was hot at that time and the dance style was popular as a result. For me, it was a matter of how to do the dances and learning the steps. I wasn't really interested though in doing that; I was more interested in my philosophy, my teaching.

I would have students assigned to me and we would be talking about whatever we were talking about during the lesson other than just the lesson. Mostly these older women were not that interested in learning more. I would teach them a little more if they needed it or wanted it; mostly they just wanted someone to dance with, companionship as much as anything.

While we would be dancing and talking, I would share with them what it was that I had been into. Some were interested in knowing about it and, as it turned, out some of them didn't like the philosophy of what I had to share.

One of the ladies made a complaint to the management that I was trying to sell her on a philosophy that went totally contrary to her

Christian religion. That put me in hot water with the management. They said I had to leave my personal philosophy to myself and couldn't talk to anybody about it anymore. That put a cramp in things, I lost interest in working there and I quit.

In August 1978, right about that time, I got a call from Bob Howingburg, a friend of mine in Houston who was an attorney (I mentioned him already as he was a student of Gurdjieff and he was the one that went to New York one day and brought back a copy of *Talks with Sri Ramana Maharshi* and gave it to me as a gift).

Bob was calling to tell me about an acquaintance of his who lived in Texas, just north of San Antonio, because he felt we had a lot in common and should meet. Walter Starcke was the guy's name; he had written a couple of books and he was going to be the featured speaker at a Spiritual Frontiers Fellowship (SFF) conference being held at Guilford College in Greensboro. This was of interest to me, and so a day or so before the conference I went to where Walter Starcke was going to be at the college.

I went a little early as I had nothing in particular to do and parked in an area not too far off the main street. I was walking down the very long sidewalk on the campus with huge old oak trees lining the way and was not too far from the main building I was on my way to, when I heard a sound from over in the bushes. The noise being made drew my attention because it was a very strange croaking. Curious, I started walking in that direction to try to understand what it was, but there wasn't anything to be seen.

There was a park bench right next to the bushes from where the sound was coming and as I walked in that direction a lady who was sitting there on a park bench reading, meditating, having her lunch or something, also heard the sound, got up and started looking too. Once we had found out it was a bird making the sound, we began to talk.

Her name was Elizabeth and it turned out that she would be attending the week–long seminars at the SFF conference along with an estimated ninety to one hundred people. She had been sitting there by herself on the park bench, so she invited me to sit down with her.

I got to asking her about her interests, what she was into and she asked me what I was there for. I told her that, although I was there to meet the keynote speaker, I had reached a place in my life that I was no longer attending anything like the conference. I had already been through all of that in my life and was really no longer seeking anything. That impressed her.

"What if you knew all there was to know about everything, but you didn't know who knows, what would you know?" I asked her. That question put her into an automatic inquiry process where she touched on "the one who knows" for the first time in her life.

I later saw Elizabeth sitting in the cafeteria with some other people and we sought out one another.

I recognized in her a woman who was truly sincere in her spiritual quest, very dedicated and open to receiving and when I talked to her, she recognized that I had something to share that was far more significant, really, than what she was getting at that conference. That's when she asked me if I took students and if I did, would I be her teacher.

I agreed, though I would put her through a few little tests along the way to make sure that she was truly not bullshitting me or herself.

One day at the SFF conference, Elizabeth asked me if she could bring some of her friends to meet me and I said, "Okay."

The next day I came back at lunchtime for us to meet and talk some more. I knew that her friends were, maybe, not going to be as interested as she was, but she had gone around and told them that she had met someone who was "very advanced" and "very spiritual," those kind of words, and that she wanted them to meet me.

I was going to meet her at lunch time in the cafeteria. I was coming through the line, she saw me, ran up and pointed out where she was sitting with her friends, so when I got through the cafeteria I could join them. It soon was pretty obvious to me that she was really the only one who was truly interested in where I was coming from; they were into all kinds of phenomena and beliefs that had nothing to do with real spiritual Sadhana (spiritual practice, ed.), so they became interested in other things and left rapidly excusing themselves saying they had other appointments. Pretty soon, it was just Elizabeth and me left there.

It all dovetailed beautifully together with Elizabeth, and I set it up to have regular times of meditation with her. So when she later wanted to bring friends to the meditation whom she thought were really sincere and truly interested in what I had to share, I said to her, "Remember what happened before - your friends that you think are interested, may not be that interested."

She said she would still like to try, so I said, "Okay, we'll see."

Claude's apartment had an upstairs and downstairs with the bedrooms upstairs and the living room, the kitchen and a little dining area downstairs. Then there was a back door that went out onto a little patio with plants.

I often would be in meditation when Claude would leave for work at his regular time early in the morning. I would quietly get up before he did and go downstairs. It wasn't a very large apartment and the living room was really a sitting room no larger than my bedroom. I would often meditate in my room on a straight armchair, but there was a larger chair I preferred in the living room that I could sit in more comfortably and for a longer period of time.

When it was time for Claude to go to work, he would come downstairs and if he noticed that I was in meditation, he would try not to disturb me. He would leave me alone and we would not have any conversation.

I mentioned earlier Caroline Hirsh, a lady who had invited me to stay in the office that she had rented in Houston just after my awakening in 1973. I had actually slept on the floor for a while and then I took over the office from her.

Well, Caroline had mount-ed a picture of Bhagavan Sri Ramana Maharshi inside a spe-cial framed box she had made herself and then given it to me. I still have that same picture. It was small, but it will always be very significant to me, because I would tune into Bhagavan's presence looking at it.

I would think about Bhagavan and read his words from his talks or spiritual teachings and I would look at his picture and consider the quality of his being and hold him in my mind. The book that had drawn me into the Phoenix book store the day of my awakening I had read so many times in Houston when I was liv-ing there and was so very familiar

Bhagavan Sri Ramana
Maharshi, circa 1942.

*Used by permission of
Sri Ramanasramam.*

with it. On that first occasion in the book store, I had been overcome by his presence in seeing the picture for that first time. It just absolutely engulfed me and I had sat in the window seat, weak and in a mode of total surrender to the energy of his presence.

It was the morning of August 24, 1978, and I was involved in my usual meditation one morning in Claude's apartment, when I had a visitation, very pungent and very pleasant, of Bhagavan's presence.

The only way I can explain it – because it's not that easy to explain – is to say that on this occasion it was more like the quality of what had happened in the book store when I had opened the book of Bhagavan and saw his picture for the first time.

Claude had gone to work on that morning and I was sitting in stillness and silence, which had a deep quality of peace and presence, more so than usual in my own meditation. I was in his living room alone except for his dog, a delightful little poodle that I used to look after in the daytime, feed her and so forth. I had already been in meditation for a long time, at least an hour or closer to two hours when all of a sudden the sense of Bhagavan's presence was there.

The quality of his presence was so familiar to me when considering him with eyes open, looking at his picture and reading his book, but this morning with my eyes closed all of a sudden his presence became very pronounced, so unusual, and there was an inner light accompanying it. My whole being was filled with this inner light. It was like his very presence was there in the room, both inside and outside of me and I was absolutely engulfed in it.

In that presence, an inner vision came to me about the work I was to do to bring Bhagavan Sri Ramana Maharshi's teaching to people, and the name of AHAM – the Association of Happiness for All Mankind - was revealed. It came to me just like an inner sound. It was not anything that I was hearing with my ears - rather with my inner ears, so to speak.

Later, I looked up AHAM in some of Bhagavan's books that I had bought. AHAM turned out to literally mean in Sanskrit both "I" in the personal sense and "I" as the principle of awareness within oneself.

Much later, when I went to India myself, I learned that AHAM was actually comprised of both the first and last letters of the Sanskrit alphabet, meaning that it encompassed the entire alphabet. The alphabet, of course, is used to describe anything in communication, and it symbolizes and encompasses everything. To me this was and is very significant.

It had been revealed to me what my work for the rest of my life was to be. There was an inner knowing, a 'definiteness' about it. It would be dedicated to introducing people to Bhagavan and his teachings, primarily to Self-Inquiry, which is his teaching.

Jumping Ahead to 2008

Things have already happened in regard to my vision that AHAM's teaching would be made known in Unity, and the Self–Inquiry training shared with those who were open and receptive in the church. Through the years Unity has been a mainstay with regard to Stan and Elizabeth traveling and introducing AHAM and the teaching in the Unity churches up and down the East Coast of the United States. Here is a brief report from Stan of an afternoon program held at the Unity Church in Greensboro.

"Everything went well. Jim went with me and took lots of photos and he himself loved being in the energy of the church and I appreciated him being present as we did the program. The church had about 120 to 150 attendees at each service, twenty-nine came to the afternoon intro program, fourteen have already registered and paid for an Awake to Awareness Retreat and four more completed registration forms... Overall, a very heart-warming day!

I would be introducing people to Self–Inquiry for them to use it as a direct meditation, as their way of awakening to the awareness within them. Self-Inquiry was to be recognized as more than just a meditation but a direct way, a higher state of meditation, a higher method, as well as a more effective method of meditating.

In the vision I could see that one day Unity would be knowledgeable of AHAM and our teaching would be made known in Unity, becoming a predominant way for Unity people to meditate, bringing people there into the pure awareness of being, or Christ consciousness, as some would better understand it.

I particularly saw Unity people because I had come up through Unity myself, but it wasn't just limited to Unity Churches across the country, I was seeing people around the world learning about and knowing about Self–Inquiry.

All of these insights came together that morning in meditation as I was immersed in Bhagavan's presence.

I had been in the meditation for at least two hours with the little dog sitting very quietly, when the bell rang, there was a knock, the dog barked and went to the door.

Claude had left the front door open when he went to work with just the screen door closed so that anybody could just open the door and come in.

Elizabeth.
AHAM archives.

It was Elizabeth who had arrived – she had already asked me if it was okay to drop by - and she called out to me. She just happened to come by that day while I was still immersed in the quietness of pure being, sitting there as I had been all morning.

I said, "The door is open, come on in."

When she came in she asked, "What's happening here, what's going on? What is this presence that I am feeling?"

I said: "Do you feel that?"

She said, "Yes, what is it?"

"I just had a visit," I think that's the way I said it. "I had a visit with Ramana Maharshi, Bhagavan."

Elizabeth said, "I can feel it."

It was still going on within me and I could also still feel it, but Elizabeth too was able to feel that presence and was bringing it up. It was not me asking her if she felt a presence, she felt it and she mentioned it to me.

I told Elizabeth about what had happened, that Bhagavan had been there this morning and that I had gotten the name of AHAM, which was an acronym for 'Association of Happiness for All Mankind.'

I had even written the name down and all that had been revealed to me, what my work was to be for the rest of my life. All of that had come to me that morning as an inner vision, an intuition.

What I had written was still lying there on the coffee table. I picked it up, showed it to her and she read it. We talked a little about it and I told her I now knew this was going to be my work and I asked her if she would be interested in joining me in this.

She didn't hesitate for a moment and said, "Yes."

So either that same day or the next day, Elizabeth came back and showed me that she had gone to her own personal bank and opened up an account under the name of "Association of Happiness for All Mankind." She had with her a bank book and a statement. She had put in $50.00 of her own money and used it to open the account.

That was the beginning of AHAM.

Dialogue on Awakening 6
The *Sense of I*

Saroja: If I meditate on you, if I think about you, and look at your picture and feel you, like you felt Bhagavan in your meditation when the vision of AHAM was revealed, if I feel you like that, do you know that? Are you aware of it?

Ramana: No!

Saroja: That I'm calling you?

Ramana: No.

Saroja: Why not?

Ramana: It just doesn't work that way.

Saroja: How does it work then?

Ramana: It doesn't work any way. It is like if someone dreams of you while they're asleep, do you know that they're dreaming of you?

Saroja: No, I don't.

Ramana: Why?

Saroja: I don't know.

Ramana: Tell me why.

Saroja: (laughter) I can't tell you why.

Ramana: Well, it's the same way, I can't tell you why.

Saroja: That's true (laughter...). So, when we call to the master, or when Ramana was there ...

Ramana: He didn't know he was being there for me. If someone is thinking about you, do you know that they're thinking about you?

Saroja: No, I do not know that.

Ramana: Why?

Saroja: I can't know that, there's no way of knowing that.

Ramana: Same thing. Bhagavan does not know when someone is thinking about Bhagavan.

Saroja: So what are the masters doing if they're not in the body anymore?

Ramana: They are in the awareness of being.

Saroja: I still want to ask a question because we have assumptions; it's not only for me. Are the masters around and helping us?

Ramana: All kinds of people have all kinds of assumptions and devotees have all kinds of concepts and assumptions about what they believe that spiritual life is or what they believe the Jnani knows or doesn't know. Those are just their assumptions. That's not the way it is with the Jnani.

Saroja: What are the masters doing when they are out of the body? Doing is not the right word...

Ramana: Who's to say they're doing anything? They're not doing anything. They're just being. A Jnani is just being, being.

Saroja: If I am calling you in the meditation, or I see your picture and I'm calling on you, whatever is revealed will be revealed through the mind, which is the instrument. Is that how it works?

Ramana: Yes, through the mind.

Saroja: So, it's our own intuition.

Ramana: I told you about Elizabeth walking into the room and saying that she was feeling something was going on, and I said, "Can you feel that?"

Elizabeth said, "Yes," and I was just as amazed as she was.

Saroja: How can she feel, if it's just like you said, imagination?

Ramana: Yes, it's just imagination. That was me having a vision of him and her tuning in and saying that something was going on.
Now, she didn't say that she knew that it was Bhagavan, She asked me what was going on, what was happening and I said that there was a vision of Bhagavan and I had written the things down.

Your own faith is what brings things into manifested reality. But it really is still going on in your own mind when it's happening.

Saroja: So when you go, it's going to be the same thing, you'll just be dissolving into the awareness of being.

Ramana: That's it. Just going back to where I came from.

Where do you go when you go to sleep?

You say: "I'm going to sleep."

So you lay down in your bed and then someone comes and asks, "What are you doing?"

"Well, don't bother me, I'm going to sleep."

Where are you going when you go to sleep? Where do you go?

Saroja: I don't know, I just go into a peaceful rest. I have no awareness of the body at that time...

Ramana: There's nowhere to go; you're just withdrawing from body-mind identification. You're withdrawing from the world; the world exists only because of the body. Have you ever seen the world apart from your body?

Saroja: No.

Ramana: No one has. It's impossible. You can't see the world apart from your body; even the dream world. You only see the dream world when you are in your dream body. You can't see a world apart from a body in which you are identified.

It requires a body to know and to see that there is a world.

Saroja: Ramana, I just want to ask one more question regarding this revelation that you had with the meditation and Bhagavan. How did you know you were manifesting him?

Ramana: By tuning in looking at Bhagavan's picture, meditating on him or thinking about him as I was reading, I could feel what to me, was him.

Saroja: In meditation when I call you, you are present for me - it's more of an impression, I don't even know how to describe it...

Ramana: When you think about me, isn't it the thought and feeling of me that comes into your consciousness?

Saroja: Yes, but it's still going on in my mind you see.

Ramana: Well, the mind is the instrument of communication.
Did we talk the other day about the seven basic truths?
The first one is that "imagination creates reality." The second one is that "thoughts are things."

Saroja: You become what you think.

Ramana: What you think about grows and then you become what you think about and then your assumptions form your world.
Imagination creates reality. Thoughts are things, what you think about grows, and you become what you think about - your assumptions are your world! All of that is taking place in consciousness.
Bhagavan often said that, "If you think of me, I am there. If you think of God, God is present."
Is God not present if you think of God?

Saroja: Yes, of course.

Ramana: If you think about God being all inclusive and you consider him to be all inclusive does that not include yourself?

If you're thinking of a master, is the master not present when you're thinking of him? The master is not his body, but the consciousness being expressed as his body.

So likewise with you, Saroja is not Saroja's body. Sure Saroja's body is Saroja but Saroja is not Saroja's body.

If you think about someone, don't they come into your awareness? Is it not in your awareness that they are present? It's them while you're thinking about them. It's not someone else while you are thinking of them.

Saroja: Correct.

Ramana: How did I know that it was Bhagavan? Because, all of a sudden, a deeper quality of his very presence came into my awareness, and it was like he was there in the room. He was in me, and he was also in the room, because Elizabeth felt him in the room.

CHAPTER 16

Early Years of AHAM (1978 to 1981)

I needed to give Frank his car back because the insurance had expired. I didn't have the money to pay for insurance and you had to park a car, remove and turn in the license plates if you didn't have an active insurance policy.

Frank had an old IBM typewriter in the basement of his Greensboro office that nobody used; it was just sitting in storage. I asked him if I could borrow it, he readily agreed, so I got it cleaned up and added a new ribbon and it worked very well. Then I started creating a flyer on the typewriter, with a name for the seminar that Elizabeth wanted me to conduct. Originally we just had that old typewriter, and eventually we bought a typewriter of our own - we didn't have a computer in those days.

When Elizabeth met me, she asked if I would be willing for her to introduce some of her friends to me and I said, "Of course." I would be happy if she did so.

One of the first was Karen. The two had met at a Dale Carnegie Course in Greensboro and became friends, and continued their friendship and communication with one another afterwards. As years ago I had been a graduate assistant to a sales course of Dale Carnegie, all of this dovetailed together; there were so many things of compatibility among us all.

Elizabeth called Karen who invited her to bring me to where she and her husband were living in the little town of Smithville, Virginia, so we could all meet. Elizabeth and I drove up there and stayed at Karen's home and I got acquainted with her and her husband.

On another occasion, Karen invited a number of her friends together at someone's home in Smithville and I gave a talk, but for her friends it was a totally different approach, something that they'd never heard about, and they were not able to fully grasp what I was saying.

Karen was by profession a teacher and also an entertainer. She was quite talented and played the guitar, sang and wrote ballads. She was really into the teaching. It was very easy for her to stand up in front of audiences and she was very good at it and able to present things very logically so that people were able to grasp the teaching. In the early days of AHAM, she functioned as my assistant and then eventually she also gave the talks which I was giving on Sunday morning when I would go out of town. She remained involved with AHAM for a long time until she spun off and started doing a Sunday morning talk with students of her own.

Elizabeth had been reading the book *Handbook to Higher Consciousness,* by a fellow named Ken Keyes (he pronounced it kize instead of keys). The book was very popular back in those days, people were buying it all over town and it was going around the country. One of the main themes was "Seven Steps to Enlightenment." She showed me the book; she wanted me to conduct a seminar based upon it, as it was significant to her. I said, "Sure, if you get some friends together." So she started calling up a lot of her friends and we began to put a seminar together.

I wasn't really interested in reading the book itself; instead I perused it and said to Elizabeth, "Well, you don't need seven steps, you can do it in one step." She liked that, but it really got to her and shocked her that I would make such a blatant statement.

Elizabeth took the flyer for the seminar to an offset printing place, had a bunch made up and started giving some out to her friends while others she put out in a book store in the Four Seasons Shopping Mall, which was near where I was staying with Claude.

The manager of the book store told Elizabeth that there was a woman who came in there quite often who would buy as many as five or ten copies at a time of Keyes's book to give away to her friends. So, Elizabeth left the flyers there with a telephone number and asked the manager to give the woman a copy when she came in. Sure enough, after the woman came into the book store, we got a call from her saying she was interested in the seminar. That was Patricia (who has ever since remained active in AHAM). Elizabeth invited her to the meditations on Wednesdays at Claude's apartment, which she started attending.

It so happened about that time that I said, "Listen, let's change the meditation to Fridays."

I intentionally changed it to Friday to see how many people would stay with it because they were young, mostly single and on Friday nights interested in going out to the bars for what they called "Happy Hour," that kind of thing, but I said, "Let's be high from meditation, instead of getting high."

As for the seminar, Elizabeth had made all the arrangements. She set up a date for it and rented a room in the Founders Hall at Guilford College. Well, there were fourteen people that attended including Jewel, Patricia, Elizabeth, Karen and her husband. For the longest time, out of that fourteen many stayed involved in AHAM.

So that's how we got started in Greensboro.

Claude was interested in being around me as long as he didn't have to make any major changes in his life. He liked talking about what I was into and he liked to be in the energy as long as it stayed a belief and a philosophy, but he wasn't interested actually in transformation for himself.

I had been staying with Claude for about three months, and it was getting to the point of stretching it a little too much, because I was not paying anything. Occasionally, someone would bring me something to eat, and would even bring food over that I'd share with him too - he was still providing me with most of my meals, as well as a place to stay, and paying for the utilities which were extra. He had not asked me to leave though I had begun to feel that I had outstayed my welcome, so that's when I mentioned that I was needing a place to stay.

Patricia had just moved into a brand new townhouse across town from where Claude lived and she invited me to move in and take a bedroom there. The room had nothing in it when I moved, and someone gave me a bedroom suite with a mattress, all that I needed to furnish it. I was living totally on the grace of God and everything was just coming and being supplied to me as I needed it.

We started having Satsang there and even began to have programs there as well. I used Patricia's address with her permission as the official address when I drove down in either Elizabeth's or her car and registered AHAM as a non-profit organization at the office of the Secretary of State of North Carolina in Raleigh, the state capital. I drew up the articles of incorporation and the bylaws of the corporation myself, setting up AHAM as a Spiritual Education Centre and as a church.

Somewhere along the line, Patricia moved to Germany. She was working over at one of the Country Furniture Stores in High Point, North Carolina and met a guy who wanted to open a distributorship, a retail store in Germany, specializing in selling furniture to US service people who were on active military duty in Europe. The move to Germany was I think originally going to be a temporary thing, but as it turned out it became permanent.

Country Furniture Store had a branch in High Point and another branch in Wilmington, North Carolina on the coast. Patricia was one of their top salespersons and somewhere back during that time, working with Elizabeth, she put together a seminar for me to do with all of their High Point employees.

Karen, Patricia and Elizabeth were all very close friends in those days and Karen had gone to work for Country Furniture Store as well as Ken, who was a guitar player and played at our Sunday talks. It was around that period of time, that Stan (a longtime member of AHAM, who owned his own newspaper company, a Black newspaper that he published weekly in High Point), called on Country Furniture Store to run an ad in his newspaper. There he met Karen who was in charge of advertising. Somewhere along the line in their conversation, they got to talking about Napoleon Hill and his book *Think and Grow Rich* (Karen may have had the book lying on her desk). Well, Karen told him about me and my history of being associated with Napoleon Hill, which made a big impression on Stan and very soon afterwards, she invited him to meet me and we became acquainted.

I was giving a seminar called the Creative Expression Workshop. In those days, I would give all the seminars myself. There were three seminars that we used to do: the Creative Expression Workshop, the Free Borne Seminar and the AHAM basic training and then we started Discover Meditation. All of these were based upon books and manuals that I wrote, had printed and put in three-ring binders.

The Free Borne was about how to live in the world but not of the world. It was a higher involvement into meditation as its basis. There was not much about meditation in the Creative Expression Workshop. It was just really more or less practical stuff, how to live in the world, how to fulfill your desires, how to accomplish whatever it was you wanted to have and do and be in the world. It was not so much a transformational program because the people in Greensboro and the new people we were introducing to the teaching were not interested in transformation. They were only interested in functional, practical things about living in the world.

Shortly after our meeting, Stan attended the next Creative Expression Workshop that I was giving. In it I was presenting a lot of the Napoleon Hill principles and he was very much interested in it. That's how he came into AHAM.

On one occasion there was a seminar in the mountains in western North Carolina where there was an Episcopalian Retreat Centre, a New Age kind of a thing and there must have been about twenty-five or thirty people going. Bill, a professor at Guilford College who taught Sanskrit and other things, was considered somewhat of a guru for a lot of New Age people who were a mixture of different ideologies and philosophies. He coordinated things and he had put together this seminar along with a couple of other people.

Jewel, Claude and I attended.

Someone had brought out a huge roll, unrolled it and put it on the entire wall and taped it up or thumb tacked it. It must have been at least twenty feet long and about six or so feet high and was waist high along the wall where you could reach up to it. The idea was to write something on that paper, anything you wanted to write; a poem, positive statement or aphorism, or draw something. It was a creative thing that everybody could participate in.

You had a name tag on which you wrote some other name than your own.

Well, on my name tag, I wrote, "YOU," as my name.

So when I came time to write on this paper whatever it was you wanted to write, I wrote at the corner on a low place on the paper, "The body is a shit factory."

Well, do you think that didn't cause a stir?

It caused a major stir.

Here were all these people with kid's Crayolas, crayons, different colors laying there on the table, and you could pick the crayon and use the crayon to write anything you wanted to write or draw anything you wanted to draw on that paper. Well, I wrote in brown crayon, "The body is a shit factory."

People would ask me, who wrote that? And I'd say, "YOU did."

When I would say "YOU did," they'd get highly offended.

They'd say: "I didn't write that!"

"No, I didn't say you wrote it," I said. "YOU" wrote it, and I was being polite.

There were very few that could see the humor. Well, before the time was up, before the week–end was up, you should have seen how many people came with their crayons and drew flowers and all kinds of things over what I had written to cover it up as though what I had written was a very offensive thing to say. It was a joke.

Claude and Jewel got the biggest kick out of it; it was hugely funny, but people couldn't necessarily see it that way.

That was my early introduction to the people in Greensboro who were involved in the New Age philosophy. I quickly became very controversial in Greensboro.

We were having meditations every Friday night and more and more people were coming and it was beginning to fill up Patricia's front room, then we started having talks at the Janus Theater in Greensboro. We would go there on a Sunday morning and clean the place up from spilt drinks, popcorn and boxes. People just dropped stuff on the floor. It was filthy and a mess. We would get it ready to have an activity Sunday morning and the owner of the theater allowed us to do it without charging us anything because we cleaned the place up.

It was a movie theater that had five small individual theaters in a little complex. I went to the owner and made an agreement to be able to use one of the theaters for our church activities which were along lines similar to Unity, a positive thinking kind of talk held every Sunday morning. A whole group that was involved in our teaching would come on Sunday morning early at about eight o'clock to clean up and get the place ready for the service at ten o'clock.

It was an alternative for people looking for something other than the orthodoxy of fundamentalist religion and gradually people began to hear about it by word of mouth. As well, we did a little advertising by way of flyers, brochures and pamphlets and it got to the point that seventy-five to ninety people were coming pretty consistently.

Karen at some point had moved down to Greensboro with her husband (though they separated and got an amiable divorce and remained friends) and got involved in the Sunday activities. She became a close friend with Ken. They were both musicians, guitarists, song writers and, on various occasions, they played quite a lot of songs each of them had written. The songs were very beautiful and they were the first musicians in AHAM.

Eventually the owner of the Janus Theatre began charging us something and that's when we knew we really wanted a place of our own.

One evening I was driving towards Patricia's apartment in her car which she let me use, because I didn't have one, and I passed by a building that had a For Rent sign. In those days South Market Street was just a two lane road with ditches on either side, but now it is a main thoroughfare in Greensboro extending considerably out of town to the airport. We were there while they widened it into a paved five lane boulevard with two lanes in each directions and a center lane that you made left turns out of. That became the first home of its own for AHAM.

It was about ten or so at night and I stopped because there was not much traffic, I backed up and pulled into the driveway where the lights shone onto the building. It was a little building and there was a telephone number on the sign, I wrote the number down and called it the next day.

The owner was a Mr. Tyson – he's passed on now – and we made an agreement with him to rent the building. The building was totally self–contained, all by itself, with a parking lot off to the side, a couple of places in front to park, and parking in the rear, right next to the intersection of Edwardia Drive. You could drive in our driveway either from Edwardia Drive or straight off West Market Street. The building next door to us was a small building too. You could drive from the back of that building next to us into our driveway at the back. It was both convenient and easy for people to find us.

We started off by making the front into a book store carrying all the same kinds of books that we carry here in AHAM's present book store in our retreat center in Asheboro, North Carolina. Of course, we carried many more books than we do now because we had larger area for inventory. We had a small office in the front and to the side of that a second office and then off of the second office there was a little counter, and a sink with hot and cold water. The counter was left by the previous tenants and it served very well for storage underneath. There were restrooms, one for women and another for men, where our office extended back several feet.

It was large enough for our needs at that time.

We divided the front from the back by putting up a curtain we had made - held on a form of a curtain rod. It extended from the ceiling all the way to the floor and you just slid the curtain opened or closed from the left and from the right where it would come together in the middle. We would leave it partly open as a passageway to go from the front to the back.

The counter, which was about six feet long and four feet wide, was set up at ordinary counter height. Behind it we kept a change box for when people bought books and underneath there was enough room to store stuff on shelves. Later we had other shelves made and eventually we found a place for shelves from businesses that didn't need them any-more. We built two book shelves ourselves and bought three of four shelves from others. We still have the shelves from West Market Street here in Asheboro (in different places, I think over at the guest house and in the dining room...)

Somewhere, we have pictures of the West Market Street Center that were taken from the outside and we may have a few views of people and events taken from the inside. These pictures were from even before Jim, AHAM's photographer, came around. When Jim started coming, we'd been around for a couple of years or so. He had moved here from Norfolk, Virginia in what they called the Tidewater area.

Jim used to keep his car parked out in front of the building where there was place for only two or three cars parallel parked. It was his favorite spot.

There was a sign that blocked the view of our place, a relatively large sign. It didn't even belong to the people who owned the building next door, but it was on their property. It advertised a construction company and we had asked the construction company if we could move their sign, but they refused, they wouldn't let us. We also asked the manager of the business next door, which was some kind of a delivery system company, if they would be willing to let us move the sign to the other side of their property where it wouldn't take away from the view of it, and would give people a better view of our building - they refused. The manager was friendly with the guy that had the sign.

So we said, "Okay, we just have to go along with it." Their sign blocked both the view to us for people coming down the street and our sign in the front window, so we got a sign put out on a pole in front that was up high enough that people could see from down the street. Still, we were holding in mind "a happy end to this movie" - that one day we would be able to have that sign moved.

One day, Jim's car - he had a very nice, clean car, a Volvo that he really loved - was parked as usual in the front of our building. A truck was coming down Market Street and the brakes for some reason went out and quit working. It was not a big, big truck but it was big enough and it was loaded with something heavy. When the driver hit the brakes, there weren't any and he was afraid if a car stopped in front of him at a signal light he would plow into it and maybe injure someone. There was a signal light on that very corner, the intersection beside the building next to us, so quickly thinking he veered off of the road, ran right into that sign, and into Jim's car pushing it all the way across the parking lot into the wall breaking a hole all the way into the building next door to us. It just totally demolished Jim's car.

The person who owned the sign had not been very friendly and refused to allow us to move the sign, but after all of this happened, he thought that maybe we had powers, as if we were witches or something and it scared the shit out of him. So when we went to him again and asked him, "Could we move the sign now?"

He said, "Yes, yes go ahead and move it, fine."

They knew that we were involved in philosophical thinking of a different nature than most people thought and believed, and our book store itself had metaphysical books - a lot of New Age books - we were selling that we did not necessarily endorse.

The sign was repaired, which was paid for by the insurance company of the truck, and then moved to where we had dug holes. It was now no longer our problem and Jim got himself another car. It was the same kind of a car, but it wasn't nearly as nice and that was always a big disappointment to him. However, the story has always made a big impression on people when we would talk about the "completion process" or "seeing the end of the movie," as fulfilling your wishes. You hold in consciousness what you want to happen and it will eventually come about. By God these processes really work!

That's just a little story about how we got started there in that little building on West Market Street.

Dialogue on Awakening 7
AHAM's Core Teaching

Saroja: It is important for this book to have a more in depth look at AHAM's teaching.

Ramana: AHAM's teaching is Bhagavan's teaching and how AHAM came into being is the story of my life. The process of my own awakening, the story of my awakening, is what we are talking about, my life as it unfolded and ultimately resulted in my awakening into the awareness of being.

So, that's what it's all about, my awakening, and then sharing with people the aspects of my awakening that would be of any benefit to them, applying my awakening in the teachings of AHAM for people to have the ability to have their own awakening.

Saroja: What kind of processes have you shared?

Ramana: AHAM, as I am seeing it, is first about Self-Inquiry.

Every person's life needs to be summed up for themselves in their recognition that the sense of I is the reference point from which they function in their own life. Their own personal story, their own history, is summed up in the returning of the sense of I back to the source from which it has taken rise, which is the pure awareness of being that they and we and all of us are abiding in.

Saroja: Yes. That's the uniqueness of AHAM's teaching of Bhagavan's wisdom, we start by recognizing that we are and then we do everything from Self, not from the mind.

Ramana: Yes. Yes! That's basically what it is.

It's the recognition of consciousness, what consciousness is and consciousness functioning as the sense of I. The sense of I requires the pure awareness out of which it takes rise. But usually, we do not recognize the pure awareness out of which the sense of I takes rise. In fact, in the beginning, we don't even recognize the sense of I. The sense of I functions, like the "finger of life" that writes our life, so to speak, but we don't recognize from where it functions.

Our union with the source through AHAM's teaching is Bhagavan's teaching, directing a person to do this for themselves, to take this inner quest of finding the location from where the sense of I rises, returning the sense of I back into its own sourcing essence, the pure awareness that all of us are. This is the one single reality, the one ocean of consciousness out of which we all rise as apparent individual waves of consciousness.

I had a very strong intuitive knowing of the significance and importance of the purpose, process and teaching of AHAM in the name itself. Now the name AHAM, Association of Happiness for All Mankind, came to me out of the blue, but we are all looking for happiness. We want happiness without the least upset, without the least taint of misery – that's what we all want.

Bhagavan says it himself somewhere in his teaching that everyone is seeking happiness, untainted with misery. That's it.

Saroja: How can one be free from the entanglements that bring us misery?

Ramana: The individual can free himself from the entanglements of life by withdrawing the sense of I - which is the root thought of existence itself - back into the pure existence of pure being. This is really what AHAM's teaching is about - how to free oneself from the entanglements of body/mind identification and identification with the world of time and space. Once you get it, you can utilize this awareness functionally and practically to be clear, efficient and effective in all endeavors and undertakings in your life in the world

That is the fulfillment, not only of the teachings of Bhagavan, but those of Jesus. My whole life prior to Bhagavan had been using Jesus's teaching in a functional and practical way. I never saw the Bible in a doctrinal way with the traditional Christian notion of Jesus's exclusivity. We may have fallen out of alignment with our true nature, yet we all are Christ-beings on our way to recalling the truth about ourselves.

Saroja: You have mentioned it many times that Self-Inquiry is not a meditation, it is a process. I think that distinction is important. Could you speak about that?

Ramana: Self-Inquiry is often considered to be a meditation, but it's important to make the distinction, to see the difference between Self-Inquiry and meditation in the traditional sense of meditation.

Meditation is always involved in duality. There's the subject who is doing the meditation and the object on which the meditator is meditating. There are always two: "I" the meditator and "who" or "what" or "that" on which I am meditating. I could traditionally be meditating on a mantra (Japa meditation), a name, a word, or an idea such as "I am a child of God," or "I am happy." It could be the breath, the guru, the teacher or your favorite god (in traditions such as Hinduism, the family god for which they have paintings or pictures) that is used as an object for meditation.

Self-Inquiry is different - it is not in duality. You can say it starts in duality, because the one who is meditating considers himself or herself to be in duality - to be with a body and a mind and living in time and space. So Self-Inquiry starts in duality but it's the process of the sense of I withdrawing back into the source out of which it arises. It's not "I" and an object; it's only the subject itself, inquiring into from whence the subject arises so that it dissolves itself into its source.

Bhagavan used to say that inquiry is the goal as well as the process for attaining the goal.

You're using the process to attain a goal so to speak, yet there really is no goal to be attained other than the non-existence of the "I" as an object and even as subject. So you're going prior to subject and prior to object, whereas meditation is on the object of meditation. So Self-Inquiry is totally different from meditation in that regard. Okay?

Saroja: It seems to me that - correct me if I'm wrong, Ramana - most techniques of meditation bring us to Self-Inquiry. I mean, ultimately, one has to go back to the Self, right?

Ramana wearing shirt
with AHAM logo.
AHAM archives.

Ramana: You see the techniques of meditation are methods of a subject meditating on an object, again, breath, guru, a picture, a candle flame, or whatever. Yes, ultimately when you have merged with the object of meditation then you have dissolved the subject into the object and you might say that the last thing that would occur is, who's meditating?

So ultimately it's correct to say that every method or technique ultimately ends in Self-Inquiry, or ends with and in the sense of I, so that the sense of I is the last thing to go.

Saroja: That's the beauty of the teaching AHAM is disseminating. We start right from the end at the very beginning, but it seems that when it's presented to most people it remains simply a notion that is difficult for people to grasp.

Ramana: Self-Inquiry seems to be difficult for most people to grasp based primarily on the habit of externalizing consciousness, which is what most people are caught in, having consciousness turn outward onto objects, onto the world of persons, places and things.

Think of it this way: think about the center of a wheel or of a circle and then think about expanding from the center in all direction out to the circumference.

Or, think of it as a sphere, a ball. Imagine you're the center of the ball and it goes out in all directions, from the center outward. The perimeter is the usual direction people are lending their attention and that habit is very strong.

When people are so caught up in the strong habit of meditating on the object, the externalized pull of consciousness, it's difficult to get a hold of where all of this begins; because we're not thinking about the beginning, we're thinking about the very activity while we're engaged in it.

Inquiry is returning attention from the periphery, the circumference, back to the center and this can happen very quickly once you begin to get it.

CHAPTER 17

Encountering Resistance

In the early days of AHAM we operated as "the Church of Happiness." We had Sunday morning talks in our own center and every Sunday we printed off the program with an article I wrote about the talk, giving it a name, and adding other basic information. Unity Church did much the same, and that was more the level that people were open and receptive to in those days.

I used to make provocative statements all the time, but it would alienate people and we would never see them again.

Yesterday (2008, *ed.*), I was being radical in insisting that suffering was body-mind identification. Back in those days (1980s), I couldn't talk that way. People didn't want to hear that you live in ignorance while you are identified with your body and your mind, and that this is the cause of your suffering. Loneliness comes from being identified with your mind and your body. That's why you're lonely. Who wants to hear that when they are just starting off on a spiritual quest! If I had told someone that in those days, it would have been like slapping them in the face.

Greensboro is in the middle of the Bible Belt, and many people accused us of being a cult; accused all the people who were regular participants of being involved in a cult, and our members had to deal with such accusations being leveled against them (We had never officially established a structure, even though we called ourselves members of AHAM).

So it happened, in the early days of AHAM, when people came to one of our activities and liked what they heard, the message that I was sharing, they would start telling their friends. But they would quickly get shot down because their friends would immediately associate, in their own minds, what the person said that they heard, with what they would call heresy, all kinds of negative notions and ideas.

Let's imagine that you had just heard of us and, instead of going to church, you came to a talk that I was giving with only thirty or forty people in attendance in a little old book store on West Market Street. Then you went back home and your friends, relatives and later your co-workers said: "That's a Cult, what are you going there for?" They'd even say, "You can go to hell for listening to that."

Even though whatever it was that you were involved in had to do with your spiritual practice and was meaningful to you, who wants to constantly hear accusations of being involved in a cult? What do you think you would have believed and thought about that?

We were renting a center - we had utilities, bills for the operation of the center, bills for books purchased, and furnishings to pay for. It took a lot of money to operate a center and we wanted people to come, because we were serving them, yet there were not many people interested in our message and taking our programs. We were not going to survive very long if there were not many people coming. That was just the practical side of it.

In 1982 we joined the International New Thought Alliance (INTA) and a number of months later Blaine Mayes, the International President, asked me to consider becoming the District President for our area.

INTA divided the country up into districts. Ours comprised North and South Carolina and part of Virginia. Blaine asked if I would be willing to serve in that capacity and go around to all of the various New Thought types of churches that had a message similar to or along the lines of INTA.

Would I be willing to put my name in nomination for District President? I agreed to it.

I don't know how Blaine learned about us and he never told me even when I asked him. Somewhere along the line one of our Sunday programs evidently got mailed to him and in reading it, he could tell where we were coming from.

I used to create a bulletin of our Sunday morning program with an actual outline of our church activities, and an article that I would write related to the talk. I did that on the old typewriter, pasting up a different cover for every Sunday.

North Carolina was in the Bible Belt and all the new thought churches there had the same kind of problems as AHAM did as far as having fundamentalist Christians projecting on them that they were a cult and that kind of thing. Therefore, our linking together was beneficial for all of us. That's what Blaine Mayes himself saw and what he presented to me as the reason he wanted me to function in the capacity of District President.

I would be free to do as I wished, and once I had put in my name for nomination, I got a letter from him officially declaring me to be the District President. I wrote him back and said: "You asked me if I would be willing to consider becoming district president - how many others were there?"

He said, "You were the only one!"

I did that for roughly three years. That must have been about 1982 and I functioned in that capacity through 1986.

AHAM is not a member of INTA anymore, although our association with it was beneficial in that it gave us some degree of authenticity.

People look for who you are associated with and in the early days of AHAM those who came to our activities used to ask: "Who are you associated with? Who are you affiliated with?

We would say: "No one. We are not affiliated or associated with anyone."

When we joined INTA, we got our name posted in their quarterly magazine; they listed in it the individual members, as well as the churches and organizations that were members or those who had made a sizeable contribution to the organization. We would carry the magazine in our center's book store on West Market Street. This gave our members something that they could say about us and gave people the feeling that we had some worldly authentication, an association that made us somewhat valid, and the message we were sharing worthwhile listening to.

Ramana giving AHAM seminar, Virginia Beach, Virginia, 1981. *Image from AHAM video.*

People could say that we were members of an organization that had been teaching this kind of thing for a hundred years and they could use that as a rebuttal to their friends, relatives or co-workers who accused them of being in a cult. Otherwise, they were not yet ready to be challenged on the level of their beliefs.

My serving as the District President of INTA in the early days of AHAM was part of cultivating the soil. It was like being a farmer who is going to plant a crop. You have to plow the field, turn the earth and get it ready to receive the seed from which the plants will grow. That's what we were doing. We were plowing the soil of consciousness in this part of the country.

As district president, I would call the directors or ministers of the various churches teaching New Thought philosophy to let them know about the International New Thought Alliance and set up a date to come and give a talk at their church. We would get acquainted, establish a relationship and a fellowship, because they too ran into the same thing we were running into in North Carolina.

I travelled during that period and a few in our group would go with me to the various other cities where I was invited to give talks. Elizabeth would usually go, or Stan when he was with us, and Karen while she was still with AHAM. I would keep my talks less radical, because I was even more radical than the International New Thought Alliance. In a manner of speaking, I had to somewhat water down my teaching and present pure INTA teaching: "God dwells in us, as us, or Christ in you, the hope and glory." I would give the talks and then ask them to consider themselves joining the alliance.

I was going out to the various Unity churches as well as occasionally the religious science organizations, but mostly Unity because of my association with it. Unity was very much a New Thought church.

In those days, there was no Unity in Greensboro, in Winston–Salem or in High Point. There were only three Unity churches in the entire state of North Carolina. There was one in Raleigh, one in Wilmington on the coast, and another in Arden which was near Ashville, up in the mountains, and that was it. Two older ladies, who lived together, neither of them married, were the founders of the Unity church in Arden, and they operated in a house that they had converted into a church. It was a nice size house, that's how they started.

In South Carolina, there was a Unity Church in Charleston, and that was all. Then, in Virginia, there was a Unity in Virginia Beach and a Divine Science church in Roanoke.

In Charlotte, in those days, the church was located in a small office complex and it was a former classmate of mine from back in the days when I was going to Unity school, who was the minister. He had been a Major in the Air Force and when he left the military he went to Unity ministerial school.

Now, they've got about six or eight or so Unity Churches in North Carolina, but that was all there were in those days.

INTA would hold a national annual conference and in 1986 it was being held in Houston. I had not returned there since I had left, but I agreed to attend with the idea of going to Houston first and from there going on to Los Angeles and spending some time with Al in developing a company, before going back to Greensboro. That's what I did.

Karen went with me to Houston. We flew out and she stayed at the Adam's Mark Hotel where the conference was being held - sharing a room, to cut down the expenses, with someone else who was also there for the conference. I stayed at my friend Bob Howingburg's apartment: he had another place - he was separated from his wife at that time, but he went to stay with her while I stayed at his place.

Bob also loaned me an automobile, and because I was from Houston and Karen had never been to Houston before, I showed her the city, taking her around to points of interest and places that I used to live. We even went by the book store to where I had been drawn and discovered Bhagavan's book (I think the Phoenix Bookstore was still in operation then). All of this was significant to her because she was interested in my history and where AHAM started.

I didn't care any longer to be the District President of INTA, so while we were there, I presented to Blaine Mayes the idea of Karen becoming the District President because she was interested in continuing on. Blaine readily agreed, and so while we were there at that conference we switched over. I resigned and then she was made the District President.

Karen had the ability to stand up in front of a crowd - a few hundred people - and talk or entertain them. That was natural with her. There were a couple of hundred people there for the conference, she met a lot of them and made a big impression. They could sense that the energy coming from her was relatively potent in comparison to those who were more in their heads and just philosophizing. But the impression she made, it kind of went to her head as well.

Because I had an awakened awareness of being, that did not give anyone else the awakened awareness of being too. People in AHAM were just novices, everybody really was just beginning, so while Karen was the most active one, in a manner of speaking, in the early days of AHAM - she functioned as my assistant and was the first person in our teaching that I trained to give programs - she didn't fully understand (nor did the other people in those days), where I was coming from.

After the conference, I went to Riverside, California where I met my friend Al while Karen returned to Greensboro. A short time after her return, she decided to leave AHAM and start her own work, yet there were commitments that had been made, programs that were already scheduled that she was going to be conducting and our church activities. Karen was functioning as the facilitator while I was away, but she completely dropped out and left without anybody to cover any of those things. Here I was in California where I stayed for a little over a month.

I talked on the telephone to Elizabeth and I said, "Well, it looks like it's fallen to you. It's now going to be your responsibility." She was reluctant because she was feeling incapable at the time, but I assured her that she was very capable. So she continued on in place of Karen. We communicated regularly during that transition time and she functioned in that capacity for many years.

Al Young had started a new a multi-level marketing company in California with a line of natural vitamins and minerals. There was one product in particular he was manufacturing that was for people who were addicted to smoking tobacco. If you took this herb consistently, about three times a day, it would cut down the craving for tobacco. It worked for a lot of people, which was one of the strengths of the line that he was selling.

Al Young was his full name, so he called the company Young Life, which was a good name in my view. Since he and I had worked together before, he asked me to consider coming out to California as he was just getting it off the ground and he needed some assistance. He knew that I had a speaking ability and that's how we had functioned together, my ability as a speaker is what had really built our companies before.

I was giving it serious consideration: Al's idea was for me to come out, we would sign up people and get it going as a multi-level marketing line. We would get AHAM people involved, giving them the opportunity to make a little extra money and it would be part of our outreach as people coming into it would learn a little bit about our positive thinking.

I returned to Greensboro from California with Al, bringing back quite a bit of his product, while some of it we shipped by regular means. Then we started presenting the Young Life program to people in AHAM who were interested in participating in it as a way of earning a little extra money, either part time or full time. Young Life was not connected with AHAM itself; it was a sideline that I was involved in, along with people in AHAM, and it became pretty active.

Al didn't have anyone to give presentations in California; there were people he had started in it, but he was giving the presentations himself. Finally, he found someone there, but because we were doing far more here than he was in California, he decided to make the move to Greensboro. We rented a place not too far from our center and a large majority of people in AHAM joined in; and it went quite well until Al and I had somewhat of a disagreement.

He and I had been in business together before and I had been a part of the company itself; this time, though, I was not asking or wanting to be part of it. I had reached a place in which I was not interested in owning things. I had gone through a transformation and I was dedicating the total of everything that I owned and would own in the future to AHAM, including all the books that I had written and would write, all of the tapes, videos, cassettes, eventual CDs and DVDs, from me and the teaching. All went to AHAM; I didn't own anything. That was the situation.

I said to Al that instead of being a part of the company with him, he could own the whole thing and just pay ten percent of what he earned to AHAM, not to me. I said by doing that, he could even write it off as a tax deduction, because we were a non-profit organization, a church actually, and so by giving to a non-profit church he could write the entire amount off.

Al, though, was not in agreement, because he didn't feel he was in full alignment with the teaching of AHAM, in as much as he had his own religious beliefs. Al was a Jehovah's Witness.

I told him, "Just consider it as a tithe."

He said: "If I was going to pay a tithe to a church then I would pay it to a church that I'm a member of, that I go to, and I don't care to a give a tithe of that amount."

I said, "Well, you can look at it as though that would be your payment to me rather than me being an owner of the company."

Still, he wanted me to be a part of the company and he was not willing to do it in that manner.

That is just how the mind can get in there and get locked into something.

I explained to him that I had already turned over everything that I owned to AHAM. But the way things happen, if you have a context, and in that context you have disagreement, a thing is almost entirely doomed to failure. He understood that, and I understood that, we tried, but there was no overcoming it because the thing also triggered off an older disagreement that he had with me in our prior time in business.

It triggered something off in him and I guess in me too, because I stood firm in my position and he stood firm in his. Because we were standing firm in our mutually, opposing positions, that became the death certificate of the enterprise. It was just a crazy situation.

He continued to try on his own in Greensboro for a while, and a number of people stayed with it, but eventually it petered out. He then moved back to California or back west somewhere and that was the end of the Young Life episode.

People felt a presence in our center in Greensboro and they would say: "My goodness, what is this place?"

They couldn't understand the kind of feeling, the atmosphere, the energy, the stillness when they walked into the bookstore. They walked in and either said: "Whoa, what is this place?" and stayed; or, they walked in and said: "What is this place!!!" and be out the door in an instant.

It was humorous to watch.

We were chartered as both a church and a spiritual training center, and in time we knew that the meditation aspect was what we were ready to expand on and make more predominant. We had a teaching from Bhagavan Sri Ramana Maharshi that was universal in dimension, significance and importance. That meant another location, so we started looking for a place to make a retreat center.

We looked in Virginia for the longest time, up in the Skyline Drive area, which is beautiful; and up the Blue Ridge Parkway area. We went quite often, traveling around, getting to know people and real estate agents, but although we found a few places that were of interest to us, for whatever reasons they didn't work out.

Two of AHAM members had found a potential place near Asheboro, North Carolina. Elizabeth and I had been on a trip to Florida and we were on our way back, so we drove through the town and met the real estate agent who took us out to see the place.

The main building AHAM, Asheboro, North Carolina. *Photo: Jim Dillinger.*

We both just said, "This is it!"

It was obviously the place and in 1992 we acquired it, moved in, and it became our retreat center. It is still our present location. After moving, we started expanding our programs.

Geographically, if you look at a map of North Carolina, we are situated almost ideally in the very heart of the state. What we have been doing is generating the consciousness that has produced a radical transformation in this part of the country, the entire East Coast of America has benefited from us being here, and I want you to know it has been an uphill task, an uphill burden the entire thirty years we've been here and it is still not easy.

The lake at AHAM, Asheboro,
North Carolina. *Photo: Jim Dillinger.*

Dr. Ihaleakala Hew Len, who taught Ho'oponopono, the Hawaiian forgiveness process, was reluctant to come to North Carolina, and then, when he did for his very first time, he was received and supported by AHAM. He came back several times and has said to Stan and others, maybe not in exactly these words but in essence, that it was AHAM that had made it feasible for him to come back and give his programs here.

We're beginning to see more local people in Asheboro (2008, ed.), but in the early days, even though people came here from all over the country, people from here did not because those involved with us locally were being shot down by their own friends, relatives and co-workers. That's still a problem.

You've got such a message of truth - why is it you just can't go in there and start sharing the message and then see people start beating the door down to get in? Well, that's not the way it works.

All of these years we have been cutting through beliefs in people's minds to get down to consciousness itself, the purity of consciousness, and to dissolve all of the mind's conditioned patterns. That is the history of AHAM. We have been doing the Herculean job of transforming the quality of consciousness in this part of the world.

Dialogue on Awakening 8

Who Is Ready for the Spiritual Path

Saroja: I see we go round and round. We do this and that and then it's like - whoops, the realization that life is taking its course. Isn't this what life is doing to all of us, putting us in situations to fulfill what we are here for?

Ramana: The highest purpose for all of us, whether we can see it for ourselves or not, is ultimately to have the awakening into the pure awareness of being. That's the highest purpose for everyone.

But in the world of people living their lives in ordinary consciousness, no one has much motivation for the spiritual quest. If anyone has had a glimpse of it - a true genuine glimpse of it - it becomes compulsive to pursue it. Then you can't really be contented with just ordinary life in the world. It's a constant pursuit. That's why there are very few who are really involved in a serious, dedicated spiritual quest, in comparison to the masses of people in the world.

On the spiritual path we have known fellow travelers, so to speak – I'm using this metaphorically – that we have met along the way; and we may say, "I've met many people," but compare those with the total masses of humanity and still you're going to find that they are far and few between. There's not that many among us.

Go into a large city, like New York City or even Toronto...

Saroja: Both great cities...

Ramana: Go walking down the street: how many people do you see who are truly into something spiritual? Most of them don't even go to church. They're not interested. They're hardly even interested in nature. They're just interested in fulfilling mundane desires.

I'm not saying that in a judgmental sense, I'm not meaning it as a put-down, I'm just expressing it as a fact that there are very few people that are actually interested in a spiritual quest. They're into material things, mundane things in the world.

Saroja: You as a master or a teacher seem to be like a vacuum pulling a few people inside, back to the source.

Ramana: There are those that are ready, willing and receptive to consider what's required and necessary in order to go back to the source. Yet, there are very few that are ready, willing and able, or capable of applying themselves to the necessary discipline.

You find that throughout the world that there are very few who are interested.

I myself was so involved in the quest, because awakening was what I wanted more than anything, that I incorrectly projected my own enthusiasm onto people, as though everyone in the world shared a similar enthusiasm for what I had found, and what I had seen. That's not the way it works, it's not the way it works at all. Still, I have kept hoping and believing over these thirty years that one day more people will really get what AHAM is all about, and we will draw large numbers of people into awakening to their true nature and abiding in the pure awareness of being, which is their pure nature.

Saroja: I was wondering if you were to comment on the Bible, would that attract more people?

Ramana: In the early days of AHAM I used to talk about the Bible, however, this didn't draw many people.

There's a famous saying: "Only when the student is ready will the teacher appear." Meaning that the student is capable of seeing and understanding what the teacher has to share, only when he or she is ready.

I felt that more people were ready than we were serving and what we needed was a way to communicate with a wider audience.

We started doing talks on Eckhart Tolle's (an awakened teacher, *ed.*) book *The New Earth: Awakening to Your Life's Purpose*, and we had two and a half times as many people when we started as we had at the end. People coming wanted to hear about it, yet they only wanted to hear a philosophy. They wanted to hear: "how I can have and be and do whatever it is I want without having to give up anything; without having to make major changes in my life. I want to have my own way, I want to accomplish whatever it is that I want to accomplish, and do it the way I want to do it, without any sacrifices on my part."

Well, that's not the way it works, but people are not ready to hear that. Perhaps only a person who has been on a spiritual path for a long time and finally come to the place where "I'm sick and tired of being sick and tired" is ready to hear about making major changes - an old soul who has had many lifetimes of seeking and many lifetimes of suffering.

People don't want to hear that they have to come to the place where they are sick and tired of being sick and tired.

I don't want to be sick and tired of being sick and tired. I want to have what I want to have; I want to do what I want to do. I want to be what I want to be, the way I want to be it. And I want to be it now! Tell me how I can do it now. I don't want to have to sacrifice anything.

You're going to have to start letting go, releasing the accumulations, the acquiring; again not so much the things themselves, but the attachment to things - and most people are caught up in attachment, as well as to the things themselves - and they don't want to let go.

I have things and I want to continue to have things and I don't want to let go of the things and don't talk to me about letting go of my attachments; my attachments are the reason I have things.

That's the way many people are in the world. So they're really not ready to even hear the message of truth. Do you get what I'm saying?

Saroja: Yes, definitely.

In AHAM we have what we call the Forgiveness Process. It follows a certain sequence, which is really about stopping, meditating and being in awareness – just seeing things for what they are and forgiving ourselves somehow, meaning accepting – it's the same thing, isn't it?

Ramana: Yes. The Forgiveness Process is fundamentally forgiving yourself for where you have been identified with something and made it problematic, where otherwise it would not have been a problem. Forgiving yourself is where you must start. You're not really able to forgive someone else unless you are able to forgive yourself. It works the other way too. You're not able to forgive yourself unless you're able to forgive someone else, because in truth, in consciousness, there is no other - Consciousness is what is.

Ramana speaking at AHAM, Asheboro, North Carolina, circa 1993. *Photo: Jim Dillinger.*

The sense of other rises out of the sense of I and in counter distinction, the sense of I is dependent upon the sense of others. The moment you give rise to the notion of "I," you feel the "I" is other than the all-ness out of which it rises, and all of the other apparent "I's," meaning all the other bodies that are houses for "I's."

"I" and "Other" give rise to the notion of duality and are the basic ingredients of it.

I speak about this in my book, There is Neither 'I,' Nor 'Other Than I,' There Is Only... - that only in pure being do "I" and "Other than I" exist together. In duality "I" requires "other than I" and "Other than I" requires "I."

You can't see "Other" without "I" and you can't see "I" without "Other." It's just so simple and basic, yet we don't look at it and recognize it for what it is.

So the forgiveness process is the recognition that I have created "Other" by identifying with "me" as a singular individual apart from the all-ness of being. I have fallen out of the all-ness of being as I have created the sense of I - the ego apart from it - and the sense of other. This is in itself the starting point and basis of suffering.

If I want to end suffering I must forgive myself for having taken on an ego and then perceiving that there is something apart from myself that is the cause of my upset. If I've created upset in someone else, I must forgive myself for having created it for them as well as for holding onto that sense of other in regard to them.

Saroja: I've experienced guilt of course, and I still sometimes do. It's so vicious – I mean, if everyone could get to experience the Forgiveness Process, my God, no more guilt!

Ramana: Yes!

Saroja: Are you really ready then when your intention is a hundred percent focused on pure awareness? Is that when you'll no longer plunge into the gutter, feeling guilty or being a victim, caught in imagined dramas? Is that it?

Ramana: Are you ready to be free, at peace and contented with your own being, with yourself? Are you ready to simply drop your position that you are a separate entity, living apart from and other than the source of being?

Once you say that you're ready, then you must be willing to demonstrate that you're ready by letting go of your sense of individuality, your sense of being a separate individual living in time and space, and remain then in and as the all-ness of being. That is being free. So the question is: "Are you ready to be free?"

The paradox is, some people find it more pleasing to remain as an individual living in and with the sense of "otherness" apart from the all-ness of being. They prefer to remain subject to differences, contradictions, opposing points of view, which they call the adventure of duality, or the adventure of dualistic living.

If someone feels that way and wishes to remain in that, it's their prerogative, their business. What they don't understand is that as long as a person remains with the sense of other, they will always be in a state in which they will be subject to upsets, conflicts, opposition and competition. Some people thrive on competition, on opposition, they enjoy that. If that's what they like, what they want, what they enjoy, they're creating that and the world allows that to be the case. Maybe they're not ready to abide in the absolute.

Some people even believe that there is no such thing as an absolute awareness in which there is no opposition, contradictions or sense of other.

You can't force anyone else into your way of seeing and knowing something to be; it's only up to them to make the choice to turn their attention in that direction.

Bhagavan said that just because the night owl does not see the sun, it's not the fault of the sun. It's the ignorance of the bird who does not come out in the day time and see the light of the sun.

In a similar sense, it is the prerogative of a person to not want to see the all-ness of being or be in the all-ness of being. The person who does not want that may not be ready for it.

I have said it often at AHAM: "it is those really who are sick and tired of being sick and tired, who are ready to hear the message." When you have reached a place in your life where you're tired of being upset - you don't wish to be upset anymore - you wish to be free, at peace and fully contented within yourself, then you're more prone to be ready to hear the message of Avaita (non-duality), that we are all one being in which there is no conflict or contradiction.

PART 5

Sacred Journeys (1984 to 2010)

Arunachala, The Sacred Mountain, Tiruvannamalai, India. The two peaks are said to embody Shakti (left) and Shiva (right), 2015. *Photo: Daniel Tigner.*

Ramana in his fifties. *AHAM Archives.*

CHAPTER 18

Arunachala Ramana in India for the First Time

Arunachala Ramana traveled to Tiruvannamalai in Southern India in the mid 1980s to pay respects to Bhagavan Sri Ramana Maharshi (1879 to 1950), who was instrumental in Ramana's second and final awakening on June 4, 1973. It happened in the Phoenix Bookstore in Houston, Texas, and, was triggered when Ramana (Dee Wayne Trammell) came across a book by Bhagavan Sri Ramana Maharshi that opened at a page showing Bhagavan's picture.

In India, almost everything was new for Ramana - the cultural practices, the food, the living arrangements, the philosophy and the town and environment itself. His first days at Bhagavan's Ashram, called the Sri Ramanasramam, the Ramana Ashram or simply the Ashram, were by Ramana's accounts, something of a shock for him as an uninitiated Westerner. He was given primitive, but somewhat favored, accommodation in the cottage that a retired English soldier had built and lived in [Major A.W. Chadwick (1890 to 1962)]. On reading about Bhagavan, Chadwick became intrigued and went to see him in 1935. He stayed in the Ashram until his death, residing in the cottage, and is buried within the Ashram grounds.

A.W. Chadwick was one in a line of Westerners who became enthralled with Bhagavan Sri Ramana Maharshi. The first was F.W.

Humphreys, a British policeman stationed in India, who met him in 1911 and wrote articles about Bhagavan in a magazine called "The International Psychic Gazette."

To give some further background to Ramana's journey, Tiruvannamalai is built around a small mountain called Arunachala, which is often referred to simply as "the hill." Arunachala was formed eons ago, perhaps as early as the Hadean Period in the earth's history, dating back more than 3.5 billion years. So the hill is from some of the most ancient rock on the earth! For many Indians, the hill is sacred, the Supreme Being manifesting as a hill.

Bhagavan Sri Ramana Maharshi, circa 1949.
Image used by permission of Sri Ramanasramam.

In the area of Tiruvannamalai in Southern India, Shaivaism, one of the four main sects of Hinduism, is prevalent. Shaivaism, itself, has many different schools and practices, as well as a vast literature, so this is only a very simplified overview, but one key feature in Shaivism is its reverence for Shiva as the Supreme Being. Arunachala, the sacred mountain, is seen as a literal embodiment of the light or fire of Shiva. In other words, Arunachala is literally Shiva, and it has attracted poets who have praised it in poems and songs, and sages who have made it a spiritual home for millennia. One of the greatest of these sages was, of course, Bhagavan Sri Ramana Maharshi, who wrote many songs in praise of Arunachala. Bhagavan saw Arunachala as being the heart of the earth, the spiritual center of the world and as his guru. Bhagavan wrote:

The Arunachaleswara Temple complex in central Tiruvannamalai seen from Arunachala, 2015. *Photo: Daniel Tigner..*

"Someone from abroad had written asking for a stone from the most sacred part of the hill. He does not know that the whole hill is sacred. It is Siva Himself. Just as we identify ourselves with a body, so Siva has chosen to identify Himself with the hill. Arunachala is pure wisdom in the form of a hill. It is compassion for those who seek Him that he has chosen to reveal Himself in the form of a hill visible to the eye. The seeker will obtain guidance and solace by staying near this hill."

Quoted from: Bhagavan Sri Ramana - A Pictorial

Biography

Tiruvannamalai is built around the hill. It is a site of many temples, ashrams and a bustling town. Its largest temple in the center of the town is the remarkable Arunachaleswara (or Annamalaiyar) Temple complex, which dates back at least to the ninth century and covers twenty-four acres. At the center of devotion within the temple is a Shiva-Lingam, a sacred stone representing Shiva, used in Hindu ceremonies of cosmic creation. Beyond Arunachaleswara, there are many other temples and special sites of worship and meditation, not just for Hindus, but for other ancient religions of India. One example is Tirumalai, an ancient Jain temple complex on the outskirts of Tiruvannamalai.

Inside the Arunachaleswara Temple complex below the sacred hill of Arunachala. *Photo: Daniel Tigner.*

Being the site of the sacred mountain of Shiva, Arunachala, and so many temples, Tiruvannamalai is a place of pilgrimage, with millions of people coming each year to festivals, to express their devotion and to do Pradakshina, a fourteen kilometer (eight mile) circumambulation of

The Adi Annamalai Temple, on the opposite side of the hill from the Arunachaleswara Temple, is an ancient temple dating back some 1200 years in its present structure. Note the peaks of Shiva (right) and Shakti (left) on the hill. Jan brought Daniel Tigner to the temple at festival time. *Photo: Jan.*

the hill that is said to bring many blessings, including release from sins, karma and suffering.

All of this was new to Ramana on his first visit to Tiruvannamalai, but his three to four month stay was remarkable for the awakened sages he met (the jnanis or self-realized beings), friendships forged, his experience of Bhagavan's presence at the Sri Ramanasramam and his experience of Arunachala. All of this shaped the future of AHAM, eventually leading to Ramana and company from AHAM returning to Tiruvannamalai, introducing Westerners to this most sacred place through a pilgrimage program, and eventually to the construction of AHAM's Indian Ashram, where Ramana (1929 to 2010) lies in his Samadhi (a shrine where an awakened being is buried), where anyone can come and meditate in the stillness of his presence.

One of Ramana's first encounters, which led to a lasting friendship, was with Ganesan, who was the manager at that time of the Sri Ramanasramam as well as Managing Editor of "The Mountain Path," a quarterly magazine devoted to the work of Bhagavan Sri Ramana Maharshi. The magazine, founded in 1964, is and was a work of literary merit, with articles that are still a source of insight and inspiration into the path that Bhagavan shared. In one article entitled "Kinder far than One's own Mother-Ramana" from January 1985, during the time of Ramana's visit, Ganesan recounts many previously unpublished and beautiful anecdotes about Bhagavan's kindness to all people and creatures, for example his great love for animals.

After Ramana's second trip to India in 1992 to 1993, Ganesan became a regular honored guest of AHAM in the United States, where he shared with extraordinary grace and generosity his direct experience with Sri Bhagavan (he is Bhagavan's grand-nephew and has memories of him as a child as well as of Bhagavan's disciples and devotees). Ganesan has also published numerous books of great interest to devotees and it was Ganesan who chose the site of Ramana's Samadhi after his passing on February 15, 2010. Such was the depth of Ramana's and Ganesan's association.

On that first trip to India, Ramana met two other notable sages: the first was Annamalai Swami (1906 to 1995), a direct disciple and devotee of Bhagavan who lived his later years beside the main Ashram in a tiny Ashram of his own. Then there was Maniswami (circa 1920 to 2006) who, at the time of Ramana's visit, was still living in the same cave that Bhagavan had lived for seventeen years from 1899 to 1916. It was here while living at the Virupaksha Cave that Bhagavan's fame began to grow and people came to know about his high state of consciousness. Ganapati Muni - an Indian poet and scholar - came and recognizing that he was a great seer or maharshi, gave him the name Bhagavan Sri Ramana Maharshi (Bhagavan's birth name was Venkataraman Iyer, but at the time of his meeting with Ganapati Muni in 1907, he was known as Brahmanaswami).

What is the power of caves that since ancient times, across world traditions, have attracted spiritual seekers? Is it just the isolation and quietude? Arunachala is the site of many special caves where sages have lived and meditated. The Virupaksha Cave where both Maniswami and Bhagavan had stayed is, however, of special significance. It contained the sacred ash remains of a fifteenth century Jnani, Virupaksha Deva, who had dwelled there.

Skandashram, another cave dwelling, was later built for Bhagavan Sri Ramana Maharshi a little higher on the hill by a devotee named Kanadaswami. Bhagavan named it after his devotee as his name 'Kanda' is translated into Sanskrit as "Skanda." That cave is part hut and part cave, as well there is a spring with clean mountain water and trees growing, including a lovely mango tree in the back against the rock wall. Bhagavan stayed there from 1916 to 1922 with his mother and brother until after his mother's death. A shrine was built for her, in what later became the present Ashram at the base of the hill, Immediately beside his mother's shrine, a shrine hall was built after Bhagavan's death, containing Bhagavan's Samadhi.

Here are anecdotes and reflections from Ramana about his first time in India.

The winter of 1984 to 1985 was my very first visit to India and to Sri Ramanasramam, in the town of Tiruvannamalai, South India. I was prompted to go there because of Bhagavan, I long had the wish to go there just because of him.

Until that time I had never been to India. I didn't know much about Vedanta (the ancient Indian philosophy of living, *ed.*). I didn't understand gurus. I really didn't understand anything about Arunachala. Although I recognized my awakening was due to Bhagavan's grace and I had gratitude for that, I had no lineage relationship that I was aware of, and I was still absolutely a novice as to what I had awakened to. I had read the *Autobiography of a Yogi* by Paramahansa Yogananda, and I had read some of Bhagavan's books - this was all that I knew about in those days.

I had been abroad when I was in the Army, but this was the first time for me to be in the Far East as a civilian. It was a totally different set of circumstances. As a military man I had been with an entire company of military personnel. This was entirely on my own and I knew nothing about what to expect.

I had written to the Sri Ramanasramam to tell them that I was coming, made a reservation and got their acceptance to come and stay in the Ashram, but I had no idea what that meant, what it entailed and the Ashram hadn't told me anything.

On arriving at the Ashram, that very first night, they put me up in Major Chadwick's cottage on the Ashram grounds. They had divided the cottage into two areas for two people to stay and one side was larger than the other. I had the small room. There were no linens, no towels, no mosquito net, nothing. They had cotton mattresses that were lumpy, because the cotton had moved around and there was a pillow that was hard as a rock. I don't know what they used for stuffing as it was absolutely like a rock.

> ### Distributing Bhagavan's Books in   North America
>
> While I was there on this first trip, I met David Godman, who was at that time working in the Ramanasramam library.
>
> One day, he and I were talking and he approached me with the idea of distributing Bhagavan's books in America. He had been given the task, to locate or contact someone to become the distributor in America of Bhagavan's books, all of the books that were written and published by the Ramanasramam. Bhagavan's books or books about him were not easily available in America.
>
> When he said that, I mean – bam! – that really got me. I said: "Yes! We would be very happy to be the distributor. We would see to it that they got distributed all over the country and in Canada."
>
> For various reasons, this did not happen right away, but years later (in the 1990s), we finally did get the distributorship for Bhagavan's books in America. During the late 1990s, we distributed quite a number of books to bookstores up and down the east coast.

In those days the Ashram, Sri Ramanasramam, was extremely rustic - I guess you can use the word primitive - and there was nothing in the way of amenities or accommodation that would appeal to Westerners.

Ramana in his mid fifties. *AHAM archives.*

It was an Ashram, not a hotel and they did not supply linens, towels, sheets, pillow cases. People coming had to bring all of those things for themselves, and then take them somewhere to get them washed and cleaned.

The first nights I was just absolutely miserable. It was hot and I was bitten by mosquitos. Their poison affects me terribly. I have a tremendous reaction to them, and one mosquito bite will do me in. After that I went about getting a mosquito net.

About my second or third day, I went to the office and asked if there was anything at all that they could do about the mattress. I didn't want to come across judgmentally or critical of them. They took me to a room where they stored the mattresses and asked me to pick out whatever I wanted there, and I picked out about four or five mattresses. I stacked them one on top of another in such a way that the cotton that had been lumpy and displaced was moved around like pieces of a puzzle fitting together - so that the valleys and the mountains would meet!

Sri Ramanasramam, Tiruvannamalai, India. Just past entrance gate, ancient Illupei tree, buildings and people. *Photo: Saroja.*

The Ashram gave me the name of a fabric store in town where I was able to buy men's dhotis and I used them as sheets to wrap my mattresses and that gave me at least some degree of comfort as far as sleeping at night. I was a mess, and it took me about ten days to two weeks to settle into the routine there, but I finally got settled in.

At first I couldn't understand things because I was not familiar with the culture. The floor in the dining hall on which you sat to eat they would wash down with manure! They would wipe up the excess water from manure, then leave it there for the longest time as the heat of the room would ultimately dry the floor.

For me, it was like putting shit on the floor! But they used the manure as a disinfectant!

Ganesan was the Ashram manager. I had seen him and I had made it known that I wanted to meet him and he had even left word that he wanted to meet me and talk to me, because he was curious as to what AHAM (Association of Happiness for all Mankind) was, that regularly every month was sending them a check.

When I met Ganesan for the first time, I said to him, "To me clearly cleanliness is next to godliness and yet, you use manure, you even put it on the floors."

He then explained to me how cow manure has a medicinal quality and that this was a traditional use of it.

This was my first visit to Mother India, to Arunachala itself, and to Sri Bhagavan Ramana Maharshi, as far as his spirit was concerned. His presence was still there in the Ashram, in the old hall in particular. The Shrine Room (Bhagavan's Samadhi) was, of course, where people went around in a devotional way, but it was just devotion. For me, it was the old hall where I felt Bhagavan's presence. I didn't need a place to meditate, but I would sit and meditate a lot in the old hall and also just in my cottage.

I had read where Bhagavan called Arunachala his guru, but for him to pay homage to a mountain and consider it to be his guru, I didn't have the slightest idea what the heck he was even talking about.

Bhagavan had said that it was the very energy of Arunachala that had drawn him to Tiruvannamalai. It is a mystery within itself that cannot be satisfactorily answered verbally, by words or made to be fully understandable by the mind.

A story is told in Shaivism, a denomination of Hinduism, about a mythical argument between the two gods - Brahma and Vishnu - that was causing turmoil in the heavens among all the gods. Shiva was the only god that had the power to resolve it and, as the story goes, he appeared as a pillar of light and then he took the form of the hill. Literally, Arunachala is Shiva.

In Hindu philosophy lingams represent Shiva, and Mount Kailash in the Himalayas is called the home of Shiva. However, both the lingam and Mount Kailash are symbols representing him, whereas Arunachala is Shiva. The hill is Shiva, not just a symbol of Shiva.

How can you say that a mountain is conscious? Yet it is. There is something about it that draws people to it. Arunachala is a mystery that is prior to the mind, it is consciousness itself. It is the center of the universe. The sense of I, the heart, the core of being is what Arunachala means, not just stands for, that's what it is.

That doesn't mean that there aren't other locations on this world that have the ability to draw people to them, but I can't necessarily speak about those, meaning I can't speak for those, I can only speak for Arunachala. And, that doesn't mean that I can say I fully understand what it all means. But when Arunachala draws you as a devotee, it's the grace of Arunachala drawing you. In other words, it's God and the grace of God saying come to me, "Come and be in my presence."

In the days when Bhagavan Ramana was living, people used to come to be with him and Bhagavan used to say: "Well, what is drawing you here?"

People would say, "You're drawing me, Bhagavan."

Bhagavan's answer to that was, "What do you think drew me here?" In other words, it was Arunachala. Bhagavan always said it was Arunachala.

In exactly the same manner, it was Arunachala that drew me. It was grace that was at work in the lives of all who have come here as devotees and that also drew Bhagavan to Tiruvannamalai. That grace is still going on, all of the time.

That was my first trip to India and I did not return until eight or nine years later, which would have been in 1992 or 1993. On that original occasion, I met two jnanis, Annamalai Swami and Maniswami.

A member of a true official Swami order, is one who has gone through a process renouncing worldliness and surrendering their life and dedicating it solely to God or to the search for Self-Realization. I met other Swamis that were very high beings, clear, pure consciousness, but not Jnanis like Maniswami and Annamalai Swami.

Annamalai Swami was one of the direct disciples and devotees of Bhagavan Sri Ramana Maharshi. He had been an attendant to Bhagavan in his earlier days and he had been in charge of the construction of the main facilities of Sri Ramanasramam. He had his own Ashram next door to the Sri Ramanasramam and I went over on my own to his Ashram and asked permission to come to Satsang, which was granted. He had a regular routine of two days a week with Satsang, very similar to what we have here in AHAM. There was a quiet time of an hour and then after it, Annamalai Swami told stories about his own life with Bhagavan or answered questions. He was very gracious and in his own child-like way, he'd explain a lot about what was taking place.

I went to be with Annamalai Swami and for the fellowship. I became close friends with a number of his devotees: Kabal from Vancouver, Canada, Mira, a little Japanese lady and Sunderam, Annamalai Swami's attendant who translated everything that Annamalai Swami had to say from Tamil into English. There was a couple who were devotees of Bhagavan that Kabal knew from Vancouver, although they had not been close in Canada. At the Ashram, they became more friendly and I became friendly with them too. We became a little knit group, kind of a family affair, and we used to do things together, go to various places where Bhagavan had been, and points of interest mentioned in the book *In Days of Great Peace*, by Mouni Sadhu. That book was somewhat popular at the time and a number of people had come to the Sri Ramanasramam because of it.

Annamalai Swami and Ramana, circa 1992, *AHAM archives.*

Mouni Sadhu was a devotee of Bhagavan and he tells the story of how he was visiting Tiruvannamalai, when he learned that there was a special event pertaining to Aurobindo in Pondicherry - so he went to Pondicherry for this function. When he arrived, the crowds were in the thousands and people were lined up for city blocks up and down Nehru Boulevard and crossing over to the entrance four and five abreast to get inside Aurobindo's Ashram.

It took hours and hours for the queue to reach the entrance of the Ashram. Then it went down five abreast to just one person who would be escorted to the room where Aurobindo was sitting and giving Darshan. People would enter one side of the room, walk across the room in front of Aurobindo to a door on the opposite side of the room, and then exit. Mouni Sadhu tells how when he walked in the room, he had the feeling he was encapsulated in a bubble of light and he walked across the room in this capsule, which was something of a protection for both him, and Aurobindo, who was evidently being protected from the people of the world. But, because the queue was so long, they had fifteen or twenty seconds, maybe thirty seconds or a minute at the most, that they were allowed to spend in Aurobindo's presence,.

Mouni Sadhu said something like: "Isn't this something! Less than a hundred miles away is the Sri Ramanasramam. Sitting with no pre-conditions, anyone could walk in, approach, ask any questions that they may have, spend as long as they wished in the presence of the Master of Masters, and leave when they felt like it."

They knew that Bhagavan would eventually answer their questions, if not immediately, eventually he would. Here was the Master of Masters with maybe at the most a couple of dozen people there at any one time.

Maniswami was living on the hill at Virupaksha Cave and I went up there regularly - for a while daily or every other day – and we established a friendship, a silent bond of mutual respect and understanding of one another.

I was held in very high regard by both Annamalai Swami and Maniswami. Both were awakened - and they knew I was awakened - but we didn't talk about it. I had gone to India to pay homage to Bhagavan, as he was instrumental in my awakening. I didn't go there for the purpose of telling people that I had awakened, so I didn't say anything to any-body about the fact that I had awakened. So, those who were not awak-ened, they didn't know; I was just another Westerner who had come to Tiruvannamalai to pay respect to Bhagavan and who, like anyone else, was just seeking. As far as they were concerned, I was just seeking.

The Virupaksha Cave where Maniswami lived had the highest energy in my view of any place on the Hill and I had been around to just about all of the famous places.

Virupaksha Deva, who was a Jnani with many disciples of his own, lived in the cave, something like five hundred years before (fifteenth century). To me Virupaksha Devi's presence is still in the cave. Bhagavan lived there for seventeen years (1899 to 1916) and then Maniswami lived in it for twenty-two years. These great beings: their presence and their states of consciousness are in that energy, and in the stillness and silence of the cave. It is quite significant and very special.

The story goes that Virupaksha had many followers, and when it came time for him to drop the body, he instructed his disciples to sit outside and not enter, to remain in silence and to not disturb him for a certain period of time. Following that period of time, they entered the cave and where his body had been only Vibhuti, sacred ash was there. It was just ashes. There was no firewood, there was nothing to burn it. It was like he had internally combusted his body. It happened as a miraculous event.

Vibhuti symbolizes the sacrifice of the body to God and here Virupaksha was nothing but sacred ash. He was a high being with Siddhis or powers to combust his body through pure sacred fire. He was not cremated.

A cremated body has bones mixed in with ash. My son was cremated at the time of his death and there was a container with his ashes, which had bone in little bitty pieces and the ashes were white looking. I've known a number of people that were cremated and the remains all looked pretty much the same.

But sacred ash is almost like powdered milk. It's not so white and it's fine like talcum powder or dust and you could just wipe it off. When Bhagavan was living there, with his own hands he fashioned the Vibhuti into the form of a mound of sacred ash and then covered it with a cloth. So, from the time Virupaksha spontaneously combusted his body and transformed it into Vibhuti, sacred ash, until this current day, people have come and visited Virupaksha Cave and taken a little of the Vibhuti and smeared it on their head. After five hundred years, the quantity of ash has, evidently, not diminished. Yes, it is an ongoing miracle!

I established a routine of going up to the Virupaksha Cave. There was an unspoken agreement that I could go up there anytime. We didn't talk that much. I met Nadia there on the Hill. She was an American, originally from New York City, and she was a friend of Maniswami. She had an extended visa and was on a long extended tour in India.

Maniswami, 2005. *AHAM archives.*

Maniswami was always saying something to her about talking so much. To me I wasn't there to talk, I was there to be in the stillness and silence. Maniswami and I would have conversations and Nadia and I too, but Maniswami didn't particularly like there to be a lot of conversations going on between us because it was almost like an open invitation for other people to come to the Cave. Since he lived there - that was his home - he wasn't much interested in the general public coming there.

He had a number of devotees who came and that's how he lived. They would drop off a little something for him and I used to do that too. Then there were occasions in which he invited me to spend the night in Virupaksha and I did that a couple of times, just meditating all night in the Cave.

On one occasion in January, 1985 - I think it might have been on the 19th - I recorded him singing Bhajan in the Cave. He sang and played his one string Ektara and, oh God, could he make music on that one string and sing. He would sing in Tamil, so I didn't know what the words meant but the quality of devotion that he put into what he was singing made it quite significant. That recording has gone all over the world and devotees have come to know about it. Of course, I gave him many copies to give out to whomever he wanted, and we ourselves have given it to many people. Maniswami and I became very close on that first trip to India.

Next to the Virupaksa Cave was Skandashram, which Skanda, Bhagavan's devotee, began building in 1916. It was more of a scenic, quieter and cool place. There was a nice breeze there as it was at a higher elevation and it was a lot cooler there than it was down at the base of the hill.

During that period of time, Bhagavan began to have many followers and devotees who joined him and lived outside and around Skandashram, and his mother and brother came also to live with him there.

In those days, a swami living on the Hill with his mother and his brother, in what you call householder fashion, was so contrary to the tradition that it started a rumor mill. People couldn't understand it. But Bhagavan was so pure, so high in consciousness, that it didn't make any difference, because he was what he was.

Dialogue on Awakening 9
Grace

Bhagavan Sri Ramana Maharshi in Lotus pose, Skandashram, 1915-17. *Imaged used by permission of Sri Ramanasramam.*

Saroja: I see that there is in me an identification with the body and mind. It's like a veil is still there and I'm not always the witness of what I do, even though in meditation - I meditate every morning - it's very quiet. I want the veil to be lifted forever.

Ramana: Now be still there a minute. If you want it to be lifted forever, wouldn't you like it to be lifted now? Does that not include now?

Saroja: Yes.

Ramana: Okay, so you want it to be lifted now. It can't be lifted forever until it's lifted now.

Saroja: Right.

Ramana: So you be quiet, be still. You're trying to lift it, you can't lift it by trying to lift it.

The true lifting of it, the forever lifting of it, the now lifting of it, is getting that it doesn't even exist. There is no veil. The only way for it to be lifted now and forever is when you get that there is no veil that is concealing or hiding the awareness that you are.

Imagine something with me. Use your imagination. Be still and use your imagination.

Saroja: Okay.

Ramana: When you travel, there are times you go to places that are not familiar to you. In other words you may go to a building, to someone's home, or say, to a conference center somewhere, in which there are strange rooms that you're not familiar with. Now just imagine that you're in such a strange place.

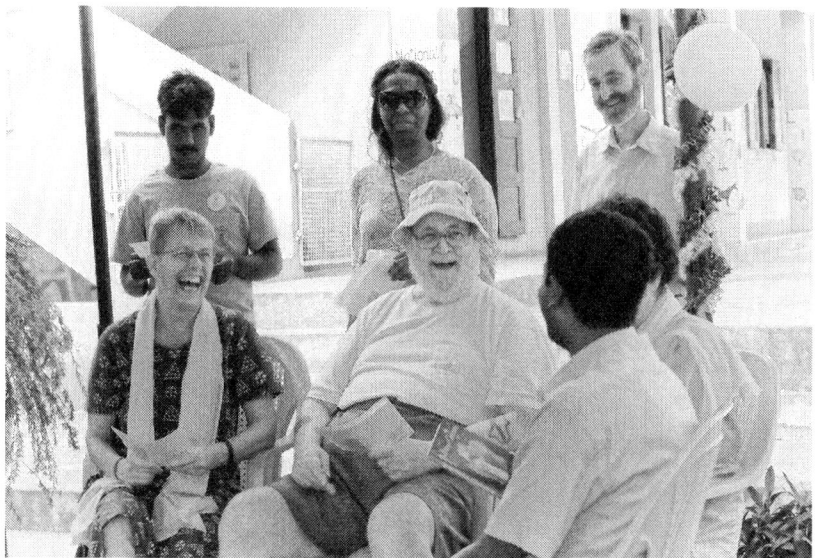

Ramana and friends, 2008. *Photo: Saroja.*

Imagine you're walking down a dark hallway. You walk very far and come to a room and open the door. Inside, it's dark, there's no window letting light in from the outside and as you walk into the room a draft closes the door shut.

Now you're standing in a room that is pitch black, you can't see anything. You wait and you look but it is so black that you cannot see anything. You hold your hand up and you cannot see your own hand right before your face. You understand? Your eyes are open, but you can't see anything.

Can you imagine this?

Saroja: Yes. I can.

Ramana: You're standing there and someone knocks on the door and asks, "Is my coat in there?" You can't even see your own hand in front of your own face. Well, what is your answer going to be?

Saroja: "I don't know."

Ramana: Exactly! "I don't know!"

And they say: "Is my book in there?"

Saroja: "I don't know."

Ramana: "I don't know." Why is it that you don't know?

Saroja: I can't see it with my eyes.

Ramana: You can't see anything. Now they say, "Are you in there?"

Saroja: "Yes, I am."

Ramana: Well, how do you know, you can't see yourself?

Saroja: I just know.

Ramana: Yes, but you can't see, so how do you know?

Saroja: I just know I am.

Ramana: Yes, you just know. You can't see yourself, but if you turn a light on, it turns out that you walked into a room of mirrors and everywhere you look around, you see your reflection. Still, before that you couldn't see, but you knew that you were.

So get in touch with how you know that you are, because it's not by seeing your body that you know that you are, nor is it by seeing your mind that you know that you are.

It's not your mind that tells you that you are, it's not your body that tells you that you are, these are both your possessions. Those are what you own they're not what you are. Being is what you are. You must be before you can even think.

Saroja: Yes.

Ramana: You say you want the veil to be removed for all time, but who says there is a veil there?

Saroja: It's just the mind trying. It's again the trying, it's again an old record trying and thinking that I'm doing things and just not relaxing and being. It's so simple.

Ramana: Exactly. Look at it here. Do you get the point?

Saroja: Yes, I do Ramana. You've been talking about that a lot, the now being always now whether it's five thousand years ago or now...

Ramana: This instance is the same instance; there are not two instances. That's very significant to get. This instance is always this instance, there are not two instances. Can you feel this?

Saroja: Yes.

Ramana: So where is this point of trying to be free of the veil? There isn't a veil, there's no veil to be free of, and there is no trying to be free.

Saroja: Thank you, Ramana.

Ramana: So are you getting it?

Saroja: Yes. It's funny listening to you because you somehow always bring the same truth in different words, but the same truth, right?

Ramana: I've always said the same thing. I've been saying the same thing for thirty-five years. It's just getting people to hear me, understand what I'm saying, what I mean by what I'm saying. It's not what I'm saying that is important, it's what I mean.

This awareness is ourselves; the awareness is who and what we are. What we are aware of is secondary to the awareness that is aware. We can't be aware of anything unless we are first, primary, the one who is aware.

White Peacock, a symbol of grace in India, on a roof at Sri Ramanasramam, 2015. *Photo: Saroja.*

But we don't see what's important because that habit of identifying with what we are aware of - looking at what we're seeing
rather than looking at the Seer - is so strong and we have held on
to it for so long. We've got to give more attention to the Seer. You
can't see anything without the Seer that sees it. It's the same way
with hearing. We give more attention to what we hear as though it's
outside of us, rather than to our Self, the hearer of what we hear.
Have you got it?

*Saroja: Yes. That's the whole trick – bringing back the attention
towards the Seer, towards the hearer, towards the Self.*

Ramana: Let me share something with you from the The
Teachings of Bhagavan Sri Ramana Maharshi. One of the ques-
tions asked by a devotee was about the guru and the guru's grace.
He wanted to know what was the guru's grace and how it led to
Self-Realization.

Bhagavan's response was that Grace is the Self. It is not to be
obtained or acquired. You only need to know that it exists.

The sun shines in its pure brightness. It's also the same with
grace. Grace is found by the proper approach. Just like the sun, it is
always shining, it is always here and now. The devotee's ignorance,
like the phantom of darkness, vanishes at the mere look of the
guru, you now are surrounded by sunlight.

The devotee asked Bhagavan: "Well cannot grace hasten the
brightness in the seeker?"

Bhagavan's response was that one of two things must be done.
You must leave it all to the Master, by surrendering to the Master
without reserve. Either, surrender yourself because you realize
your inability and your need for assistance, the Higher Power to
help you. Or, the other thing you can do is to investigate into the
cause of misery. Go into the source and thereby merge in the Self.

Either way, you will be free from misery. God or guru never forsakes the devotee who has surrendered.

The devotee himself then asked: "What is the significance of prostrating to the guru or to God (as they do in India)?"

Bhagavan response to that question was that prostration signifies the subsidence of the ego. It means merging oneself, the ego, the sense of individuality, the sense of I into the source. Now God or the guru cannot be deceived by one's outward genuflexion, bowing and prostrating. He sees whether the ego is there or not. Okay?

Saroja: Yes. Thank you, Ramana.

CHAPTER 19

Satsang (Spiritual Talks)

Arunachala Ramana's first journey to India in 1984 to 85 marks a pivotal point in his ideas and approach to his teachings. Earlier questions about his spiritual lineage seem to dissolve. From this point onward, Ramana, and AHAM, clearly belong to the lineage of Bhagavan Sri Ramana Maharshi.

In both AHAM centers - Asheboro, North Carolina, USA, and the AHAM Ashram, Tiruvannamalai, India (purchased in 1999) - there is a room devoted to meditation and giving Satsang, spiritual talks, where Ramana would respond to questions from spiritual seekers from around the world. In India, the room is called the "Sanctuary." Ramana would be seated front and center, behind him, on the wall, a picture of Arunachala, the sacred hill, to the right a large photo of Bhagavan, and to the left a large photo of Jesus. This is Ramana's complete lineage, and that of AHAM.

While Ramana was on a visit to India in the late 1990s, the giving of Satsang came about naturally, as Ramana responded to the needs of seekers for guidance both in the process of Self-Inquiry, and other areas of their Sadhana or spiritual practice.

"Sat Sanga," in Sanskrit, the language of the Hindu scriptures, is translated as "holy association," "keeping company with God," or associating with one who has

299

directly Awakened to God-consciousness, or to the true
Self (definition from AHAM website).

*Over time, these talks became more formal and structured, but even
then, they sometimes overflowed and continued far beyond the formal
schedule. Saroja, who conducted the interviews with Ramana for this
book, participated in various "table talks" or informal Satsangs with
Ramana, that went on for five or six hours. Such talks could happen at
any time - Ramana made himself unconditionally and whole-heartedly
available to whomever had a question or need to share.*

*Satsang continued until the end of Ramana's life. He gave his
last Satsang on February 2, 2010, from the AHAM Ashram in
Tiruvannamalai, India, two weeks before dropping his body. In the
video of that talk, Ramana's passion for sharing and his love and joy
are evident, but it is also obvious that his body is struggling.*

*Ramana's anecdotes about his personal life, are few in this final
chapter. One gets the impression that his own life stories were no longer
of much importance to him. He saw his personal story, as told in this
book, as significant only inasmuch as it might help us to understand the
spiritual journey, its pitfalls and discoveries, its trials and tribulations.*

*Above all else, Ramana's life after awakening was a reaching out to
everyone and anyone who might benefit from his experience. Everything
he did had that purpose, as is clear in what he tells Saroja about the true
motivation for this book:*

> The personal history of someone really has nothing to
> do with truth. It doesn't really deal with what's impor-
> tant: The only important thing is the spiritual essence.
> All that I have told you about my life - as it unfolded and
> ultimately resulted in my awakening into the awareness
> of being - has been to share aspects of my awakening
> with those who would find it of benefit to them in their
> own awakening.

Maybe some readers will feel they have had similar experiences, or that their life has been somewhat like mine, and it might give them the feeling that, "Well, I can do it, too!"

So, I'm sharing this story - and it's important that it is authentic and true - but it is still not who I am. It's a history of the body-mind.

Even though my personal story may be of interest to people, having the spiritual awakening and abiding in the state of realization, I no longer consider personal history as having anything to do with actual enlightenment. It's the spiritual quest that is important. Personal history may be about what leads up to enlightenment, but it is all in the past. We don't live in the past and we don't live in the future, we really only live this moment.

Even reading this history is taking place in the present. So what really needs to be included here - so that people don't buy into the story so much – is the truth that all of us live only in this instant. This moment is what counts, it is the only reality.

In 1992, Ramana returned to India with Elizabeth, who was the key trainer in AHAM until her retirement eighteen years later. On the way, they stopped in Europe and stayed as guests of Patricia in Germany. Patricia, Rick, and a few others from AHAM, also joined them in India. From that year until his death (2010), Ramana made an annual pilgrimage to India. Many other people from AHAM went as well.

Here are a few anecdotes from Ramana of the journey in India, followed by an account from Elizabeth.

On my return to India in 1992, eight years after my first trip, Elizabeth went with me and we stopped and stayed with Patricia in

Germany, then went on to Tiruvannamalai together. Patricia - who has tremendous compassion and generosity - picked us up at the Frankfurt airport and took us to the little town of Kaiserslautern, where she lived and worked as a tour guide, and also took us as her guests on a number of whirlwind tours of Europe.

Her tour company had huge and very comfortable buses with as many as fifty people riding in each. We went to Paris, London, Rome, Pisa, Naples, Sorrento, and Nuremburg. We mainly visited old churches, many which were bombed out, and then rebuilt after the war. We had a tour of the Vatican. On one of the tours, we went to the Basilica of St. Francis of Assisi (Assisi, Italy), the ashram - you could say - where St. Francis's body is entombed - none of the places we visited in Europe, including St. Peter's Basilica in Rome, could compare with it. The Shakti energy at St. Francis's tomb, the consciousness, was still present. In my view, St. Francis was a saint, not only in the Catholic tradition, but he would be considered as such in Hinduism.

Patricia. *AHAM archives.*

On arrival in Tiruvannamalai, I immediately re-established my relationship with Maniswami and Annamalai Swami. I introduced Elizabeth, Patricia and others to Annamalai Swami, and we started going to his Satsang.

My first time in India, I had met an Australian who lived up on the Hill. His name was Narakuthi Swami, which, as I understand it, means "jackal" in Tamil. He was a very independent guy and we hit it off well together. He became involved in reconstruction work on an ancient water tank on the hill that was crumbling and breaking down. Rebuilding it was very helpful to the local people who used the tank to hold water for drinking as well as for bathing and washing their clothes. AHAM assisted him financially in doing that.

From the very beginning in 1978 at AHAM, we made a pledge of tithing about ten percent of our income to a fund for contributing to spiritual work. This was about the principle of prosperity and devotion. We tithed to other organizations doing charitable work – God's work, as we called it. We had earmarked a certain amount for the Sri Ramanasramam. They didn't know who we were or anything about us, other than that every month they received a donation from us. One of the things we did was to meet Swamis, finding those who were dedicating their lives to spiritual work. Then we took from our tithing to subsidize them; sending them a regular small stipend.

Among the Swamis was a group with Swami Ramanananda, whom I had met in the book depot at the Sri Ramanasramam. I was talking to the manager about a book and he was giving me a hard time: Swami Ramanananda happened to be there, and interceded on my behalf. I was grateful for that.

Another Swami, Amananda, was visiting Sri Ramanasramam. He was a young, friendly, little guy, with a room not too far from my own, in the men's section. The way the Ashram was laid out, I had to pass in front of his room on my way out. Every time I would leave, he would be right there, and immediately come out and question me, "Where are you going?"

There were times that I would have just preferred to be on my own, but every time I went out, he wanted to go with me. In many ways he was helpful, because he could manage in English and translate with people.

A number of times, we did Pradakshina, circumambulating the hill. I had to be very careful about drinking the water, and Amanada Swami, who knew I couldn't drink water that he could drink, looked after me. One time, I didn't have water with me. He knew a place with a relatively small, but nice house that had a clean well. While we stopped to get a drink, a young man came out and invited us in for tea. Then we completed our walk.

Elizabeth, Ramana and Swami Ramanananda. *AHAM archives.*

On a second Pradakshina, we again stopped and had water there, and again the young man invited us in. While he was serving us tea, the owner came. It was Swami Ramanananda, who had helped me in the book store. He was living here all the way around on the opposite side of the hill to Sri Ramanasramam. He could speak good English and we established a relationship, a friendship, and he invited me to stop in any time that I wanted.

It was in the mid 1990s when we began a Pilgrimage program and we continued it every year afterwards.

Sri Ramanasramam gave permission to us to bring groups of people - it was a unique arrangement. We owe Bhagavan Sri Ramana Maharshi's family a debt of gratitude for maintaining the Sri Ramanasramam and making it a place of pilgrimage, where all of us could benefit from Bhagavan's presence. It has been no easy task that they have done throughout the years.

Elizabeth and I usually went in November and a group would come for a month at a time beginning in November, another in December, and a last one in January. Then we usually went back to North Carolina in February, or a little later.

On the first pilgrimage, there were a couple of gentlemen from Georgia - attorneys - Elizabeth had met them when she was traveling in Georgia. They were active in AHAM back in those days. One of them had a real culture shock and did not know how to handle it. They were relatively affluent, so money was no problem for them, and they ended up staying in a five star hotel in Madras, so they didn't stay long in Tiruvannamalai. It was then that we began to look into a place of our own, so we could have our own meals, more or less of a Western nature, plus much more comfortable accommodation for the people that were coming.

We started the process of registering AHAM as a non-profit organization in India, and the two attorneys gave us legal guidelines on how to go about it. They didn't know Indian law, but understood basic law, and so they came up with various ideas and actions required to start up

AHAM as a non-profit charitable organization, very similar to our charter and how we operated in the U.S.

One of the towers of the Arunachaleswara
Temple complex at the center of Tiruvannamalai
seen from the street. *Photo: Daniel Tigner*

People wanting to make the pilgrimage to India came to our AHAM Centre in Asheboro, North Carolina, for a week-end in preparation. We learned how to prepare people, telling them what to take with them and what to expect when they got to India - understanding the culture, and how to behave in an appropriate way so as not to inadvertently offend anybody. We taught people how to sit and eat on the floor, using metal trays in place of banana leaves that were used as plates in the Ramanasramam. We had a manual with material from a book about Shaivism culture that we used with permission from the author. People enjoyed doing this as they felt prepared and it was very helpful to them. It went so well that the Ramanasramam asked Elizabeth if she would be willing to write up a little brochure that could be given out to Westerners to prepare them in the same manner that our people were being prepared by us.

Once people arrived in India, we showed them around to places of interest, and then they were pretty much on their own, other than on the days that we would meet and I'd answer their questions. Later on, the pilgrimage program became quite extensive. There was an agenda, a day-by-day and week-by-week schedule for the period of time that the people were there. There was also free time, but people were there not just as tourists, they were doing Sadhana, their spiritual work. We did that for a number of years.

People asked me questions about Bhagavan's teachings, which were of course AHAM's teachings; in particular, about the proper way to practice Self-Inquiry. Word began to spread, as our people met Westerners not in our group, that someone was sharing Bhagavan's teachings on how to practice Self-Inquiry. People started to come and sit outside of Elizabeth's room. They would sit on the portico and listen through the door to my answers. More and more people congregated outside Elizabeth's room to listen, and people asked if it was all right if they invited friends who wanted to attend. I said okay. Eight or ten more came the next week. It expanded to the point where there were more than we could handle in Elizabeth's room, so it was better to have it in my room, which was larger.

We weren't calling it Satsang at that time. We would just say we were going to have a gathering, a silent time, and then I would take questions. On that day, I walked into the cottage, and I couldn't believe it. I saw shoes lying all over; the room was full - something like thirty-five people there - we were absolutely cheek-to-cheek - I was not anticipating this.

As no one had the authority to give Satsang in the Ramanasramam, Patricia went looking for a place and found a building that used to be the old post office, and that's where we had the next session. There were about sixty or seventy people, the place was packed.

We were the first Westerners to start doing Satsang in Tiruvannamalai. God knows how many people are doing Satsang there now!

The Ashram was very accommodating; they made it possible for us to store our trunks in their storage room, next to the kitchen, off the main dining hall. We packed our trunks before leaving, then someone picked them up and put them in storage for us. When we'd return later in the year, they brought our trunks out to us. We had started to accumulate things, which we made available to other people. As well, people would purchase what they needed for their stay, and then when they left, they would donate it to us, because they didn't want to take things that they had no real use for back home.

We began to look for a facility of our own. We rented two houses in the same neighborhood as the Ramanasramam. You came out the Ashram's front gate, turned left, continued to the second road, and turned right. There was a gulley or a ditch there. It was then a kind of zigzag down that road. We rented there until we built our own Ashram.

The first property we purchased was farmland. It was set back from - and without direct access to - the road. There was a farmer's agreement that you could cross one another's land to get to your land in order to farm. But there were some shenanigans taking place during that period of time and we learned that we had paid far too much for the property. About the second or third year after we had purchased it, the main electrical company came through and built high voltage towers, electrical lines right in the middle of the piece of property of the young man we had purchased part of our land from, crossing into the corner of our property. The lines ran between our property and the hill, cutting our view. It seemed possible that the person who sold us the properties knew that this was going to happen.

Friends attending Ramana's fifth Death Anniversary (2015) at the AHAM Ashram, India. *Photo: Daniel Tigner.*

There's a misconception that many people have as to what it means to live in the awakened awareness of being. It does not mean that you're not susceptible to being stolen from, ripped off, unscrupulous characters taking advantage of you, or that you're omniscient, all knowing. All it means is that you know the Self and that everything is an expression of the one pure consciousness of being, the consciousness that you are. Everything and everyone is an expression of the Self that you are.

There are many kind and generous people who have been taken in by con artists. It can very easily happen to anyone. It happens in the world all the time. And when you have awakened to the pure awareness of being, you live in a state of vulnerability. It makes you more vulnerable,

Kumarasamy during construction of AHAM. *AHAM archives.*

not less, because you see people suffering and you don't want people to suffer. You want to do whatever you can to alleviate their suffering.

It was in 1998 that Kumarasamy (who later became one of our trustees) wrote to me in America. He had been to the library at the Ramanasramam, picked up one of our newsletters or my book, and sent me questions as a devotee. I responded. He also wanted to know if, when I came to India, he could have an audience with me. I forgot about it, but one day after Satsang, an Indian gentleman asked to see me. He presented me with the letter that I had written to him. He was very gracious. He asked me if AHAM would be interested in a place he knew of, that the owners were interested in selling.

I was curious, so he came by and showed me the plans, the actual blueprints. It was very impressive. He then made arrangements with the owners and two of them came by in their car and took us out there. That's how we found our AHAM India Ashram.

It had been under construction, but they were no longer working on it. It was a shell with concrete walls, dirt floors and all grey looking. The two main buildings had already been built - what we now call our Satsang House and our Guest House - but the compound walls had not been built, and it was just open, but we could see the potential. The basic structure for the Ashram was already there. It was ideal for what we wanted. We already owned property, but this place offered the potential of being more quickly usable.

Charlotte. *Photo: Jim Dillinger.*

Charlotte was in charge of the construction and she did a masterful job. She was there every day during the seasons that we came, and then we also had one of our trustees oversee it. Paneer came on staff, and he put together all the builders, a trustworthy group of painters, carpenters, masons, plumbers, electricians, all of it. Charlotte would be there every day, and I would come and spend much of the day with her, just to give her moral support. It took three years to complete the work.

We had a grand opening for the AHAM India Ashram in November, 2001.

I have told you about the energy, presence, stillness and silence found in the Virupaksha Cave on the hill. Well, a number of people who have come to the AHAM Ashram and sat in our meditation sanctuary have said that the stillness, silence and presence they have felt in the Sanctuary was almost the equivalent to what they felt in the Virupaksha cave.

The Sanctuary in the AHAM Ashram, Tiruvannamalai, India. Front left is a picture of Jesus, center, Arunachala and right, Ramana Maharshi. *Photo: Daniel Tigner.*

Sitting in my chair in my room with the curtains open, I can look up to the hill. One day, a group of us had gone to the summit of Arunachala. Annais was one of them. I was sitting in my chair by the telephone, looking through my telescope at them. They were waving a towel, so I knew it was them, and we were talking using a Walkie-Talkie. That was before cellphones were used here.

The telephone rang. It was Annais's mother, Clyde, in America. It was early in the day here and a Tuesday evening in the USA. I took the Walkie-Talkie and put it onto the telephone, saying to Annais, "Here's your mother." I switched back and forth from hearing to the speaking so that Annais could talk with her mother. They had a conversation from the top of the hill into our center in America. That was the first time that someone spoke from the summit of Arunachala to someone in America.

Elizabeth – A Pilgrimage to India

Elizabeth, Ottawa, Canada, 2001. *Photo: Saroja.*

I had really wanted to go to see Arunachala, I had a strong pull, but with big responsibilities at the Centre, it just didn't work out, until, one day, I was talking to Patricia about it, and she said, "What about if you set a date?"

I set the date and I started putting money into a savings account, not knowing how it was going to work, but within two weeks, someone offered the entire amount for me, as well as for Ramana, to go to India. I didn't realize it until afterwards, it is Arunachala that takes care of the timing of when you go to India - we don't.

That first year (1992 to 93) Ramana and I, Patricia, Rick, and two other fellows that were a part of AHAM, came and stayed with us at the

Sri Ramanasramam. We had a light kind of program, a gathering with Ramana once a week, just checking in with him, but it was mostly about our being at Arunachala and the Ashram. Ramana said to us: "You have everything here. We're here with the hill and Bhagavan; there is no need for me to do anything."

Those first four months in India were about "getting ones sea legs," as Ramana would say, learning all the customs, doing things in harmony with the environment and the culture - how, for example, when you give and receive money, you always use the right hand. We always followed Ramana as to the protocols, the best way to show respect in the temples, that sort of thing. The first year; he was our guide walking around the hill.

I was learning what to do and what not to do. You needed to boil water for twenty minutes before you drank it, and I actually had a time when I didn't do that, and got sick for about a month.

In America, we shared our experience with people; they got interested and that's when the pilgrimage program was established. I put together the program and people going on the pilgrimage came to our center for an orientation. We covered how the Sri Ramanasramam operated, the cultural dos and don'ts, and how to prepare to go to India. We even booked their flights, so they could fly together, and guided them about what to do when they arrived.

Because of the orientation, people didn't feel the repercussions like I did on my first trip to India. The videos I had shown them, along with the stories I shared, told them what they were going to face, so it wasn't a huge giant speed bump for them to go over. "Elizabeth told us this was going to happen, and it sure is that way, you know."

When they got there for the pilgrimage, they stayed at the Sri Ramanasramam, which was gracious enough to let us have eight people for a month at a time. I took them around the Ashram, introduced them to the President, who at that time was Ganesan, letting them get their feet wet. When we went into the dining hall in the first days, we always went in together - all of those type of things.

I will never forget one guy was sitting there with loose shorts on and his legs up, because he couldn't quite get them to cross, when one of the little geico lizards ran across the floor, went right up one leg into his shorts up and down the other leg and out. It was those crazy things that happened. We guided people every step of the way, until they started to know where they were going, then they were pretty much on their own.

What I had as feedback from Sri Ramanasramam was that they were very happy with the way that the people were respectful. We all wore white, followed the customs – not showing the ankles for the women and the shoulders and things like that. Everything was being honored and because of the respect we showed, the Ashram approved of us doing it each year. The manager even asked me if I would write a book about all of what I was telling our people, so that he could give that to Westerners or other people that came.

Elizabeth and Ramana, circa 2008. *AHAM archives.*

Ramana met with us twice a week. I'd set it up in my room in the Ashram for him to give a talk. That was the program for a number of years.

For Ramana, it was just about respecting and honoring being at the Sri Ramanasramam with Bhagavan and Arunachala.

Patricia had set up a meeting in Ramana's room. When we arrived we saw shoes all over the ground and when we walked in there were about thirty to thirty-five of us in the one little bedroom. At that point, it was obvious that we needed to find another place, because there were going to be even more people. So, the next time we met at the old post office, which was a large hall, and more than sixty people came. Ramana's message is quite radical; some people gravitated to it and some of the people had a hard time with it. You either really liked him or didn't like him: there was no middle way with Ramana.

The years in India were wonderful for me, because I was away from my responsibilities as the only trainer at the time in our center in North Carolina. I could travel, really regroup, recharge and create programs that took Self-Inquiry and applied it in relationships and different areas in life. After an idea came through, I would give it to Ramana, and he would fine tune it the way he did. So it was a good creative time.

A beautiful part of India was meeting devotees who had been with Bhagavan Sri Ramana Maharshi - like Ganesan, his grand-nephew, and some of the Swamis, like Maniswami and Annamalai Swami. We'd have Satsang with Annamalai Swami twice a week, sitting with him in silence.

My years at Sri Ramanasramam were very precious to me because I really established a relationship with Bhagavan. Up to that point, the teachings that I had received were mostly through Ramana, about the very practical, everyday use of Self-Inquiry. In India, I started getting in touch with the devotional quality, melting into the heart, hours of meditation in the old hall, walking around the shrine and going up on the hill, spending lots and lots of time basking in the stillness and silence.

Dialogue on Awakening 10
Some Final Words

Saroja: What is the point of seeking enlightenment, if it is to just disappear into existence? What is the motivation to be enlightened if, when you leave this body, you just disappear and become one with the whole?

Ramana: Let's say you don't reach the state of pure awareness. Let's look at it from that perspective. Are you enjoying life in this dimension?

Saroja: There are pleasurable moments, but I can't say that this is really, truly fulfilling.

Ramana: In other words, the truth is there's no happiness in this dimension. There's no happiness in this world of time and space. Is there?

Saroja: No.

Ramana: There may be brief moments, brief intervals when everything happens to be going pleasantly, when everything is going the way we would like it to go, but we can't have any guarantee it is ever going to go the way we want it to go, and along with the pleasure, there is also pain and suffering.

What's occurring around the world?

People are starving to death; they are displaced. On the TV News you see pictures of people carrying all their belongings on their heads, children and families going down the roads, refugees trying to get somewhere, trying to get out of the killing, to get away from it all. Now, even in Canada...

Ramana and Saroja, Ottawa, Canada 2001. *Photo Elizabeth.*

Saroja: There are people living in the streets.

Ramana: Yes. And in America there is poverty, the poor, people living in the streets. Then on the other hand, there is so much greed for power and control by those who only are interested in what they can acquire and obtain for themselves. Everyone, in this world of time and space, is living to some extent at the effect of these conditions.

Look at what happened to the early Christians. What does History tell you?

Saroja: Persecution.

Ramana: Yes, persecution. Persecution, hatred, hostility and war have been going on since the beginning of man's history. Who wouldn't want to be free of all of that if they knew that there is a way to be totally free, rather than just partially free?

So, what is the purpose of realization? Why would one want to be realized?

Saroja: Yes, it's very obvious.

Ramana: Enlightenment is the process of disassociating from body-mind identification to the extent of freeing oneself from the ignorance of living in and as the body, as though the body is who and what we are. Does that answer your question?

Saroja: Yes, I have another question. Can you actually consciously choose to come back in a body, to help people?

Ramana: Once you have become complete in your realization and abidance in the pure awareness of being - when that fully and finally occurs - there no longer is a separate entity living with a *sense of I* and looking at so called others. There is no "I" and "You" in the pure awareness of being.

In other words, God - we'll use the word "God," if that doesn't trigger off all kinds of concepts; or call it the Supreme Being, the One Reality, Absolute Truth, Divine Wisdom, whatever words that you want to use to describe the source and essence of pure being itself - is all-inclusive. How can there be in the all-inclusive any separate individual apart from it. Do you get it?

Saroja: Yes, I get it. If I may formulate the question differently, is there a possibility of re-birth or not?

Saroja: In order to have a body, you have to have identification; you have to be identified.

Ramana: Yes, identified with the body as being a separate self.

Saroja: A separate self...

Ramana: The sense of being a separate, individual being, but look and see - is there such a one?

Saroja: No, there is not. It's just an illusion. Somehow, it's almost like we are puppets in the hands of God. Whatever is happening, we are just a vehicle of expression for the source, but not really the maker, the doer of things.

Ramana: Maybe this analogy will help. Imagine you have gone to a play with actors and actresses playing roles.

Saroja: Yes.

Ramana: People are dressed in various costumes, playing whatever role that the script calls for. When the actor is good and playing in an excellent production, then you, as a member of the audience, no longer consider their actual identity in ordinary life. They may even be famous, but while they are engaged in that role, you no longer remember them in their identity, but rather you are identified with the role they are playing. Right?

Saroja: That's usually what happens, yes.

Ramana: But, they are not their character in the play, they're just playing the role of the character.

Saroja: Yes.

Ramana: In exactly the same manner, you're caught up in and identified with the role of Saroja, when, really, it is the Supreme Being playing the role of Saroja.

Saroja: Yes ... it's hilarious sometimes... (laughter)

Ramana: So, while you are playing the role of Saroja, you might say that you are forgetting your true identity, who you really are, the Supreme One.

Saroja: Yes.

Ramana: Well, what is self-realization?

Saroja: Realizing that you're just playing a role and letting it be, enjoying the show.

Ramana: Exactly. You are not the role that you appear to be and that all along you have considered yourself to be, but in truth you are just like Moses and Jesus who, after realization, said, "I am that I am" and, "I and my father are..."

Saroja: "One!"

Ramana: Exactly. Not two, not different, not someone else. Are you getting it?

Saroja: Yes, Ramana.

I am so grateful that we could do these interviews: that you made time to be with me and answer these questions, allowing me to share this experience with everyone around me - and perhaps even the whole world. Sometimes, I don't find the words to really say what I would like to say. The awareness that "I'm not the body," but "I have a body" is becoming clearer in me every day. It has become absolutely anchored in me. I know that I cannot be otherwise than in the awareness, yet I'm not thriving in it like you do. You have this awareness at all times. You are a truly <u>Happy Man</u>, but I still get caught in emotions and thoughts. I'm not liberated completely like you are. There's what I call a BUT, something that keeps part of me somehow clinging to misery.

Ramana: I understand what you mean by what you're saying, where you are still identified with your emotions, as though those thoughts and emotions have control of you. Certainly, you don't go around saying, "I am awake, I am awake, I am awake." Mind or the Ego saying so would be totally inappropriate and give you even more trouble and more difficulty than you may feel you're in now.

Instead, you must constantly and consistently keep your attention focused on the source of your awareness rather than on what you are aware of.

Here - do you see what I'm holding?

Saroja: Yes, a flashlight

Ramana: Do you see the light ray, when I point the torch around in my room?

Saroja: Yes, I see the ray of light wherever you point it.

Ramana: The torch can light up anything where you shine it, but the torch cannot light up itself. Do you understand what I'm saying?

Saroja: Yes.

Ramana: Your consciousness is like a torch that lights up everything that you give your mind to, but consciousness cannot itself light up. It's like a torch, lighting up the sensations and the feelings in your body and in your mind. Do you see what I'm saying?

Saroja: Yes, I do.

Ramana's resting or Samadhi, a place of
meditation and Self-Inquiry.

Photo: Saroja.

PART 6

Completion: Remembering Ramana (November 1, 1929 to February 15, 2010)

Flowers around the photo of Ramana at his Samadhi.

AHAM archives.

Performing the Puja rituals on the fifth anniversary
of Ramana's passing. *Photo: Daniel Tigner*

Stan: My Journey
with Ramana

Stan, 2015. *Photo: Daniel Tigner.*

Stan, who is currently serving as the spiritual and executive director of AHAM, shares his journey with Ramana and his devotion to the teaching of Self-Inquiry.

In 2009, Ramana and I were in the parking lot of AHAM's bank in Asheboro, North Carolina - Ramana needed to have some papers signed - when he told me, "I don't think I am coming back from India," I said,

"Let us hope that's not true," but I saw how serious he was - When I say, "serious," I don't mean it was heavy, that there was any upset with it, but that he felt very certain.

When he left for the airport on his way to India in November of 2009, he got into the vehicle, looked at me and said, "Goodbye, Stan," I said, "I will see you again," but I had the feeling that this might be the last time.

Ramana's health was failing; he had a kidney removed in 2007 and other complications. Then his health seemed to improve, but he had cancer, which he had known about for a year or two - and, as far as I knew, it hadn't gone into remission. Ramana himself could feel that it was still there in the body. In December of 2009, his legs swelled and he had to be taken to the hospital. He got out, but he had to be taken in again, so we knew then that it was serious. I talked to him alone only once while he was in India, a month or two prior to his passing on February 15, 2010, and I asked him, "Do you want me to come to India? I will come."

"No, Stan," he said. "I want you to stay in Asheboro and keep on doing the work, taking care of the organization."

In my heart, I have always been devoted to Ramana. My devotion has expressed itself in getting on with the work. Ramana and I worked together hand in hand and he said a couple of times that he could feel my devotion to the dissemination of the teaching, to the truth. My devotion did not express itself in the way of rituals, bowing down - although I had no problem with that. I noticed when people bowed down to Ramana, so I asked him whether that was what I should be doing. I'll never forget what he said, "No Stan, bow your ego down. Bow down to yourself, your true Self. The spiritual egos love to bow, and often times it is just a show." Still, after he and I had been in a process together - and some gigantic releasing had occurred for me - I did bow down in front of him.

Ramana and I were about twenty years apart in age, but we had very similar upbringings with strong parental guidance and discipline, and the work ethic. We liked many of the same things, the same food; and we had similar backgrounds in sales. We talked the same language to a great degree and that made it easier in the beginning years for me to keep my involvement in the spiritual work.

I met Ramana on September 11, 1981 - a defining moment for me. I signed up, sight unseen, for a class that he was teaching on a Thursday night. AHAM operated out of a book store in Greensboro, North Carolina, and I was running a newspaper in High Point, about twenty to thirty miles from there. I was very much into Napoleon Hill: Hill's books were my Bible - and I was told that Raman was his protégé (at that time his name was Raman, not Ramana). It was unheard of for a publisher to miss Press Day, which was Thursday at that time - and I had never in eight years in the newspaper business missed it, but that night I did. I said, "Hey, I've got to go," even though I had some misgivings, because Napoleon Hill with someone by the name of Raman didn't make sense to me.

Out he came in a plaid jacket, red shirt, and high-water pants (we called it that when you wore your pants high up from your shoes) - it was not stylish. "Good evening, my name is Raman," he said. "I am your trainer. Let's get something straight, this is not my training, this is your training."

I sat in the front row - the first time I ever sat in the front row to hear anyone - but I was gearing up to meet someone who had been with Napoleon Hill. Ramana walked up to me, put his face close to mine, looked at me and said: "Why don't you love yourself?"

Oh, shit! I started tightening up, and I thought, *how can I ease out of here?* But I was in the front row, and I could not leave without making a scene.

"I know you think that fulfilling all of your desires is going to make you happy," Ramana continued. "I know you think that, but let me tell you something: If you haven't found happiness within you before you get all that stuff - you think that you're miserable now, you haven't seen misery. I know, because I had it all and I was miserable! The thing of it is, after you get all that stuff and you're still not happy, you have nowhere else to go, nothing to look forward to, and it is miserable."

330 Ramana American Mystic: Memoirs of a Happy Man

I did not want to hear it, but it hit me in a place that I could not avoid; it hit me to such an extent, that despite my resistance and wanting to run away - something inside me had been touched that I couldn't run away from. That was my introduction to Ramana.

It was only a week or two before I met Ramana that I had read the last chapter of Napoleon Hill's final book, *Grow Rich! With Peace of Mind*: That book somehow prepared me for the next step with Ramana.

For many years, my own journey was a roller coaster ride up and down, because of my personal tendencies and my identification with seeking, which was strong. I didn't realize how strong it was. I was intentionally seeking money and relationships – to be honest, not so much relationships - I was

> **Napoleon Hill** had been counselor to a couple of US presidents and one of them on his death bed asked him something to the effect: "Dr. Hill, you have been with me through all kinds of situations - and your advice has been very helpful and valuable - Can you give me one more piece of advice?"
>
> Napoleon Hill replied, "Mr. President, ultimately - nothing matters." Ramana said that Hill meant - "no thing matters."

chasing women. I was seeking - as I see it now - freedom, but I didn't know what freedom was. I thought freedom was having more - financial independence. I had the grandiose purpose of becoming the most successful publisher ever, getting big. It was not about quality or real meaning. At the same time, the newspaper I was publishing (and others I had been involved in previously) was geared towards human rights. It was a black, African American, oriented newspaper, primarily serving the black consumer market.

One day, I walked into my office in High Point and Ramana was sitting there. All he said was, "Come on, take a ride with me."

We went to a lake nearby and walked, hardly saying anything, until we sat on a bench. Then he looked at me and said, "It's time for you to expand your purpose in life. It's time for you to start serving a higher calling."

I had no idea what he was talking about intellectually, but inwardly I could feel something and I started crying. I had no idea why I was crying - a chord had been struck inside me. We sat there for two or three hours - not continuously talking - just sitting. "Your purpose right now serving the black community is great and is much needed," Ramana said. (There were so many human rights abuses at that time). He continued, "Your real purpose includes everything you are now doing, but goes even beyond race and color, beyond all of that."

The interesting thing was that I had never questioned serving in the newspaper business; only recently, had I begun to ask myself about some of the things I was doing and whether I was really serving my purpose. What Ramana said, though, was not something I wanted to hear. I had a lot invested in terms of opinions and beliefs, as well as money and time. I knew the newspaper business and I was good at it. I was co-director of the North Carolina Black Publishers Association, and I had received awards - that kind of thing. I didn't like being in that "I don't know what to do land." It was not comfortable at all.

Ramana told me, "Just let it sit, don't try to do anything about it." So it sat. He had told me I needed to get involved in AHAM, not just taking programs, but for me to be a 'buddy' (a sort of personal trainer for people who took programs in AHAM), so I started volunteering. This was a period of uncertainty in my life and in my spiritual clearing. Luckily, I had some people in my life who were instrumental in my being able to stay with the process of spiritually or consciously working on myself. I was spending as much time in AHAM as I was in my work. The more I got involved, the less I was able to keep my attention on the purpose of the newspaper. Finally, I had to close it up.

When I dissolved the paper, I was in a lot of debt. Some of my creditors forgave the debt, but even with that, people said, at the time, that I might have to declare bankruptcy. I said, "No, I'm not going to do that." I owed people money and I didn't know how it was going to happen but I said, "I'm going to pay you back." And I did, it took a long time, but I got completely out of debt. I sold imported cars for about three or four years: BMWs, Porsches, Hondas and Audis. I had fun and whenever the upper management tried to promote me, I said, "I don't want to be the boss any more, I don't want any responsibility."

Stan and Ramana saying hello. *AHAM archives..*

I was putting a lot of time into AHAM and I was also tithing to it. In 1988, I went full time with AHAM. I did not have any source of income and AHAM was not able to pay anything, but I had saved quite a bit of money and one of the people from the AHAM family, who wanted to support me giving my time and attention to AHAM, said, "Come and stay at my house, you won't have to pay anything."

In 1991, shortly after we opened the meditation retreat and training center in Asheboro, North Carolina, I moved there along with Ramana and Elizabeth. A couple or so years later, I began to serve as AHAM's outreach director; I was on the road often giving talks to organizations – many churches. I remember times when I was in church during my younger years hearing the preacher reciting the words of Jesus: "For he that hath, to him shall be given: and he that hath not, from him shall be taken even that which he hath." (Mark 4:25, King James Version). When I first heard that, I quite frankly thought that Jesus was cold-hearted. I didn't have anything and he was going to take it away. I just didn't get the meaning, but through Ramana I came to understand that Jesus was talking about consciousness. If I only have a penny, but I have the feeling of enough, then more will be given. But, if I have a million dollars, and I don't feel I have enough still, that which I have will be taken away. It has nothing to do with the amount, it has to do with consciousness.

Being involved in the work of Self-Inquiry had given me a much deeper understanding and respect for Jesus. AHAM's teachings brought Jesus's teachings to life and we were well received at Unity churches. They saw us as sharing the Self, the Christ within, God within, in a way that people could hear, not offending against their love for Jesus.

Another saying of Jesus is, "But strive first for the kingdom of God and his righteousness, and all these things will be given to you as well." (Matthew 6:33, New Revised Standard Version). It was Ramana Maharshi who shared how to find the kingdom of God through the process of Self-Inquiry, taught at AHAM in the Intensive Self-Inquiry Training (ISIT). This program is in two parts: Self-Inquiry Training, and, Neutralizing Your Negative Past. It has really expanded over the years and serves more people than ever. The program is a great degree different than when it was introduced and there's been a definite three hundred percent improvement in its delivery, facilitating people more easily to get the essence of the teaching.

Ramana had said that we were stirring the pot of consciousness, and if we kept stirring it by working on ourselves, clearing our own consciousness, it would lighten the work for everybody and then people would be naturally drawn to AHAM. They would come in and bang, they'd get it. Back in the early days, Ramana used to say that one day people will come and in their first program awakening would occur. What we are finding now is that the people coming to our programs are indeed "getting it" much more quickly than in the early days of AHAM.

Steve - who recently became a Resident Staff Member and has been taking care of our web outreach to younger folks as well as the broader population - got involved in AHAM at age 31, the same age that I did, and he is getting the teachings light-years faster than I did. It's like the teachings are obvious to him. In one of my first programs in AHAM, my 'buddy' was Ramana. I called him every day. For me, understanding the teachings was a big struggle, but I think that more and more people are ready now.

Years before he died, I remember Ramana saying something that has helped me in my work: "I'm not looking for devotees and AHAM is not looking for devotees. I am here to make Buddhas," he said, "Everyone needs to take more responsibility for their own transformation and not depend on a trainer or a guru. AHAM is not here for you to become dependent. Yes, depend on us for support, for the training, and to be with us in conscious company-fellowship, but you have to make a commitment to your own spiritual path." That's why Ramana was so tough, so that we didn't become dependent.

I tell people what I have told Ramana: There are three men in the world that I honor most; my father, Martin Luther King and Ramana. My father - growing up where we lived - did miraculous things to provide for us. Martin Luther King did a lot to give a greater degree of freedom to this body, as a black man. It was Ramana though that gave me the real freedom - the freedom that is beyond this body.

Vivian: Taking Care of a Master

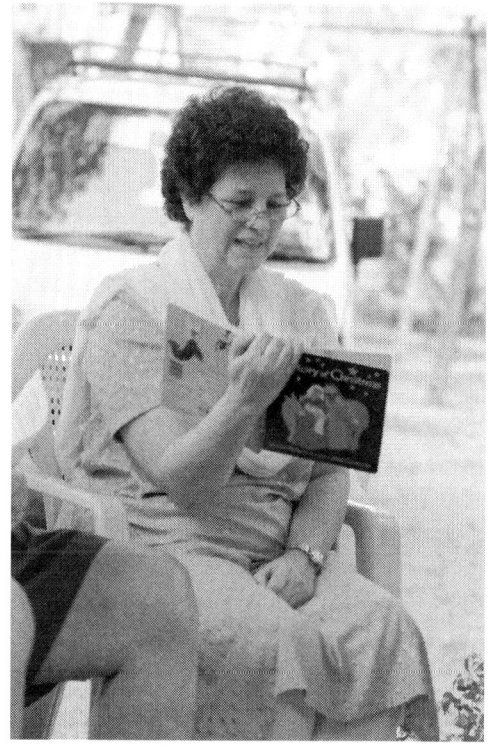

Vivian reading to children (2008) at the Arunachala
Village School (www.avillageschool.com) Tiruvannamali,
India, which AHAM enjoys supporting. Ramana is sitting
beside her. *Photo: Saroja..*

*Vivian was Ramana's caregiver for a number of years, and was an inti-
mate witness to his last weeks and to his passing from the body on February
15, 2010.*

On March 18, 1994, I went to AHAM for the first time and when I got on the property, a man told me I had to go register. He was a big, hippie-looking guy with a pony tail. I had no idea where I was going, but just walking past him, I knew I was in the right place. Shortly afterwards, I was introduced to him in the kitchen and I shook his hand. I didn't know who he was or what he was; sitting next to him at the bar in the kitchen, there was a feeling of unconditional love that I had never felt before. I didn't want to leave his side.

Students at AVS listening. *Photo: Saroja.*

It was Ramana and from then on there was awe and love for his being. It was almost like when a little animal opens its eyes for the first time and whatever it sees first, it thinks is his parent. That's what it felt like. It was like my life began that day, the beginning of real living. I trusted Ramana exclusively with my life. I could tell him anything and not feel ashamed – anything! I could tell him my darkest, deepest secrets and he would never judge. Never!

Seven years later, on July 13, 2001, I moved to AHAM. It was where I wanted to be.

There wasn't anything I wouldn't do for Ramana. I knew that he was sharing the truth and there were times when resistance might come up, but I still knew it was God speaking and I had to take responsibility for the resistance. That was how it was throughout the whole sixteen years that I knew him.

I gradually started taking care of Ramana a little bit and then Ramana had a kidney operation in 2007, and I stayed with him in the hospital after his surgery. It seemed from that point on, I was the predominant caregiver. Charlotte took care of him a little before that with the medication, but after the surgery, he really needed more assistance. Then Ramana insisted on my coming with him to India, because he knew that I wanted to take care of him - his body.

I had always been in a caregiver role in the past, but somehow it was always a "doer-ship." With Ramana, when it started out, there was a feeling of being special, but that all left me - it became a pure giving and it was like I couldn't give enough.

I questioned if what I was giving was enough! One time I asked Ramana, "What is my role?" There was still a feeling of having to prove myself. Ramana said, "Well, you're taking care of me." I knew it was important, but it wasn't until the last three weeks or so of his life, that I really felt its importance - totally.

He would say to me, "You're a good kid!" I resisted him calling me that and so I asked him about it and he said, "Jesus would say, 'Bless my child.'" That's how he meant it, "Bless my child."

So, I finally accepted he would say that - He just wanted me to appreciate what I do. He would always say, "I appreciate you so much..."

I'd said, "You don't have to say, thank you. I know you appreciate..."

But he would say, "I just want you to know how much I appreciate you." Then I would have tears, because why is he saying that to me? God doesn't have to say that.

There was a lot of creativity that came up with Ramana. Everything was an adventure. We always had fun when we went to the doctors, the dentist or wherever. Afterwards, we'd always go for lunch. It was a wonderful time just to be with him and of course with his hearing aid, music would be too loud, and I would have to ask people to cut down the sound. I was required to be assertive. For example, in the hospital, I had to get the nurse to have things checked, or get them to wash the floor, because they were washing the floor with dirty water. I had to speak up.

Watching television with him every night, I became his ears. He had to take out his hearing aid to wear the headphones to hear the television. "What did they say?" he'd ask me. Or, sometimes he would explain what was going on. Everything he said was purposeful. We would watch an hour and a half movie and it could take three hours because we would stop often.

Everything with Ramana had a purpose, a lesson. He didn't say anything that was not significant. When I had resistance I had to break through it, I had to surrender. When I did, things worked out perfectly. There was no effort. If Ramana called me, even though I would tell him I was in the middle of something, he would say, "I know that you have things to do, but this is important." Then I would end up staying with him for an hour or two. It was all to break the identification with what I was doing. He did that with both Jan and me.

I would look for excuses to go in, to be in his presence. It was like being with Bhagavan Sri Ramana Maharshi. Massaging Ramana's feet, I would envision massaging Bhagavan's feet - there was no difference. In the last weeks in India looking after Ramana, I hadn't really gone to Sri Ramanasramam too much and I really didn't have a pull to even walk around the hill (Arunachala).

Ramana said, "You're with Bhagavan, when you're with me."

I learned not to tell Ramana what to do, I learned to ask him, "Do you want something?" because he didn't like to be told to do something. I got to know him and his ways, which is why he liked me being with him. I knew that when you took something you put it back right where it was, he was particular.

He taught me the simplicity of things and he showed me how to be thorough. The last two weeks of being with him I was his secretary. I had to write emails for him, and every single word had to be correct, nothing left as a question. That was difficult for me to learn. Now I realize the importance of not missing anything, being fully clear on everything, like opening an envelope. Ramana would open up the short end. Why open up the long end when you have the short end? Take less time, but go slower and do not rush, because then you don't make mistakes. How to explain the simplicity? Just be simple, just be present.

Vivian, beside Ramana, taking notes during Satsang, 2008.
Photo: Saroja.

I learned in India - one of the things Ramana always shared - was just be with what is in the moment. He was in the moment. You didn't say, "We'll see how it works out," because he would say, "No, that's the future." He was always bringing me back to now.

When I asked him what would my role be when I went back to AHAM in America, he said, "Just be, that's all - and what has to be done will be revealed."

The day following Ramana's passing (February 16, 2010)), Pachiamma, who took care of Maniswami (Ramana's good friend and also an awakened being) for many years and Vivian stand at Ramana's Samadhi. Vivian may be singing the song "Arunachala Shiva." *Photo AHAM archives.*

Ramana had said, "I don't know if I'll be coming back to America." There was a feeling even before we left for India that this might happen and looking back, little things indicated that he wouldn't be coming back. When we came back from the hospital in India, in January 2010, Ramana announced to the community that he would not be returning to America, that he had cancer. We had looked at all kinds of alternatives, his going home by boat, this and that, but it wouldn't have worked out. So he just had to stay. It felt like Bhagavan had kept him there by Arunachala, and arranged it so he couldn't travel anymore.

In the last few weeks I was with him 24/7. I started reading to him and that was a fulfillment of something that I had wanted to do - reading to people in the hospital, but never did. So that was a completion. I slept on a mattress on the floor in his room, because he had to get up every hour and a half. I learned not to sleep so much; just being aware. There was a lot of assistance people didn't know that he needed. He shared with me the pain he was in. He had a lot of pain medication, but it just didn't work. I could see the pain he was in and I assisted him whenever he needed it.

Until the last day or two before his passing, I didn't know whether he was going to come out of it and say: "Okay! Here I am!" He was full of surprises and he hadn't lost his sense of humor. We thought it would be months that Ramana would still be with us, so we called the air conditioning people to see where we could put an air conditioner; we sent Charles to look at a hospital bed the Friday just before the Monday that Ramana passed and entered into Mahasamadhi (the great and final Samadhi of an awakened being at death – ed.). We had a commode made. We used to sit him in his chair to go down into the bathroom, so we had a ramp made, and handles in the bathroom. This was all done in the week before his death. It was as if we had no idea it was so near, although he was in agonizing pain.

I always wanted to be with him in his last moments. I had no idea what that would be like, but he made sure that I didn't go off track. He pointed out things with increasing intensity, making sure I let go of what was not true. He was very much more intense with me those last weeks. He wanted to make sure I got it. The last week I was sitting next to him and he did the Self-Inquiry with me. In our last conversation, Ramana said to me: "Where are you?" And then we just sat for about fifteen minutes. That was all. That was the last actual thing with him.

When he passed from this body, I knew that my role had been completely fulfilled and taking care of Ramana was my main purpose for being here. I had the feeling that we had known each other before and something had been completed.

Ramana spoke in the middle of the night, he was semi-conscious, but he was always aware; I know he was aware. He would just start talking and so after a while I thought I had better write some of it down - it didn't always make sense - but I wrote down whatever I could hear.

On the Wednesday night, five days before his passing, I heard him crying, "Vivian, help me." I knew it was only the body suffering. By a grace I just kept remembering who he was - and who he was, was not in pain. It was just the body. I was able to be with him fully and allow him to go through whatever he had to go through. I just prayed to Bhagavan to let him complete, to be finished. Take him.

It was really a beautiful experience. I could feel the intensity and three times during the night I felt like I was going to pass out, there was so much energy. When Ramana was going through all of this, it felt like it was clearing through me - some kind of transmission - that the Vasanas (karmic tendencies or imprints – ed.) were being burned up in my body to such a degree that I was just going to pass out. So, I just stayed with Self-Inquiry. letting it be, and then it passed. There has been a significant change within me since then.

I had never been with a dying person - so I just watched and observed what happened to his body. After he dropped the body, we sat him up in the reception area and I put some pillows and stayed the night on the floor beside him.

There was quite a joy when Ramana finally was finished, because his body suffered too much for so many years - why stay around? He had already given what he had to give, so it was time. He kept saying he had enough. There was a better place for him. One of my first reactions was that with Ramana being buried in Tiruvannamalai, the world would now know who he was. He was a bridge between the East and the West, between AHAM in America and AHAM in India.

I didn't go to sleep at night without thanking Bhagavan for being able to take care of Ramana.

I still talk to Ramana as though he were here – and, in fact, he's very much present. In my early years in AHAM, I used to read about what it would be like to be with a master. I found out: Ramana was and is a master!

Ramana coming out to the portico for Satsang,
Jan adjusts the digital camera, 2008.

Photo: Saroja.

Jan: Completion - Arunachala Ramana's Passing

Jan and Ramana enjoying children at the
Arunachala Village School, 2008. *Photo: Saroja.*

*Jan is the manager of the Arunachala Ramana AHAM Ashram in
Tiruvannamalai, India, where she witnessed the unfolding of the last
months of Ramana's life. In this account, she shares not only how she met
Ramana and came to live in India, but her perceptions of Ramana's passing
- the atmosphere and feeling of that time - with love and deep appreciation
of Ramana.*

In May of 1996, I took a job with a company that moved me across
the country (from the San Francisco Bay Area in Northern California to
Reston, Virginia) for my work. For the first three months I traveled back

and forth between California and Virginia, buying a new house and selling my California house; and I became pretty involved in the business, working eighty or more hours a week. The second week after arriving in Virginia I learned of AHAM at an Intro in a Unity Church and a year later I encountered AHAM again. Then I started going to AHAM in Asheboro, North Carolina, running down there every free moment I had.

It was as if I was holding two lives together, and I needed to move in the direction of AHAM. I took a year's leave of absence from the company and then resigned. I went back a year later to a retirement party for one of my bosses and he said there were three or four people that had retired shortly after I had left; as if they were finally allowed to follow their passions. My former boss said, "You did everything we needed for you to do and more; and we didn't know exactly what we were going to do with you, because you were over-qualified for what we really needed." My leaving was perfect!

I had gone to college in the late sixties in San Diego. I didn't finish it and I lived a so-called hippie life - odd jobs and counter culture - I was not into drugs or any of that stuff, but I wasn't into ordinary life either. I was definitely searching. I didn't know it was a spiritual search - I just knew I was searching. I loved nature, so anything that got me out of doors made me happy. I tried many things, but nothing ever held me until AHAM. It was like a moth being drawn to a flame. There was no going back.

I came to my first AHAM weekend program in November of 1997. The week-end course was called *Discover Meditation* – and I remember Ramana answered one of my questions. I had said that something was just a habit and he had said, "No, that's not right." Afterwards, I was determined to figure out what he was saying and why it hit me so strongly. A switch inside me got turned on. I didn't know why, I loved being around Ramana, even if he was tough and I was nervous and uncomfortable around him - I just loved being with him.

In January of 1998, I attended a second AHAM program, and one month later I assisted in a *Discover Meditation* Program held in the

Washington DC area. I was sitting on a bench outside the retreat center and I could see Ramana. I thought, "Gosh, look at this big man" and, I said to myself, "its okay, its okay." At the end of the weekend, someone was backing up in a huge van and Ramana was in the driveway directing him, "No, go that way. No, go this way." It all seemed so ordinary and I was thinking, this wasn't really my idea of what a guru or teacher was supposed to be.

Ramana Washing Car, Ottawa, Canada 2001.
Photo: Saroja.

I came here to Tiruvannamalai, India for the first time in 1999 and stayed for four months. The second time I came for four months and stayed a year, then I came back for six months and it turned out to be three and half years. I returned to America for a year and a half, then came back in the Spring of 2006 - and except for a couple of trips back to the States - I have been here ever since. It's been, altogether, twelve years in India.

In the last couple of years of his life, Ramana had lost a lot of physical energy and physical robustness, but his being and his presence wasn't diminished in any way. I can see now, that all these years, Ramana was hanging in as long as he possibly could, so he could be here for us. In one Satsang talk, I remember Ramana saying that he was a "wuss for pain." As I watch old videos and reflect, I see that he wasn't a wuss in the slightest – there was a great discomfort and pain in his body and he stayed behind it. Near the end though, those last weeks, the pain was far beyond the point of being manageable.

The AHAM logo carved into the wood of door panels at the AHAM Ashram, Tiruvannamalai, India.
Photo: Daniel Tigner.

After his return from the hospital in late January of 2010, he was no longer mobile, but he had even had a haircut and his life presence was still big. He gave his last videotaped talk on February 2, 2010 - thirteen days before his death – at the AHAM Ashram, Tiruvannamalai, India. In the first portion of the talk, he shares with us what was happening to his body and then he reminds us of the highest purpose of life:

> Namaste.
>
> Again, it is my pleasure to be able to be with you all.
>
> It's been somewhat of a rough ride I might add, for whatever that's worth. We just take each leap as it happens, take each phase of it as it presents itself.
>
> The doctors gave me a different medication yesterday for the discomfort, the pain – but, it's not yet doing the job, so we will just keep holding [in consciousness] that

they will come up with something that is beneficial in that regard. This is certainly giving an insight and a deeper understanding as to what it really means to be free of the body, to recognize what is the high purpose of life. And I am very happy to share it with you, at least for those who are really open, ready, and receptive to receiving it.

I'm sure all of us here have at one time seen various poses, photos, pictures of Bhagavan. You notice that he wasn't so much into clothing. He didn't have an outstanding wardrobe. I wonder why that's so? I wonder why it is that Bhagavan Ramana was not into clothing.

Bhagavan Sri Ramana Maharshi, 1940-42, near path going up the hill to Skandashram. *Used by permission of Sri Ramanasramam.*

One of my favorite pictures is of Bhagavan sitting up on the hill on a big rock, and the first time I had the opportunity to come here, I wanted to find that rock - to sit on that same rock that Bhagavan sat on with one leg crossed over the other, a water pot next to him and his staff. Those were his only worldly possessions, a water pot and a staff. If anyone were to come along and say, "Bhagavan, I sure would like to have your water pot," he would have just readily given it to him - or his staff or anything of that nature -simply because Bhagavan didn't own anything. He had already, readily, released, given up ownership of everything, including ownership of his own body.

Now, let's take into consideration for a moment, if you will, that Bhagavan had given up ownership of everything. He didn't own anything and he didn't want anything – and, yet, paradoxically, he was the owner of the entire universe. Kings and Queens, Maharajas and Maharanis, came and bowed at Bhagavan's feet. They gave him all manner of gifts that he did not even accept or receive. He would accept them and give them to the Ashram, but he, himself, did not accept or own anything. Would you say then that Bhagavan, in a manner of speaking, was already finished with life in this world? Do we get this?

He had totally completed life in this world. In other words, you could say that Bhagavan Ramana had reached the highest level of consciousness that can ever be reached in this plane of existence; and his life was a demonstration of it, a pure, perfect demonstration.

Now, he readily stated with devotees - who would ask him about their lives and how to live their lives - "Do whatever you are inclined to do." It was maybe not exactly in those words, but meaning that. Do whatever you feel inclined to do, live out your life, complete your life. But, for those who have the wisdom to see: understand that the highest purpose of life is to complete life in this lifetime - free of all possessions, free of all wants, free of all needs.

Ramana passed on February 15, 2010 at about 9:15 in the evening. That last week of Ramana's life, we all sensed that the end was getting near, so everybody was staying close by. Vivian and I talked at great lengths and we decided that until it was final, we were going to continue making preparations to care for Ramana in the long term.

Ramana's room, AHAM Ashram, Tiruvannamalai, India. Visitors often sit here for meditation. *Photo: Daniel Tigner.*

The windows in Ramana's room open onto a veranda and we had chairs out there and lots of old friends came in the morning, sat and meditated, and then came back in the evening for an hour or two. The quality and the presence there was special. One of our good friends, an Indian man, simply said, "Bhagavan is here."

The very last day, that evening, his breathing was heavy and less and less. I would go in every half hour and check on him. Around 8:30 in the evening, Vivian called me on the cell phone and said, "His breathing has changed," so we all moved in quickly and sat there in quiet meditation.

We could hear his breathing continue to change, slowing down, and there was a rattling sound in his chest. The breath came with big gaps and you wondered if another breath was coming. Then, all of a sudden, another one didn't come. It stopped and everything was so peaceful and still. We all just sat there for a while, knowing it was the last breath. The quality of presence and stillness was more profound than I have ever felt - ever! It was beautiful!

Arunachala Ramana's Samadhi - Creating a Sacred Place for Meditation

In both spiritual and secular traditions from around the world, the final resting place of a saint or a sage (also an artist, a scientist, or a great leader) is thought of as holding a higher energy - an imprint of the person's life and consciousness - that we can feel, meditate on, attune to and be inspired by. In India, the resting place or tomb of a Jnani or an awakened being, called a Samadhi, is especially valued. The preparations and rituals followed are meant not only to honor the Jnani, but are done with the intent to create a sacred space, to ensure that spiritual seekers can always come there as a place of refuge, contemplation and elevation of their consciousness.

Here Jan recounts some of the main rites following Ramana's passing and the preparation of his Samadhi.

The Puja or prayer rituals for Arunachala Ramana started off with the ritual washing of his body. This was done on the front porch with all sorts of different liquids like turmeric and sandalwood powders, oil and rosewater - I don't know how many different things. Then a clean cloth was wrapped around his body and flower garlands from Bhagavan's shrine placed on his body that were brought by Sundaram, the President of Sri Ramanasramam, and Ganesan.

A big hole, seven feet by seven feet and six feet deep was dug to bury Ramana's body, just outside of Ramana's bedroom. After it was dug, Mani, from the Sri Ramanasramam asked, "Did you find any rocks?" and the folks who dug the hole said, "No." He said, "Very good." This was taken as being a good sign.

The bottom of the hole was lined with loose bricks (to allow drainage) and the walls lined with bricks that were filled with mortar. Ramana's body was put in a huge sac that a tailor had come out to measure and stitch the week before.

The hole for Ramana's Samadhi is being lined with bricks, February 16, 2010. AHAM archives.

Ramana's body was fairly heavy, and although he had lost weight in the last couple of weeks of his life – when someone leaves their body, it is said that because there is no one conscious inside holding it up, it becomes what we call "dead weight." Swami Ramanananda was considering the best way to lift Ramana, but someone said, "Oh, there's enough of us to lift him down into the burial pit." So then Ramana's body was carefully lowered so that he didn't get dropped, and then we started filling the pit with salt, Vibhuti (sacred ash), many piles of flowers, earth and leaves - all layered in appropriately – while we sang the sacred devotional song, "Arunachala Shiva."

Ramana's body needed to be sitting upright and facing Arunachala and then a stick placed above his head at the top of the pile to mark the spot where a Shiva-Lingam would later be placed (in Bhagavan's lineage, the Shiva-Lingam, represents consciousness). That's all that happened that day.

. There was a second Puja ten days later. The first ten days following death allow a process of accepting and acknowledging the death. It is said that the soul is still there and in the ten days it is also able to let go. For Ramana, though, there was no letting go, it was already done - Ramana was already complete, there was nothing for him to let go of. But we in AHAM had a relationship with Ramana's mind and body to let go of, and it was truly a very special time for us, because, at the same time, there was a real knowing that Ramana hadn't gone anywhere.

In a ten-day Puja, a householder feeds the crows. For a Jnani, you feed Sadhus. You feed twenty-seven, fifty-four or one hundred and eight Sadhus - we fed fifty-four Sadhus. Granite stone slabs were set in place for the top layer of the Samadhi and the Shiva-Lingam laid down just over the top of Ramana's head. The second Puja consecrates the Shiva-Lingam and it is washed in all sorts of fluids. Although it's just an object, there is a noticeable energy around it. The cloth that wrapped around the Shiva-Lingam was, itself, from Bhagavan's shrine, a gift from the Sri Ramanasramam.

You normally don't pass cloth from Samadhi to Samadhi unless the person is a true devotee, which Ramana was. That cloth is now in a special place in the sanctuary at AHAM.

In this part of Southern India, there is a third Puja at the end of forty-eight days. It further consecrates the Shiva-Lingam and the space, fully establishing the consciousness there. At that time a roof was built over the Samadhi.

Every day, throughout the year, we have an early morning Puja at Ramana's Samadhi. Ramana's presence is always there - but the daily prayers and cleansing is an act of devotion and love that keeps the environment charged for those of us that are still in the body and can experience it.

Vivian and Jan watching the placing of the Shiva Lingam on Ramana's Samadhi in the second puja. Swami Ramanananda is at the right corner of the Samadhi.
AHAM archives.

356 | RAMANA AMERICAN MYSTIC: MEMOIRS OF A HAPPY MAN

Once a year, a special Puja is performed, on the annual day of death or Aradhana. In the West, we may remember someone on their birthday, here a death anniversary Puja honors the spirit.

I can see why Ramana's being in Tiruvannamalai when he dropped his body was important for our understanding of AHAM's lineage, the basis of what we have and the teaching of Self-Inquiry. Ramana always said that the AHAM Indian Ashram was a Bhagavan Centre.

The Samadhi is a treasure, and I feel blessed and lucky to oversee the sacred task of preserving this space, ensuring that presence of Ramana remains strong in the Samadhi as well as in his room and the Sanctuary. We have left them just as they were when Ramana was here. The Samadhi is for people to sit and meditate – Saroja came and spent some time there and has written an account of her experience.

Ramana's presence is so strong, it's sometimes almost overpowering. There is perfection in how all of this has worked and how, in hindsight, everything was just perfect, done exactly the way it was intended to be.

Ganesan Speaks about Arunachala Ramana's Passing

Ganesan at the fifth celebration marking Ramana's passing, February 15, 2015. Note the flower decoration behind him. *Photo: Daniel Tigner.*

On April 7, 2010, about two months after Ramana's passing, Saroja spoke with Ramana's good friend, Ganesan, about their relationship and Ramana's last days. Former President of Sri Ramanasramam, a respected spiritual teacher, and editor of "The Mountain Path", a journal devoted to the work of Bhagavan Sri Ramana Maharshi, Ganesan has unique insight into the significance of Ramana dropping the body near Arunachala.

Ganesan: Namaskar (a respectful greeting in India, like Namaste, ed.). I am happy you are having this interview with me about Ramana, who I still like to call Ramana Baba.

Saroja: You were a significant part of Ramana's life, and you played an important role during his interment, helping ensure that the prayer rites, the Pujas, and the burial were done in the right way for a Jnani or awakened being. How did you meet Ramana?

Ganesan: Ramana came to Sri Ramanasramam in the 1980s. I was in charge of publications at that time, I saw that he was deeply interested in the teachings of Ramana Maharshi, and so we had very frequent talks whenever he came to Tiruvannamalai. Then in 1991 or 1992, I went to the AHAM center in Asheboro, North Carolina. My Indian hosts contacted AHAM, and then took me there, and every year after that, I have returned on AHAM's invitation.

Saroja: What drew the two of you together as friends?

Ganesan: Ramana had started the institution of AHAM, which exclusively taught Bhagavan Sri Ramana Maharshi's Self-Inquiry process, and I was fascinated that nearly two thousand Americans had come to know about Self-Inquiry through AHAM. Without Ramana, and his creating AHAM, I don't know how that would have been achieved. So, I've always had admiration for him.

The way he trained his students and the way he answered questions on Self-Inquiry and on Sadhana (spiritual practice, ed.) amazed me.

In the last few years, we became closer. He'd ask me personal questions concerning dropping the body? I made it very clear to him that an old devotee of Bhagavan drops the body at Arunachala. That would be my personal wish - that Ramana, if possible, if Arunachala permitted, should drop the body there. In my last visit, he joked that he was coming to Arunachala with a one-way ticket.

Saroja: Do you mean when you saw Ramana on your last trip to the AHAM center in North Carolina, in July of 2009?

Ganesan: Yes. We had discussions then, and he said he was not able to win over pain and hunger. I told him that if you accepted pain and hunger, you could win over them. At that time, he said he was coming here to India to definitely drop the body.

Saroja: He said that to you?

Ganesan: Yes, yes.

Saroja: Oh, so he knew!

Arunachala. *Photo: Daniel Tigner.*

Ganesan: When he arrived here in Tiruvannamalai in the fall of 2009, he called me and we had a discussion which, as usual, he started with a harsh and dominating tone - I just listened.

Saroja: That was his way of loving us – his tone of voice.

Ganesan: Yes, that I know – that's why I didn't talk back or defend or argue. But, just as he has a trick, I also have a trick - to keep silent!

"Ganesan," Ramana said. "You have told me how to win over the pain, but I have still not been able to do that. Please help me."

I went near him, held his hand, and told him, "Surrender to Arunachala - surrender everything to Arunachala and it will do it for you. When you are so honest as to admit that you cannot do it, surrender - it is the only way."

I reminded him of an anecdote Bhagavan told about a passenger on a train who was carrying his baggage on his head. I said to Ramana, "Why are you carrying your baggage on your head? Surrender everything: your discipline, your longing to guide people, everything. Surrender not being able to bear pain and hunger."

Ramana listened very patiently.

Saroja: Your conversations were in Ramana's room in the AHAM Ashram in Tiruvannamalai?

Ganesan: Yes. When I said to him to surrender to Arunachala, he did not answer, but there was no negative response from him either. Instead, he made a request, "Go and stay in AHAM in North Carolina as long as you want. Your needs will be looked after by AHAM." I have personally loved every member of the AHAM center, especially those managing it, helping Ramana to maintain the integrity of the institution. So I am always happy to go to AHAM in the USA.

After some time Ramana added, "Ganesan, you and I are giving the same teaching. We are taking the horse to drink water: you take the horse and I also take the horse, but the only difference is that you give freedom to the horse to drink or not to drink.

I told him that yes, I knew.

He went into silence and then, suddenly, he started talking again. "Ganesan, I have realized now that no one can make a horse drink water, unless it wants to drink." When he said that, I felt then he was able to see, and he was being blessed by Arunachala to see this truth within himself.

In the next few days, I could not go, but I heard that Ramana was sitting for sixteen hours in his chair. People were coming and sitting next to him. Anurada, my secretary, had said to Jan and Vivian that it would be better for the windows to be open and for visitors to sit on the veranda, rather than next to him. They opened the windows and Vivian said, "He's not opened his eyes, he cannot see Arunachala." I don't know if he was unconscious or conscious - but his eyes were closed.

Anurada replied, "How does it matter if Ramana cannot see Arunachala? Arunachala can see Ramana."

I feel this was not just a light statement – Arunachala had blessed him. Arunachala was all the time seeing him. All this had a great significance for me.

On the last day, when I went in, Ramana was lying down, with no symptoms of experiencing pain. I loved that. I think it was 9:30 in the evening or so that he left the body - I was there until 5 o'clock or 5:30 in the afternoon. Vivian and I were very near Ramana, when suddenly a wave of real joy came and we both started laughing aloud like children, without even noticing what others might think about it. I looked at Vivian and she nodded. There was such joy!

Ramana was in peace: that's how I interpret myself and Vivian laughing loudly. That's not a situation to laugh: No sane being will laugh in the presence of a dying man. This indicates that Arunachala had blessed him. For me it is very significant.

Ramana had confessed that he had completed all that he wanted to do. He had no more desires – the only thing he was really attached to was AHAM – he stated, "There is nothing more for me to do – I am ready." Ramana dropped the body in silence and in calmness, a sure sign that Arunachala had blessed him. That is my personal point of view. I cannot prove it, I cannot quote any reference for that, but I felt it very deeply within me and I was so happy to participate in the burial ceremony.

Saroja: Ganesan, could you tell us about what happened right after Ramana left the body?

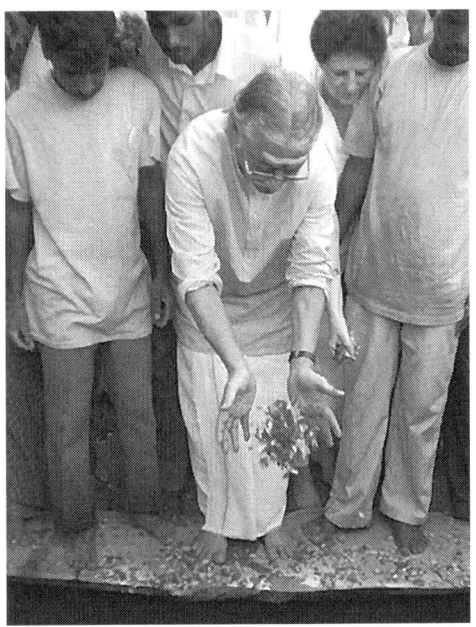

Ganesan putting flowers into the burial chamber of
Ramana, February 16, 2010. *AHAM archives.*

Ganesan: Ramana was in line with Bhagavan's direct teaching, with the potent support of Jesus Christ's teachings - because Bhagavan, himself, got Self-Inquiry from Jesus Christ. After Ramana dropped the body, his body was made to sit in the reception area. There was a cloth that went around his chin and it was tied to a nail to hold up his head. The way the cloth was placed made it look exactly like a cross. It was not an apparition or anything like that, but Ramana was totally dedicated to Bhagavan and equally to Jesus Christ.

Saroja: You know more than anyone about the traditions, how the body should be interred. Please say something about the Pujas and how Ramana was buried and what the rites represent.

Ganesan in a moment of prayer by the burial chamber of
Ramana, February 16, 2010. *AHAM archives.*

Ganesan: The explanations about the significance of the Pujas any-one can give - I don't know if they are true or not, they may be just giving us mental satisfaction - but I insisted that Ramana should be seated in Padmassan (lotus position, ed.), and the ritual washing be done, the pour-ing of water and milk – everything of ritualistic significance, because, one of the last things he said to me before he went into sixteen hours of silence was, "Ganesan, believe me, if I were not born a Westerner, I would have been one of the sadhus (mendicants) going around the hill and would be sleeping in the open space here." His inner longing was to be a true renunciate, attached to Arunachala. He could not do that, but he allowed Arunachala to take hold of him, which is an equally great surrender.

Anurada and I had already discussed with Vivian and Jan what to do when Ramana dropped the body, and Swami Ramanananda was also helpful. So when Ramana's body was interred, Everything was harmonious. It was beautiful. Food was brought from Ramanasramam. I felt Bhagavan blessing our Ramana with Prasad (food given as a religious offering, ed.) and we chanted Arunachala Shiva. On the forty-eighth day, the Mandala Puja, I was there with Anurada, and we again chanted Arunachala Shiva and there was such a sense of fulfillment. I am very happy that I was associated with Ramana and that I could be there as a true friend in his last rites, I am very grateful to him for that and to every member of AHAM.

Robert Adams (1928 to 1997); an American author and devotee of Bhagavan Sri Ramana Maharshi) used to say; "All is well that ends well."

Ramana's death was so peaceful. There was no sense of sorrow – that somebody had died. To be honest, I felt very happy.

Arunachala, the hill on the right, as seen from the roof of the AHAM Ashram. *Photo: Daniel Tigner.*

I thank Ramana for having fulfilled - or allowing Arunachala to fulfill - his inner desire to drop the body at the foot of Arunachala. I had said to him to surrender to Arunachala. He surely had done that and he became silent. He had the great honor of getting interred in the sacred ground of Arunachala itself. Somehow that gives me great fulfillment.

"My involvement with people - anyone and everyone who is open and receptive - has been just to be an instrument for them to discover within themselves their own true nature."

Arunachala Ramana

Saroja's Experience of Meditation in Ramana's Samadhi

Saroja at the Sri Ramanasramam in 1998. *Photo by Passerby.*

In 1998, Saroja had been staying at the Sri Ramanasramam when she encountered Arunachala Ramana at the first Satsang he gave in Tiruvannamalai. Over the years, she heard fragments of Ramana's life story. Finding the stories captivating and instructive, one day in 2008 she gathered the courage to ask Ramana if she could interview him for a book about his life. At first he hesitated – as he attributed little importance to a person's biography – but seeing it might be helpful to seekers, he acquiesced. So Saroja began the series of more than twenty interviews with Ramana that took place over the last two years of his life.

On her return to the Arunachala Ramana Ashram in Tiruvannamalai, India, in 2014, Saroja immersed herself in a daily meditation in Ramana's Samadhi. Her experience is described here.

Five years had gone by since I had last been in Tiruvannamalai, India and stayed at the Arunachala Ramana AHAM Ashram. My last visit was the winter of 2009 - I left just weeks before Ramana dropped his body. I am grateful to have been able to read to Ramana the first five chapters of his memoirs (the same text that you, Dear Reader, now read) and to have received his blessings to bring them to publication.

I can't tell you enough how happy I was to be again in the AHAM Ashram at the foot of Arunachala. The first impression was the strong and clear energy within the Ashram compound, and the stillness around the Samadhi. The feeling of sacredness and of Ramana's presence is dense, tangible and unexpected (the intensity is always a surprise to me, each time I arrive from being out in the world).

As you may know, a Samadhi traditionally is a place where the body of a high being, an enlightened one, is buried. It is considered to be a sacred place, a place of communion with oneself and where a devotee can pay his respects. I planned to meditate there each day during my stay and I was not sure what to expect. It felt like the beginning of a journey.

The next morning and every morning after that during my two-month stay, I woke up around four in the morning and sat and meditated at the Samadhi for a good hour and a half; after that I would often go sit in Ramana's room. Initially, I found myself paying a great deal of attention to the aches and pains in different parts of my body during the meditation; in short, I was preoccupied about how to be comfortable. Interestingly enough, pretty rapidly the aches and pains subsided, and I was able to simply witness anything I would normally qualify as discomfort.

Saroja helping with the morning Puja
at Ramana's Samadhi. *Photo: Jan.*

We may all have underlying, primary thoughts and tendencies. Mine came up loud and clear during these meditations. One was the thought that something is missing, I am not complete, I am not enough – a feeling that I needed to keep looking. Linked to that overriding dissatisfaction with myself, there was a desire to have a great experience, a kind of a peak experience that would transform all my life forever. These underlying thoughts were pretty constant. Papaji, another master in the lineage of Bhagavan Sri Ramana Maharshi (I had been with Papaji until his death and then met Ramana), had given me the mantra "Om Tat Sat" to repeat when thoughts came. I used it along with the Self-Inquiry process in my Samadhi meditations.

Saroja with basket of flowers for morning Puja
at Ramana's Samadhi. *Photo: Jan.*

The first few weeks, I was alert in the meditation - not falling asleep.
Then I started to fall asleep and that really bothered me. I started asking Ramana to help me not to fall into unconsciousness, but to remain
alert and present. To prevent falling asleep, instead of sitting the entire
time, I started doing Pradakshina, walking around the Samadhi at a slow,
meditative pace. That helped me to stay alert. As I walked, I would sometimes speak out loud to Ramana, expressing all of my concerns, worries,
questions, expectations, fears, likes and dislikes and preferences - all that
my mind was bringing up - and most importantly releasing, giving away
and surrendering it all to Ramana, Arunachala, and existence. The exer-
cise - so to speak - of surrendering, showed me that all that was needed
was to simply be with what was in the moment, experiencing everything

without doing anything about what was going on, allowing and feeling every thought, every perception – everything!

In the first weeks, I kept expecting to see Ramana appear and we'd have a conversation, but at one point I began to simply feel his presence, not only at the Samadhi, but everywhere – the Samadhi, though, was a kind of vortex of energy, the focal point of that silent presence. An especially powerful way that I experienced the energy of the Samadhi was through participating in the morning Pujas. On three occasions I did the five washings of the Shiva-Lingam and the top of the Samadhi. Afterwards, the whole day I was filled with so much energy, joy and bliss that it is hard to describe.

Toward the end of my stay, I remember going for a walk and thoughts starting to arise. I recall allowing the thoughts to continue and become a nice movie in my mind. Even though I chose then to daydream, this event showed me what I have always known somewhere, that there is an underlying awareness that is always conscious of everything. I simply need to listen and abide in that awareness. I realized that – as many masters have told us - that there is nothing to do. At the same time, the inner spiritual work requires of us an ongoing, moment-to-moment vigilance.

When I returned to the West - physically departing from Arunachala, the AHAM Ashram, and Ramana's Samadhi - beyond any emotion, I felt simultaneously full and empty. I have treasured my time at Ramana's Samadhi, at the foot of Arunachala. What a precious blessing!

I would like to encourage everyone reading this book - who feels a connection with Ramana - to come to Tiruvannamalai, to Arunachala, to visit the Sri Ramanasramam and the AHAM Ashram and to experience the gift of meditating at Ramana's Samadhi.

Namaste,
Saroja

Arunachala Ramana, 2008. *Photo: Saroja.*

Glossary for American Mystic

The glossary provides short and basic definitions of key terms used in this book. A much more in depth glossary is found in: A. Ramana. *Radical Realizations and Frequently Used AHAM Terms*, Asheboro, NC, AHAM Publications, 2004.

Abiding in Self - Remaining continually in self-awareness, the witnessing consciousness that is prior to all thoughts, emotions, sensations and identification with the body-mind.

AHAM (Capitalized) - An acronym for the "Association of Happiness for All Mankind," founded in 1978 by Arunachala Ramana.

aham (small letters) - A Sanskrit word meaning "I," "Self," or the "sense of I."

Being at Cause - Seeing that you are the source and cause of all that is happening in your life, and are fully capable of taking responsibility for it, versus Being at the Effect of.

Being at the effect of - Believing in outside causes for the problems or things you find disagreeable or upsetting in your life; blaming other people or events for whatever is wrong. When you believe you are "at the effect of" outside forces, you feel powerless and victimized.

"Bullshit"(slang) - An effective and direct term that was sometimes used by Arunachala Ramana to cut through maneuvering, subterfuge and self-deception, so to clear the air and stop any tendency to hide or to lay down a smokescreen around a topic, situation or issue.

Completion - In spiritual work, bringing to fulfilment, conclusion or closure any process or situation. Completion, in the greatest sense, means to become fully self-realized and liberated in this lifetime.

Conscious - Being aware of your own existence, your Self, the environment and world around you.

Conscious Company - Fellowship with people who are consciously engaging in spiritual work.

Devotee - One who has ardent feelings of devotion or affection toward God, the Higher Self, or the Guru.

Duality - Believing in and living life based on the concept that the world has solid, objective reality independent of your consciousness of it.

Ego - All the thoughts and feelings of being a self-contained person (the body-mind, a personal self, born into time and space, growing old and dying)who has learned to protect a separate identity and to assert themselves as apart from others and the world. The ego is identification with a false self as opposed to the real Self discovered through Self-Inquiry and spiritual work.

Guru - A personal spiritual teacher. From Sanskrit: "the dispeller of darkness, giver of light."

Happy End of the Movie - Vividly envisioning and feeling that which you wish to be, do and have as already having manifested or as presently manifesting in one's life. A 'wish-fulfilment' technique using the power of imagination.

I AM - Is Pure Consciousness; it's the name of the reflected light of pure being, Self, God, the source. In the Bible, it is the declared name of God (Exodus 3:15).

Identity - Who or what someone is considered to be. It is especially what someone names or calls himself/herself, and thinks himself/herself to be; the set of characteristics that one recognizes as belonging particularly to himself/herself, and which is believed to constitute or make up his/her individual being or self.

Jnani (Sanskrit) - One who is awakened or self-realized.

Liberation - The joyous release from body-mind identification, felt as peace, freedom and happiness.

Non-duality - The one single Existence, in which there is no "other." It is true Knowledge and Wisdom of the unity of Being.

Pradakshina (Sanskrit) - Circumambulating or walking around a shrine or a sacred place.

Prior to - Awareness that is prior to thoughts, emotions or sensations.

Puja (Sanskrit) - In Hinduism, a prayer ritual.

Sadhu (Sanskrit) - An ascetic or holy person.

Self-Realization - Realization of your true nature.

Sadhana (Sanskrit) - Means spiritual practice, in which you strive to attain spiritual purification, perfection or Self-Realization.

Samadhi (Sanskrit) - The transcendental and natural state of pure awakened being.

A Samadhi - The tomb of a sage or Jnani. A Samadhi is often empowered as a place of meditation.

Satsang (Sanskrit) - A meditation gathering with a self-realized being, in silence or with questions and answers to spiritual questions.

Self-Inquiry - The direct method or process to the realization and abidance in the Self, brought forth to the world by Bhagavan Sri Ramana Maharshi. Self-Inquiry is making a profound investigation into the true nature of one's inner being.

Self-Realization - Is awakening to and abiding in the true Self.

Senior Prom - A graduation dance for high school students.

Sense of I - Is the life principle: the feeling of "being alive," known and felt by all living beings.

Siddha (Sanskrit) - Spiritually perfected being.

Siddhis (Sanskrit) - Often refer to special powers such as telepathy or clairvoyance possessed by a Siddha.

Surrender - In one's spiritual practice, surrender means letting go of the ego-mind into the Self. It is relinquishing your position or point of view to the Truth or to a higher, clearer and more appropriate perspective.

Swami (Sanskrit) - One who has gone through a process renouncing worldliness and surrendering their life to the search for Self-Realization.

Tendencies - Inclination to think and act in a predetermined or habitual manner based on conditioned patterns recorded in the mind.

Vedanta (Sanskrit) - Means, "the end of knowing." It is a system of philosophy based on the Upanishads, which are commentaries on the ancient Hindu *Vedas* (sacred writings).

Vibhuti (Sanskrit) - Sacred ash.

References, Suggested Reading and Websites

Arunachala Ramana Books

A. Ramana. *There is Neither I, Nor Other Than I, There Is Only....*, Asheboro, NC, AHAM Publications, 2006 (first published 1997).

A. Ramana. *Consciousness Being Itself,* Asheboro, NC, AHAM Publications, 1995.

A. Ramana. *Handbook to Perpetual Happiness,* Asheboro, NC, AHAM Publications, 1997 (first published 1981).

A. Ramana. *Freeing Yourself From the Prison of Your Mind,* Asheboro, NC, AHAM Publications, 2005.

A. Ramana. *You Already Are What You Seek,* Asheboro, NC, AHAM Publications, 2006.

A. Ramana. *Living Free,* Asheboro, NC, AHAM Publications, 2002.

A. Ramana. *Radical and Frequently Used AHAM Terms,* Asheboro, NC, AHAM Publications, 2004.

AHAM Contact Information

AHAM Website: www.aham.com

Contact AHAM USA:

Via Phone:(336) 381-3988
Via Email: generalmail@aham.com
Via Post: (AHAM) • 4368 NC Hwy 134,
Asheboro, North Carolina 27205 USA

Contact AHAM India:

The Association of Happiness
for All Mankind (AHAM) • 255 AHAM Road,
Tiruvannamalai 606 603, Tamil Nadu, South India.
Phone: 04715 237383
Email: arunaham@vsnl.com

Videos of Arunachala Ramana and Osho

Spiritual-Video.com

Website: www.spiritual-video.com

On this website you will find audio-extracts from interviews
with Arunachala Ramana used in *American Mystic: Memoirs
of a Happy Man*, many videos of talks given by Arunachala
Ramana, as well as discourses by Osho.

Bhagavan, circa 1949. *Photographed by G.G. Welling, used by permission of Sri Ramanasramam.*

The Writings of Bhagavan Sri Ramana Maharshi

Ramana Maharshi. *The Collected Works of Sri Ramana Maharshi,* Sri Ramanasramam, Tiruvannamalai, India, Twelfth edition 2014.

Ramana Maharshi. *Who Am I? The Teachings of Bhagavan Sri Ramana Maharshi,* Ramanasramam, Tiruvannamalai, India, Eighth edition 2010.

Writings about Living with Bhagavan Sri Ramana Maharshi

There are many accounts of living with Bhagavan. This is only a selection of a few important books.

Brunton, Paul. *A Search in Secret India*, 1935. This book introduced many Westerners to Ramana Maharshi.

Cohen, S.S. *Guru Ramana*, Sri Ramanasramam, Tiruvannamalai, India, Eleventh edition 2012 (first published 1956).

Chadwick, Major A. W. *A Sadhu's Reminiscences of Ramana Maharshi*, Sri Ramanasramam, Tiruvannamalai, India, first published in 1961.

Ganesan, V. *Ramana Periya Puranam (Inner Journey of 75 Old Devotees)*, available as a free download from AHAM (www.aham.com/RamanaPeriyaPuranam)

Ganesan, V. *Glory of Ramana Maharshi*, Sri Ramanasramam, Tiruvannamalai, India, First Edition edition 2008.

Ganesan, V. *Moments Remembered, Reminiscences of Bhagavan Ramana. Compilation of individual experiences of many devotees of Sri Ramana Maharshi*, Sri Ramanasramam, Tiruvannamalai, India, 1994.

Osborne, Arthur. *Ramana Maharshi and the Path of Self-Knowledge*, Sri Ramanasramam, Tiruvannamalai, India, 2006.

Mouni Sadhu. *In Days of Great Peace*, George Allen and Unwin Ltd., United Kingdom, 1957.

Picture Books

Bhagavan Sri Ramana Maharshi, The Restored Photographs, Volumes One, Sri Ramanasramam, Tiruvannamalai, India, 2005.

Bhagavan Sri Ramana Maharshi, The Restored Photographs, Volumes Two, Sri Ramanasramam, Tiruvannamalai, India, 2006.

Dillinger, Jim (author, photographer). *Arunachala Sacred Mountain Of South India,* Asheboro, NC, AHAM Publications, 2007.

Grenblatt, Joan and Matthew (compiler and designers). *Bhagavan Sri Ramana, A Pictorial Biography*, Sri Ramanasramam, Tiruvannamalai, India, 1995 (first edition 1981).

Websites of Interest

AHAM: www.aham.com/

Bhagavan Sri Ramana Maharshi Ashram: www.sriramanamaharshi.org

Books, videos and resources on Bhagavan and his lineage: davidgodman.org

Annamalai Swami: realization.org/p/annamalai-swami/annamalai-swami.html

Neville Goddard: realneville.com

Daniel Tigner (editor of American Mystic):
www.danieltigner.com; www.essences.ca

Email: daniel@danieltigner.com

Saroja G. Poilblan (who interviewed Arunachala Ramana for American Mystic): www.sarojaresource.com

Email: sarojaramana@me.com

Spiritual-Videos: www.spiritual-video.com

Recommended Spiritual Biographies

Carson, Clayton. *The Autobiography of Martin Luther King, Jr.*, Warner Books, 1961.

Godman, David. *Nothing Ever Happened* (A three volume biography of *H. W. L. Poonj, aka Papaji)*, Avadhuta Foundation, Lucknow, India, 1998.

Gurdjieff, G. I. *Meetings with Remarkable Men*, Martino Fine Books, 2010 (English translation A. R. Orage, 1963).

Osho, *Glimpses of a Golden Childhood, The Rebellious Childhood of a Great Enlightened One*, Rebel Publishing House, Cologne, Germany (latest edition 2008).

Peters, Fritz, preface by Henry Miller. *My Journey with a Mystic (about the author's journey with Gurdjieff)*, Tale Weaver Publishing, 1986.

Swami Muktananda. *Play of Consciousness: A Spiritual Autobiography*, Siddha Yoga Publications, 1978.

Yogananda, Paramahansa. *Autobiography of a Yogi*, Self-Realization Fellowship; Reprint edition 1998 (first published in 1946).

Books by Authors Mentioned in American Mystic

Annamalai Swami. *Annamalai Swami - Final Talks*, edited David Godman, Annamalai Swami Ashram, 2000.

Baker, Mary Edy. *Science and Health, With Key to the Scriptures*, Christian Science Board of Directors, 2011 (first published 1875).

Burnstein, Morey. *The Search for Bridey Murphy*, Doubleday, New Edition, 1989 (first published 1956).

Cerminara, Gina. *Many Lives, Many Loves*, Devorss & Co, 1981 (first published circa 1958).

Fillmore, Charles. *Metaphysical Bible Dictionary*, Wilder Publications, 2012 (first published 1931).

Fillmore, Myrtle. *Christian Healing*, Unity, 2005 (first published 1909).

Freeman, James Dillet. *The Story of Unity,* Unity Books, Unity Village, Missouri, USA, 2007.

Freeman, James Dillet. *Love is Strong as Death, Moving Through Grief,* Unity Books, Unity Village, Missouri, USA, 2000.

Goddard, Neville. *Neville Goddard: The Complete Reader* (compilation), Audio Enlightenment, 2013.

Hill, Napolean. *Think and Grow Rich,* unedited version, Napoleon Hill Foundation, 2012 (first published 1937).

Hill, Napolean. *The Law of Success in 16 Lessons,* Wilder Publications, 2011 (first published 1928).

Hopkins, Emma Curtis. *High Mysticism - Studies in the Wisdom of the Sages of the Ages*, Wise Woman Press, 2010 (first published circa 1940).

Huffman, Robert W. and Irene Specht. *Many Wonderful Things,* DeVorss & Co, 2nd Printing 1958.

Jones, James Breckenridge. *If You Can Count to Four*, original edition 1957.

Keyes, Ken, *Handbook to Higher Consciousness*, Love Line Books, 5th edition, 1993.

Paulsen, J. Sig. *How to Love Your Neighbor*, Doubleday, 1974.

Starcke, Walter. *The Double Thread*, Guadalupe Press, 1989.

Sugrue, Thomas. *Story of Edgar Cayce: There is a River,* A.R.E. Press; Revised edition, 1997.

Swami Chidvilasananda (formerly Malti), *Enthusiasm,* A Siddha Yoga Publication, South Fallsbour, New York, USA, 1997.

Tolle, Eckhart. *A New Earth: Awakening to Your Life's Purpose,* Penguin, reprint 2008.

Webb, Ripley. *The Eternal Pilgrim,* Asheboro, NC, AHAM Publications, 2004 (Original publication in London, England just after World War II).

Wilson, Ernest C. *If You Want to Enough - A Book of Memoirs,* Quality Press, 1985.

Books on India

Osho. *India My Loved: A Spiritual Journey,* Rebel Publishing House, Pune, India, 1997.

Shivani. *"Arunachala" (Tiruvannamalai) An Endless Experience*, ISBN 978-81-7525-860-0, Shivani Publishing, 2007.

Pattanaik, Devdutt, *7 Secrets of Shiva*, Westlake Ltd, New Delhi, India, 2011.

Made in the USA
Middletown, DE
19 December 2018